PASSION FOR LIFE

JOHN JAMES AND MURIEL JAMES

PASSION FOR LIFE

Psychology and the Human Spirit

A DUTTON BOOK

DUTTON

Published by the Penguin Group
Penguin Books USA Inc., 375 Hudson Street,
New York, New York 10014, U.S.A.
Penguin Books Ltd, 27 Wrights Lane,
London W8 5TZ, England
Penguin Books Australia Ltd, Ringwood,
Victoria, Australia
Penguin Books Canada Ltd, 2801 John Street,
Markham, Ontario, Canada L3R 1B4
Penguin Books (N.Z.) Ltd, 182–190 Wairau Road,
Auckland 10, New Zealand

Penguin Books Ltd, Registered Offices:
Harmondsworth, Middlesex, England

First published by Dutton, an imprint of New American Library,
a division of Penguin Books USA Inc.
Distributed in Canada by McClelland & Stewart Inc.

REGISTERED TRADEMARK—MARCA REGISTRADA

LIBRARY OF CONGRESS CATALOGING-IN-PUBLICATION DATA:
James, John, 1946–
Passion for life : psychology and the human spirit /
John James and Muriel James.
p.   cm.

1. Spiritual life.   2. Self-actualization—Religious aspects.
3. Motivation (Psychology).   4. Transactional analysis.
I. James, Muriel.   II. Title.
BL624.J43   1991
248.4—dc20   90-21515
                                                              CIP

Printed in the United States of America
Set in Cheltenham Light

Designed by Steven N. Stathakis

To our teachers, students, colleagues, clients, friends, and family who entered into genuine dialogue with us.

ACKNOWLEDGMENTS

In addition to the men and women who are profiled, quoted, and acknowledged in this book, there are many others who have been helpful to us. Clients, teachers, students, colleagues, and friends have all encouraged us to write this book. Some of them may not know how important they have been in our lives and for the development of our theory, especially:

Javier Alborna	Harland Hogue
Chauncey Blossom	Sy Horowitz
Kaye Burke	Ian James
Jacquie Butler	Duncan James
Clayton Cobb	Jean Johnson
Arnold Come	Sherman Johnson
Dale Cooper	George Kandathil
Ann Dilworth	Kathleen and Ben Kaulback
Arthur Foster	Robert Leslie
Michiko Fukazawa	Pat Loughary
Jan and Locke Gibbs	Charles McCoy
Victor Gold	Gail and Lynne Miller
Bill Harvey	Shunji Nishi

Ruby Peregrine   Maria Teresa Romanini
Werner Rautenberg   Louis Savary
Hans Reudi-Weber

Our special thanks to Betty Fielding and Sue Hughes who showed their support and affection by reading and commenting on much of the manuscript. As "one picture is worth a thousand words," we also thank the photographers, artists, and graphic designers who added life to our words.

We are deeply appreciative of our spouses, Ibis Schlesinger-James and Ernest Brawley, for their ideas, inspiration, encouragement, support and tolerance throughout. Without them, it would not have been possible.

We also have sincere appreciation for our agent John Brockman, his associate Katinka Matson, and for our editors Gary Luke and Matthew Sartwell at NAL/Dutton, for believing in our ideas and the value they might have for others.

To thousands of our colleagues in the International Transactional Analysis Association with members in eighty-three countries, we thank you for the innumerable hours you spent listening to our ideas and theory of the inner core and the human spirit.

Now we offer this book with the hope that the concepts will be useful to you in increasing your passion for life. With this in mind, we look forward to hearing from you, our readers.

JOHN JAMES   MURIEL JAMES
Lafayette, California   Lafayette, California

CONTENTS

3. PASSIONS OF THE SOUL

4. THE URGE TO LIVE

5. THE URGE FOR FREEDOM

6. THE URGE TO UNDERSTAND

7. THE URGE TO CREATE

8. THE URGE TO ENJOY

9. THE URGE TO CONNECT

CONTENTS

10. THE URGE TO TRANSCEND

11. MISSION OF THE HUMAN SPIRIT

PASSION FOR LIFE

INTRODUCTION

❦

Just before the dawn, faint glimmers of light appear in the sky. As the earth turns on its axis, its many creatures stretch and start to awaken. Then the light brightens as the birds announce the coming day. Our waking minds change focus from the land of dreams and fantasy to a world that demands intelligent choices, a world pleading for love.

The choices required of us come from having a strong passion for life. A passion for life is more than a nebulous feeling of optimism and love of living. It is the commitment to life that motivates us to do our best and strive to make a positive difference in other peoples' lives. It is the determination to fight for what we believe in and to fight against suffering, injustice, and the waste of natural resources. It is the decision to transcend barriers that inhibit our best efforts. It reflects a commitment to be and to do more than we believed was possible.

Having a passion for life means being excited and involved in what is and what can be. It is like waking up and feeling full of energy. It is like falling in love and being full of joy. It is like being imprisoned and suddenly set free.

This book offers a theory that encourages this attitude. The theory moves beyond the understanding of the physical and the psychological self to a broader concept of the human spirit or the spiritual self. It includes concepts of how the human spirit functions when it is free, how it can be related when it is not free, and how it can be developed more fully.

This spiritual self interacts with the physical and psychological selves; it also has its own unique qualities and powers. These powers arise from seven basic, universal urges. All peoples experience them at all times and places, yet each individual person experiences them in unique and personal ways. Although various conditions influence the intensity and expression of these urges, they constantly push from within to be expressed in one way or another. When these urges are active and free-flowing, we experience a passion for life.

In this book we are not focusing on the past as much as on the present and future; we are not focusing on pathology but rather on health; we are not focusing on problems but more on possibilities, including our potentials for creativity, self-generated ethics, and goals which are motivated by the positive urges of the human spirit.

Many people, however, are uncomfortable with the word "spirit" or any of its derivatives. In the early nineteen seventies, the words "spirit," "spiritual," and "spirituality" began to be used in new ways. Until then, the words seemed to belong primarily to religious organizations that disagreed on the meaning of the words. However, a vast humanity began stretching those terms as a part of their search for something more than tradition was offering. Non-theologically oriented people were speaking about their lives and using humanistic or transpersonal words to express their searches for meanings and ultimates. Although their definitions were sometimes as elusive as the theologians', a pre-dawn light seemed to appear.

Now, in the light of early day, it has become clear that many people are yearning to explore the spiritual dimensions of life and to find words and concepts to discuss their experience and understandings. *Passion for Life* is our attempt to provide such a theory as well as a language that can be used to discuss it.

THE DEVELOPMENT OF THE THEORY ————————————

The process of identifying and verifying this theory of the human spirit and its seven universal urges has taken over twenty years of careful study, research, and observation. Over the years, we have taught and tested this theory of the human spirit in workshops, seminars, and lectures in many parts of the world and to people with different professional interests and diverse cultural backgrounds.

To augment our knowledge while writing this book, and as another way to check on the universality of the theory, we scoured the libraries of theological seminaries, Stanford University, and the University of California. Our endnotes show many of the resources we consulted and the ideas we found most relevant to this subject.

Although the works of many writers have contributed to our conclusions, three writers have been highly significant in the development of our ideas: Martin Buber, Viktor Frankl, and Eric Berne. Some of their basic principles are interwoven into our theories.

The writings of Martin Buber have, for many years, given us a philosophical foundation for understanding the potentials of dialogic relations and the spheres of existence in which we may encounter the Eternal Thou. Although we did not know him, his concepts touched us to the core.

Viktor Frankl's theory of logotherapy has also been important to us with its focus on the search for meaning and the defiant power of the human spirit. We are grateful that in the 1960s Frankl was a guest speaker for a series of lectures sponsored by our institute in the San Francisco Bay Area; in return, we presented our theory of the interaction of logotherapy and transactional analysis at his institute in Vienna.

The psychological theory of transactional analysis developed by Eric Berne has also provided an important foundation to our understanding of personality. Both of us studied with Berne, knew him well for many years, and have included elements of his theory in many of our writings. In *Passion for Life*, we use transactional analysis yet move beyond it—to explore the powers of the human spirit that come from within the inner core of the spiritual self.

The preliminary concept of the human spirit was first published in 1973 and was subsequently refined in several other publications.[1] *Passion for Life* represents an expansion and further development of these initial ideas.

A PERSONAL NOTE

In case you want to get further acquainted with us, we want to share a few words about what it is like for us to work together as a mother-and-son team. In this society where family ties are often broken or frayed, some people question the dynamics of relatives who work together. Yet for us, it has been a blessing.

For many years we have wanted to complete the research and write this book. We are delighted with the result. Several elements in our lives were conducive to the process of writing this book together. In the first place we live about two miles apart, in a small suburb outside of San Francisco, and thus we could meet, discuss, argue, and write with some regularity and convenience.

We also had some common university experiences. Both of us earned degrees from the University of California and master's degrees from different theological seminaries in Berkeley. I, John, followed the traditional pattern of going to the university after graduating from high school. I, Muriel, did not begin my higher education until I was in my thirties, after fifteen years of working and raising children. However, in the process, we both studied with a few of the same professors and this gave us a common foundation for understanding and arguing through some important points presented in this book.

Sometimes we have worked on joint projects. For example, for several years we co-directed the Oasis Center, an education and counseling center for adults, a day-treatment center and residential group home for adolescents, and a professional training institute for professionals in many fields. Currently we are directors of the James Institute, an education, psychotherapy, and professional training center in Lafayette, California. In the summer, we often co-lead week-long intensive workshops. Between our joint projects, we go our separate ways as speakers, trainers, psychotherapists, and consultants.

In the process of writing this book together, we have confronted each other with every idea that is included. We have talked and debated about how each idea is true, or partly true, and how we sometimes interpret things differently because of differences in our age, sex, education, interests, or experience.

Therefore, what we present in this book is not just theory—it also reflects what we have learned in asking each other the questions we now pose to you. Sitting across the kitchen table, day after day, we have not let each other off the hook. We have not agreed with each other out of expediency. We have chosen to question each other directly, and in the process, have learned more about the urges of the human spirit and the passion for life.

We know, of course, that our knowledge and understanding—as well as yours—will continue to grow. This book is only one very small step in an ongoing process over the centuries to understand the power of the human spirit.

JOHN JAMES AND MURIEL JAMES
Lafayette, California

1

A PATH WITH HEART

TO BE HUMAN IS TO KEEP RATTLING THE BARS OF THE CAGE OF
EXISTENCE HOLLERING, "WHAT'S IT FOR?"

—ROBERT FULGHUM[1]

❦

A UNIVERSAL HUNGER

Have you ever experienced a transcendent moment when everything seemed so magnificent you wondered how you could make
it last? Or how you could re-create it? Or have you ever wondered
after a long day at work if your efforts really mattered and asked
yourself, "What's the point of it all?" Perhaps you have been in a
relationship in which you felt discouraged and wondered to yourself, "Is this all there is?"

A universal hunger pervades the world. It is the hunger to
get more out of life, to give more back, to be more involved, and
to find more meaning. This is the hunger of the soul searching for
"something more."

Everyone is searching for something more. Some search for
feelings of personal significance, trying to find ways to feel unique
or important in who we are and in what we do. Others look for a
"place in the sun" where they feel they belong and are secure. Still
others yearn for a close relationship with someone or more freedom
within a relationship. Some long for good health and more vitality,
for the chance to learn something new, to be creative, or to have

more fun, because these experiences would bring more meaning to life.

Sometimes the yearning for something more motivates us to look beyond our daily routines, to break out of stagnant, going-nowhere situations. At other times it is disconcerting and distracting because it highlights what is missing in our lives. Yet in spite of this discomfort, the yearning remains and may begin to feel like what is called a spiritual hunger.

The word *spiritual* means different things to different people. For some, it means to be concerned with religious questions or aspirations or a sense of union with God. For others, it refers to some special aspect of life not normally experienced in the everyday. In German there are two words that highlight these different meanings: *Geistlich* refers to spiritual matters that reflect a religious orientation; *geistig* refers to spiritual matters without a religious orientation. We are using *spiritual* to refer to *the essential or central nature of life—to matters of ultimate concern*—which to some people have a religious dimension and to other people do not.

Regardless of the orientation, when we are aware of spiritual hunger, we become more attentive to what is ultimately important and focus on essentials more than superficialities, on the basic nature of life rather than the surface reflections. We listen to our deeper yearnings rather than allow ourselves to become easily distracted by the tasks or events of the day.

Spiritual hunger can be intense, like physical hunger: you feel as though you're starving and search for ways to be filled. A sixteenth-century mystic called this "the dark night of the soul." Or spiritual hunger can be a mild, nagging discomfort that arises when life seems to be going fairly well yet, for some reason, you feel dissatisfied and want more.

Because we want to avoid discomfort, we often ignore or deny our spiritual hunger. Some deny it because they do not want to believe in anything spiritual because they associate the word with ignorance or with religious practices in which they don't believe. You may recognize the hunger but ignore it because other things seem more pressing. However, the body often expresses what the mind refuses to recognize. Poor health, boredom, loss of energy, a continuing sense of loneliness, and deep depression can be symptoms of spiritual hungers that have been denied or ignored.

In today's fast-lane, high-tech world conditions are continually changing, uncertainty and chaos abound, values are frequently questioned, and life sometimes seems absurd. Relationships are often fragile, economic pressures continuous, and the desire to get ahead so demanding that life easily gets out of balance or becomes ossified. When it does, we know, at a deep level, the hunger for more meaning. Look around. Everywhere you'll see people who are spiritually hungry. It is as though they were waiting for the sunrise, waiting for a new day when basic human yearnings can be fulfilled.

THE SEARCH BEGINS

The yearning for ultimate significance, for more challenging activities and deeper relationships, motivates us to begin a spiritual search. *A spiritual search is one in which we passionately reach for goals that have personal meaning and enhance life.*

Many spiritual searches begin with a yearning to understand God or some higher power, or to come in contact with deep inner resources. All kinds of people have gone on these kinds of spiritual searches. Aborigines of Australia have gone on "walkabouts"; North American Indians have gone on vision quests. People of many cultures have gone on pilgrimages or retreats, and they still do.

Any kind of personal crisis that disrupts life like an explosion and jolts us into awareness can be a catalyst for a spiritual search. An accident or a serious illness can do it. Being drafted into the military just out of high school, being raped, becoming pregnant at an early age, or losing an important relationship, which leave us feeling unwanted, bereft, or at loose ends, frequently have this effect. When we feel as if we are drowning in grief or pain and trying desperately to keep our heads above water, we may cry out, "Why is this happening to me?" This cry can signal a search for deeper meaning.

A spiritual search can start with positive experiences. The awe we feel when viewing the natural grandeur of Mount Kilimanjaro, Mount Fuji, Mount Everest, or the Matterhorn can do this. Sometimes our search starts when we are awestruck by what people have created. The Parthenon, the Sistine Chapel, the ancient ruins of Machu Pichu—through them we get in touch with the beauty, mystery, and meaning of the past and begin to look for more.

When we travel to Tikal and see the altars in front of each Mayan temple or stand in front of the Wailing Wall in Jerusalem or observe the faithful bathing in the Ganges River of India or the pilgrims walking to Mecca, or hear the devout praying in the Vatican, we may be inspired to begin our own quest.

The search may also start when we see something wondrous, such as the birth of a baby, or it may begin with a new awareness of our potential and gifts that we can develop and give to others. However it starts, each spiritual quest is unique regardless of where it leads.

A PATH WITH HEART

The challenge of a spiritual search is to find and follow a path with heart. Each of us goes down many paths in the journey through life. There is the path we travel as we grow up, including the joys and challenges of family, friends, and school. There is the path we take as we move from being dependent on others to becoming more reliant on ourselves. There are paths we walk holding hands with those we love and the career path we plod wearily or with excitement.

Each path has a course or direction; each challenges us to clarify our values and discover where our preferences lie. Along the way, we often encounter problems that invite us, or force us, to make unexpected changes. We head off in directions we never anticipated and do things we never imagined. Sometimes we realize that we have taken a path going nowhere.

There are many paths in life we can take, many ways we can live. Anthropologist Carlos Castaneda has advice for when we stand at the crossroads making our choices: "Look at every path closely and deliberately, then ask ourselves a crucial question: 'Does this path have a heart?' If it does, the path is good; if it doesn't, it is of no use."[2]

A path with heart is a course of action that calls us to respond with passion—to act on the basis of a positive emotional and intellectual commitment to someone or something. It calls us to devote positive energy and enthusiasm to an activity or a cause that has personal meaning.

A path with heart calls us to expand our horizons. It invites us to move beyond our self-centered activities and act in more ethical, loving, and compassionate ways. A path with heart brings out the best in us. It calls us to be more than we are and to do more than we have done. A path with heart is one that encourages us to evolve, to use ourselves to the utmost and not be content with just coasting through life.

To be on a path with heart may mean to stand by a personal commitment to someone, even when it requires time and energy and brings little in return. Or it may mean standing up for what we believe is ethical and right, even in the face of criticism or inconvenience. It can also mean enjoying life instead of seeing only the serious side. The path may lead to work in the healing professions, to create beauty that nurtures the soul, to design ways to decrease some of the drudgery in life, to protect the environment, or to stand up for human rights.

These kinds of paths are directed toward humanistic goals and may or may not be related to religious beliefs. However, because the desire to take them comes from the core of the human spirit, traveling these paths can be part of a spiritual search. This was true for zoologist Jane Goodall, whose long and intense search began in childhood with a deep interest in animals. This interest grew into a passion to understand chimpanzees by studying them in their natural habitat. In getting to know them, she discovered they communicated in complex ways, had social structures and hunting habits, could use tools, and, like people, had unique personalities. Her almost thirty-year search on a path with heart now leads her to try to protect the chimpanzees' living routines from being disturbed by the many tour groups that come to Gombe National Park in Tanzania.[3]

For some people, a path with heart leads to a focused search for God. In fact, most major religions are based on the life and insights of someone who went on this kind of spiritual search, sometimes against the common religious beliefs of the time. Moses, Buddha, Jesus, and Muhammad were four of the most significant.

Tradition tells how Moses, on his path with heart in about 1260 B.C., led the ancient Hebrews out of slavery in Egypt into the Sinai Peninsula wilderness. There, in their new freedom, they learned how to become a self-determined people.

Siddhartha Gautama, later called Buddha, chose a path away from the security of family and material possessions to search for something more. His travels and meditation led to the enlightenment that comes from seeing the world as it is, not as one wishes it to be.

There are many stories in the life of Jesus that relate to his efforts to stay on a path with heart. From as early as age twelve, he went to the temple in Jerusalem to talk with the wise teachers. In his time in the wilderness he struggled with temptation and reaffirmed his mission of teaching love.

Like the other great religious leaders who preceded him, Muhammad was critical of the religious practices of his day. He searched for Allah (God) in the solitude of a mountain cave until he had a vision in which he heard the archangel Gabriel proclaim him to be a prophet. This vision and subsequent revelations became the foundation of the Qur'an, the holy book of Islam.

Religious leaders such as these are very rare, but each of us, like Moses, confronts a crossing of the Red Sea in our journey from slavery into freedom. Each of us, like Buddha, yearns for something more and needs to take time to reflect on what that "more" is. Like Muhammad, we each hope for a clear vision that will lead to a strong sense of mission and purpose in life. And, like Jesus, we also struggle to understand the nature of love so that we can share it with others.

For many people, a path with heart involves an integration of their religious beliefs into their lives and work. This is the goal of Charles Schulz, the creator of the worldwide popular comic strip "Peanuts." Schulz finds ways to reflect the human condition in cartoons of a dog and a group of four- or five-year-old children.

Snoopy, the beagle, always dreams of fame, as do many of us; Lucy represents a universal, defiant spirit who angrily wants to control others and believes that she alone is right. Charlie Brown is that part of us that is innocent about life yet suffers from loneliness, feels inadequate, and is sometimes ridiculed. In addition, each of us from time to time may worry or feel insecure like Charlie Brown while on our search for something more. And like Linus, who clutches his security blanket and addictively sucks his thumb, we may hang on to what we imagine is secure while we search for something more. This message comes through clearly in one cartoon of Linus on his knees praying, with the caption: "Security is knowing you are not alone."[4]

Whether or not we have faith in God or some higher power, security can come from knowing we are not alone in our spiritual search. We are *all* searching for something more, all seeking to find a direction we feel called or positively compelled to take.

HEARING THE CALL

A path with heart is one that we feel called to take. The sense of being called can come from the quiet, inner voice of our own yearnings, or from a loud, insistent one that challenges us from a newscast or a pulpit; from the curses of the downtrodden, or the wailing of a child. Frank Borman, after his flight to the moon on *Apollo 8*, was moved by a call from earth:

> WHEN YOU'RE FINALLY UP ON THE MOON, LOOKING BACK AT THE EARTH, ALL THESE DIFFERENCES AND NATIONALISTIC TRAITS ARE PRETTY WELL GOING TO BLEND AND YOU'RE GOING TO GET A CONCEPT THAT MAYBE THIS IS REALLY ONE WORLD AND WHY THE HELL CAN'T WE LEARN TO LIVE TOGETHER LIKE DECENT PEOPLE?[5]

The search for ways "to live together like decent people" is one call we need to hear. It may include cleaning up the poverty of inner-city ghettos, cleaning up corruption in government agencies, or cleaning out the drugs in our schools. The call may be to clean up our own personal lives. We might need to learn more about our inner conflicts and confusions, to give up our addictive behaviors, to resolve problems with loved ones and build new ways of relating. Or the call may be to take care of ourselves physically.

We may be called to break free and develop our potential strengths, to move into the excitement of learning, the challenge of creativity, or the joy of authentic relationships. We may be called to create something of beauty, such as a garden that nourishes the spirit, or something that is useful, such as a house that provides comfort and safety. We may be called to heal the sick or to share joy with those we love.

We may even hear more desperate calls and seek ways to respond to natural catastrophes, worldwide hunger, exploitive po-

Many paths to take

Some destinations are unknown

*Some paths
are comfortable*

*Some paths
are uncharted*

Ways to a path with heart

KOZO RAKKAKU

*Some paths expand
our horizons*

DIANE M. REED

*Some paths
have special meaning*

MURIEL JAMES

*Some paths lead
to a search for God*

litical or economic conditions, terrorism, or war. Perhaps we will be beckoned to save some form of endangered species by hearing the call of the Peregrine falcon, the African elephant, or the Blue whale. Or we may feel called to save the planet—its waters, deserts, and rain forests—from further pollution and destruction.

Without exception, every cosmonaut and astronaut has come back from space dedicated to protecting our colorful, shimmering earth. Cosmonaut Yuri Artyukhin expressed it:

> IT ISN'T IMPORTANT IN WHICH SEA OR LAKE YOU OBSERVE A SLICK OF POLLUTION, OR IN THE FORESTS OF WHICH COUNTRY A FIRE BREAKS OUT, OR ON WHICH CONTINENT A HURRICANE ARISES. YOU ARE STANDING GUARD OVER THE WHOLE OF EARTH.[6]

To stand guard over the whole earth is a spiritual journey that requires us to solve seemingly insurmountable problems. We can only do this by taking a path with heart.

❧ RECOGNIZING A PATH WITH HEART

Some people like to explore on their own. Others like to know where they're headed. The following are optional exercises that are designed to help you apply the ideas in this chapter in a more personal way.

❧ START WITH CONTEMPLATION. Contemplation involves sitting quietly and focusing on a particular subject. Read each of the following quotes, then reflect on what each could mean to you personally, or what questions each raises in your mind.

> NEVER MEASURE THE HEIGHT OF A MOUNTAIN, UNTIL YOU HAVE REACHED THE TOP. THEN YOU WILL SEE HOW LOW IT WAS.
> —DAG HAMMARSKJOLD[7]

> IT IS NOT ENOUGH FOR ME TO ASK QUESTIONS; I WANT TO KNOW HOW TO ANSWER THE ONE QUESTION THAT SEEMS TO ENCOMPASS EVERYTHING I FACE: WHAT AM I HERE FOR?
> —ABRAHAM HESCHEL[8]

GOD SAYS TO MAN, AS HE SAID TO MOSES: "PUT OFF THY SHOES
FROM THY FEET"—PUT OFF THE HABITUAL WHICH ENCLOSES YOUR
FOOT, AND YOU WILL KNOW THE PLACE ON WHICH YOU ARE NOW
STANDING IS HOLY GROUND.

—MARTIN BUBER[9]

THE SENSE OF PARALYSIS PROCEEDS NOT SO MUCH OUT OF THE
MAMMOTH SIZE OF THE PROBLEM BUT OUT OF THE PUNINESS OF
THE PURPOSE.

—NORMAN COUSINS[10]

THE MINUTE A PERSON WHOSE WORD MEANS A GREAT DEAL TO
OTHERS DARE TO TAKE THE OPEN-HEARTED AND COURAGEOUS WAY,
MANY OTHERS FOLLOW.

—MARIAN ANDERSON[11]

❦ WANTING MORE. The yearning for something more is universal, and yet what we want often differs from person to person. What do you want more of?

Does it reveal a passion for life or merely a desire for greater comfort or convenience?

❦ A PATH WITH HEART. Think of times in the past when you felt as if you were on a path with heart. What were you doing? What made the experience so important for you?

Are you currently on a path with heart? If so, is it in one that has to do with your relationships with others, your career, some form of social action, or your own physical, intellectual, emotional, or spiritual development?

Are you feeling called to do something new with your life lately? Or are you feeling a sense that there is something important you want to do? If so, what is it, and what are you waiting for?

❦ GOING ON A SPIRITUAL SEARCH. Are you currently involved in some kind of spiritual search? If so, does it have a religious or nonreligious orientation? What is it and what are you searching for? Do you feel passionately involved in it?

❦ ANSWERABLE AND UNANSWERABLE QUESTIONS. List below some of the questions you have about your spiritual search. Then mark the questions that are of highest priority to you. As you continue through the book, you may want to turn back to these questions occasionally and see if you are finding some answers.

2

BEHOLD! THE HUMAN SPIRIT

THE ONES WHO COUNT ARE THOSE PERSONS WHO—THOUGH THEY
MAY BE OF LITTLE RENOWN—RESPOND TO AND ARE RESPONSIBLE
FOR THE CONTINUATION OF THE LIVING SPIRIT.
                                                        —MARTIN BUBER[1]

MIGHTIER THAN THE SWORD

One thing we all have in common is the power to control a large
part of our lives. Napoleon meant this when he said, "the sword
and the spirit are the two mightiest forces in the world, yet the
spirit is the mightiest of the two."[2] What is this spirit that is so
powerful?

The word *spirit* is used in many ways to refer to an animating
principle of life. People with high energy are often called spirited,
so are dogs and horses. In business and sports the word is used
for a group attitude, a "team spirit." In courts "the letter of the
law" is sometimes contrasted to "the spirit of the law." When a
heated discussion is being held, it is "a spirited debate." Charles
Lindbergh flew his monoplane, the *Spirit of St. Louis* across the
Atlantic in 1927. His was an adventurous spirit that is typical of
many people who forge new paths.

In another sense, the spirit of the times is one of the most
powerful forces controlling the destiny of a people. For example,
the spirit of 1776 symbolized a revolutionary period in the United
States when the desire for political freedom was high and the spirit

of the people was mobilized to achieve it, just as the spirit of *perestroika* led to dramatic changes in the Soviet Union in 1989.

An individual's spirit, as well as the spirit of a people, is an amazing power to behold.

This chapter focuses on the human spirit—how to recognize it, and how it is linked to our personalities and to other sources of power. Although we can lose touch with the spiritual part of ourselves, its defiant power can break through in wonderful and awesome ways.

THE HUMAN SPIRIT

The human spirit is the vital animating force in a person that can move a person beyond the normal confines of life to a sense of wholeness and holiness. As a vital force, it is alive within each of us; as an animating force, it moves us to action.

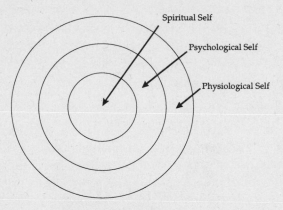

THE INTERACTIVE SELVES

The human spirit expresses the energies that come from the spiritual self. This is the deepest self; it is the innermost core of being. It acts through our bodies and personalities—and sometimes in spite of them. Just as each of us has a physical self and a psychological self, so each of us has a spiritual self. These three selves are not separate: the physical, psychological, and spiritual selves are interactive and parts of the whole.

Whether or not we are conscious of the spiritual self, and whether or not we are open to its power, the spiritual self is at the center of our being. It is a permanent reality that underlies all of human existence and is part of the natural inheritance with which we are born.

This spiritual self is *universal* because it is common to all. Yet, it is also *personal* as each of us expresses it in our unique way. Each of our bodies differs in everything from our DNA structure to our physical appearance; each of our personalities is also unique; so too each of us expresses the spiritual self differently.

Some people believe that the existence of the human spirit is a matter of conjecture, others that it is a matter of faith. Still others are convinced that the human spirit, or spiritual self, is very real, in spite of its being a nonphysical reality. To us, the human spirit, sometimes called the "soul," can be experienced, understood, and expressed.

Like gravity, the spiritual self cannot be seen or touched, but it can be known. We know gravity exists for all people and exerts its influence at all times—we count on gravity to keep our world in order and our feet on the ground—yet most of us can't explain exactly what it is or how it works. So, too, the spiritual self at the core of our being influences us at all times. The ways we express our inner spirit reflect the powers of the spiritual self and are the focus of this book.

PSYCHOLOGISTS AND THE SPIRITUAL SELF

Many people in the Western world consider the concept of the spiritual part of a person to be archaic, "not scientific." The concepts of the soul and spirit are usually ignored in most psychological and medical training programs. Generally speaking, physicians have been expected to deal with the body, psychologists with the mind, and the clergy with the soul or spirit.

Historically, these "specialists" have often been critical of each other. Those concerned with minds have often denied the importance of bodies, and those concerned primarily with body or mind have often rejected the concept of the human spirit and spirituality. Sigmund Freud, for example, claimed that what was called "spirituality" was actually repressed sexuality.[3]

There are, however, some notable exceptions to this attitude found in the writings of several fathers of modern psychology. Carl Jung wrote, "Like every other being, I am a splinter of the infinite deity."[4] Alfred Adler believed that the soul is a psychic organ and that a person is a unity struggling for wholeness.[5] Wholeness, according to Viktor Frankl, comes when the somatic, psychic, and spiritual are integrated. Human existence, to Frankl, is spiritual existence.[6] And, according to Gordon Allport, "A mature personality always has some unifying philosophy of life, although not necessarily religious in type, nor articulated in words, nor entirely complete."[7]

Each of these theorists believed in a spiritual dimension of life, yet none of them took the next step and developed a theory of the human spirit and how its powers can be experienced and expressed. In this book, we take that step. We set forth a new theory related to psychology that moves beyond it to a more basic understanding of the inner core of the self.

Whereas most psychological theories are based on models that focus on people's blocks, impasses, or shortcomings, the theory of the spiritual self is based on the assumption that the basic inner urges that people have are positive motivating forces. These spiritual urges are all essentially healthy. They ebb and flow from time to time and depend upon the person's priorities, yet when these urges are released, life becomes more meaningful and vital.

This theory of the human spirit deals with the deeper aspects of human motivation, including our potential for creativity, self-determined ethics, and other goals that give life meaning. In the past, many psychologists have been rather at a loss to know how to deal with people's spiritual or religious concerns. And people with religious or spiritual backgrounds have often been unable to understand what psychology has to do with spiritual concerns.

This theory bridges that gap and serves to unravel some of the mysteries in each realm. It provides those interested in psychology a way to understand the spiritual dimensions of life and provides people who have religious or spiritual orientations a way to understand the wonders of the human spirit interacting with the innumerable wonders of the world and life.

THE NATURE OF PERSONALITY

One theory of psychology that can help us to understand the nature of personality is Transactional Analysis, often abbreviated as T.A. It was developed by psychiatrist Eric Berne who, like most psychologists, focused on the power of the personality but not other sources of power. We have expanded this theory.

In basic T.A. theory, the personality is thought to consist of three ego states, colloquially called the Child, the Adult, and the Parent. Each ego state has a consistent pattern of feelings, thoughts, and beliefs that correspond to a consistent pattern of behavior.[8] The theory uses a diagram of three stacked circles to illustrate the structure of the personality. The bottom circle is called "the Child" and represents the unique inner child within each person. The middle circle represents the thinking, analytical part of the personality called "the Adult." The top circle represents the attitudes and behaviors of parent and other authority figures that each person incorporates into his or her personality at a very early age. This is called "the Parent."

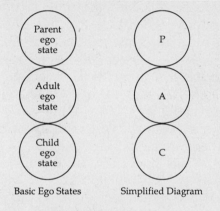

Basic Ego States   Simplified Diagram

PERSONALITY STRUCTURE

Everyone has a Child ego state that reflects genetic inheritances and all the natural impulses of infants. Every child is born with a spiritual experience of the mystery of life. Watching a baby, we can see its little body and face in moments of deep peace. We can see the baby's awe and wonder when it begins to look around to see light and shadows, sky and birds, and smiles of those who care. This look of awe is a reflection of the spiritual self that, in each of us, is in the Child ego state.

The inner Child naturally wants what it wants when it wants it, and that is usually right away. In healthy families, children learn how to postpone immediate gratification for longer range benefits. They learn how to be polite and thoughtful of others, how to cooperate and share, how to learn and work, and how to compete and succeed. In other words, they adapt to their environments.

Many adaptations are very useful as they enable us to survive and live in society with some measure of acceptance. Other adaptations are not useful, as when children overadapt to parental authority and continually say "yes" when they want to say "no." The power of the human spirit can be stifled by overadapting.

One common early childhood adaptation is related to the religious beliefs within a particular family or culture. From an early age, many children are taught that the spiritual path is to participate in religious rites, seeking God through worship or prayer. Others are taught that the whole universe is integrated and holy, and that religious rites are not as important as respecting the whole earth. Still others are programmed to ignore or reject anything with a spiritual connotation.

When we are in the Child ego state, we think, feel, and act as we did when we were children. We experienced liveliness and enthusiasm, sadness and withdrawal, anger and rebellion, compliance and politeness. Some frequent Child expressions include "I wish," "I want," and "I won't." The Child part of our personality allows us to be emotional, spontaneous, and outgoing—to touch and feel and experience people and things.

This inner Child has great value when used appropriately to express feelings of affection and sexuality, curiosity and creativity, delight and charm, self-protection and joy. It is natural for this Child to try to pretend to be strong while looking to a higher power for love and protection, and to offer up the trusting prayers of childhood.

Probably, it is the Child in us that experiences the transcendent moments that sometimes occur during worship or other religious rituals or in extraordinary experiences that lead to an oceanic sense of oneness.

However, as adolescents or adults, we may question our childhood beliefs and reject them or try to understand them in new ways. To do this, we may use the Adult ego state, the part of the personality that is oriented to current reality and to the objective gathering and organizing of information. It estimates probabilities. The Adult often asks, Who? What? Why? Where? When? and How much?—not as a parent might in order to be judgmental, nor as a child might to be self-serving, but to help clarify things and get accurate information with which to make decisions.

With the Adult, we can make objective, meaningful decisions related to the "here and now" instead of based on preconceived notions stemming from Child feelings and adaptations or from Parent traditions and prejudices.

Being grown up is not the same as being in the Adult ego state. Many grown-ups act like children or like parental dictators, and even little children possess an Adult ego state. When we are in the Adult ego state, we are observing, computing, analyzing, and making decisions based on facts, not fancy. The Adult is unique in each person because everyone has different information and experiences.

The Adult does not always make accurate decisions, because it may not have enough facts to do so. Yet when using the Adult ego state, we work as objectively as possible with the facts we do have.

The search to understand how and why things work as they do especially interests the Adult in us. We can use it to study the deeper meanings behind sacred teachings. Furthermore, when we have religious insights or other kinds of transcendent experiences, we may use the Adult to try to figure them out. The development of an ethical position, recognizing the dignity of all people, also comes from this part of the personality. The ethical Adult will seek ways to solve the problems of mankind and will try to unravel the mysteries of the spiritual dimension of life.

The Parent ego state contains the specific attitudes and behaviors incorporated from external authorities, especially one's parents. However, any significant parent figure experienced in childhood can be incorporated into the Parent ego state, including grandparents, older siblings or other relatives, even housekeepers, neighbors, and teachers.

Inwardly the Parent ego state is heard by the inner Child like tape-recorded messages that are replayed. They contain the "shoulds" and "shouldn'ts," encouragements and expectations, guidance and rules about feelings, thoughts, and behavior that were modeled for us by our parenting figures. Family, cultural, and religious traditions are also passed down generation to generation through the Parent ego state. Many parents teach their children religious traditions that have been used for centuries.

Naturally, some Parent tapes may conflict with others. In preparing for an important meeting, a person may hear an internal Parent tape that says, "Speak up," and another that argues, "Don't talk back." Or if one parent in a family is Catholic and the other is Jewish, their children may have conflicting messages about religion. Many of our inner conflicts reflect contrary ways of thinking and behaving that we witnessed in our parenting figures.

Parents may encourage expression of our deeper yearnings or may be critical of them. An internal Parent might say something like, "Follow your heart and do what you believe in," or it might say, "Don't be stupid and waste your time like that." What we say to ourselves has an enormous impact on how we feel inwardly and what we do outwardly.

Outwardly the Parent is expressed toward others in critical and controlling behaviors or nurturing and encouraging acts that are similar to those we perceived our parent figures using when we were young. When in the Parent ego state, we are likely to voice opinions like those we heard our parent figures use, such as "Children should be seen and not heard." We might give the same encouraging advice to others that our parents gave us, "Don't worry, it's going to be all right." Or we may be critical of those with different cultural values and traditions, saying, "You can't trust the kinds of people who came from that background."

For better or worse, strong Parent personalities are legion in organizations in which doctrines and dogmas are important. People who are not open to other people's ideas operate primarily from the Parent ego state and often treat others as if they were children. They may act like authorities who believe they have all the answers for dealing with other people's problems, or they may act self-righteously opinionated and be disinterested in what others feel, think, or believe.

People with positive Parent qualities are especially noticeable in organizations such as hospitals. They care about others and give useful support and guidance, sometimes using skills learned from their own parents. They may be deeply committed to putting their faith into action and in helping others find ways to make the most of their spiritual journeys. Managers, teachers, counselors, and others who are willing to stand up for what they believe and do so in constructive ways often demonstrate positive attributes learned from parent figures.

At any time, one part of the personality may be more active than other parts. When the Parent ego state is energized, an urge to help others may seek expression. When the Adult ego state is energized, an urge to understand and be self-determining is likely to be high. When the Child ego state is energized, an urge to enjoy, to be free, and to transcend everyday routine may be most active.

Well-balanced personalities have three essential qualities that make them effective. They display caring and justice (Parent qualities), they are open to fun and humor (Child qualities), and they strive for understanding and competence (Adult qualities). They display personal attractiveness and responsiveness, an ethical responsibility, and the ability to enjoy life. Healthy people blend all three ego states into harmonious and unique formulas so they are not overly emotional, not too judgmental and pushy, and not exclusively serious and computerlike.

THE INNER CORE

All ego states can be transformed when the spiritual self is expressed through them. When Transactional Analysis was first being developed, the diagram of three stacked circles was enclosed in an oval. The oval represented the body; the three stacked circles the personality. A major addition to this theory was made in 1973 when the concept of an inner column was added to represent the human spirit at the inner core of the self.[9]

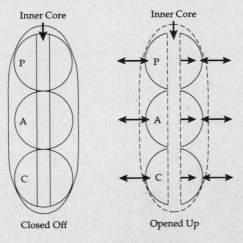

EGO STATES AND THE INNER CORE

The inner core houses the spiritual self and is expressed in positive and hopeful ways. Ideally, all three ego states as well as our physical bodies can be open to the spiritual self, the positive power at the core of the human spirit. When the Parent is open to the inner core, we express positive caring and nurturing qualities found in the best of parents. When the Adult is open to the powers of the inner core, we make decisions based on facts, which also take into account other people's feelings and well-being and protect the environment rather than exploit it. And when the Child is open to the energies of the inner core, we express ourselves with the attractive childlike qualities of affection, warmth, and curiosity. Playfulness and loving feelings enliven and strengthen our relationships.

When you are in touch with your spiritual self, the power that comes from the inner core can transform your personality. Someone who wishes to be dead may suddenly find the power to fight for life, one who feels trapped and inadequate may suddenly find the power to break free from negative circumstances and self-images.

The physical body can also be transformed by the power from within. The commitment to stop smoking or to give up alcohol or drug abuse often requires a spiritual awakening. When the power from the inner core is blocked, we feel impotent and unable to control our lives. When it is open, we can experience a spiritual dimension in all of existence.

COSMIC AND HOLY SOURCES OF POWER

The spiritual dimension of life is also associated with two other sources of power: the cosmic spirit and the holy spirit. *The cosmic spirit is the creative force that is revealed in the order of the universe and underlying unity of all things.* This cosmic order is often referred to by scientists who study physics, astronomy, biology, and other forms of science. Albert Einstein, for example, was awed by the laws of nature, which, he said, "know no dogma or God conceived in man's image," but, rather, reflect "the cosmic religious feeling" and "reveal an intelligence of such superiority that, compared with it, all the systematic thinking and acting of human beings is an utterly insignificant reflection."[10]

Until very recently, cosmic laws of nature were thought to be eternal and unchangeable. This deterministic Newtonian way of thinking left no room for changes caused by human will and purpose. In 1920, however, the concept of new physics or quantum mechanics that began to change the way physicists and others thought about the cosmos was developed. No longer was the cosmos 100 percent predictable. Scientists had discovered that subatomic processes occur at random and that these processes can also be affected by human intervention.[11] For example, the way we are damaging the ozone layer, which protects the earth, or cutting the forests that replenish the air, shows how human intervention can change the earth we live on and thus affect the spirit of the cosmos.

Instead of an objective scientific approach, most of us experience the cosmic spirit more subjectively through personal experiences with nature and life. We can feel caught up in awe when observing the order and oneness of the universe. The sheen of light on a lake, the glint of sunset through a forest, the moon tipping dreams from its crescent are but a few of the wonders of the cosmic spirit. According to theologian Paul Tillich:

> THROUGH STARS AND STONES, TREES AND ANIMALS, GROWTH AND CATASTROPHE; THROUGH TOOLS AND HOUSES, SCULPTURE AND MELODY, POEMS AND PROSE, LAWS AND CUSTOMS; THROUGH PARTS OF THE BODY AND FUNCTIONS OF THE MIND, FAMILY RELATIONS AND VOLUNTARY COMMUNITIES, HISTORICAL LEADERS AND NATIONAL BEING, IDEALS AND VIRTUES, THE HOLY CAN ENCOUNTER US.[12]

Many naturalists and nature lovers have written about this order and sense of oneness. John Muir, for example, an early crusader for the establishment of Yosemite Valley as a national park, put it succinctly: "When we try to pick out anything by itself, we find it hitched to everything else in the universe."[13]

This unity of all life is a basic belief in many cultural traditions. In Navajo Indian tradition, for example, "the world is thick with deity. Every natural force, every geographical feature, every plant, animal or meteorological phenomenon has its particular supernatural power."[14] Traditional Navajo people strive to live in harmony with every element of nature. They treat the Mother Earth sparingly, disturbing it as little as possible. They respect the animals and plants, not killing or using more than they need; when they do cut or kill out of necessity, they thank the spirit of the plant or animal for helping sustain their people.

The Navajo culture is an example of how the universe is revered and both cosmic and natural forces are given spiritual meaning. In most cultures, whether literate or nonliterate, from the earliest to the present, there has always been a strong interest in trying to understand and explain a spiritual presence that underlies existence. Both animate and inanimate objects have been believed to have spirits, and contact with these spirits has been sought through spirit houses, totem poles, kachina dolls, sand paintings, shields, effigies, masks, fetishes, rituals, and prayers.

To some people, nature itself is holy. To other people there is a force greater than nature, which they believe to be a divine power. This power is referred to as spirits, gods, or a God whom they worship. For example, the oldest religion of Japan, Shintoism, is based on a belief in the *kami,* which is the Japanese word for *gods* or *spirits.* A Shinto creation myth tells that the age of the kami began when the cosmos emerged out of chaos, and that now there are as many as eight million eight hundred gods.[15]

An even older tradition is Hinduism, which is also rooted in the belief in many spirits and both male and female deities. Chief among them are Shiva and Vishnu. Vishnu is the benevolent one who incarnates himself in various forms to straighten things out in the world, while Shiva is the creator, preserver, and destroyer of the universe. Another important deity is the goddess Devi or Shakti, called upon for tapping the creative energies within oneself. The people of ancient India were sometimes said to be "intoxicated by God" because they interpreted life from a spiritual perspective instead of from a historical or economic point of view. To them, the ultimate reality was Brahman, the "self" in all life forms.

Like the Hindus, the ancient Greeks and Romans believed there were many gods. There were the great gods who inhabited Mount Olympus, the major deities of the sports arena and state cults, as well as the minor deities of the home. These gods and goddesses were believed to have both human and superhuman traits. They were believed to be able to influence the weather, confuse friends and enemies with trickery, be placated by sacrifice, and transform themselves into animals or people at will.

By the first century B.C., Roman rulers called themselves gods and goddesses and were deified either before or after death.

Julius Caesar was the first Roman to have this dubious honor, followed by Augustus Caesar, his wife, and family.

The concept of there being only one god emerged briefly under the rule of the Egyptian pharaoh, Akhnaton, who identified himself with Ra, the Sun God. Many have speculated that this early form of monotheism influenced Moses, who was said to have been educated in the pharaoh's court in about 1260 B.C. The Old Testament credits Moses with bringing to the ancient Jews the belief in Yahweh as the only God of the Hebrews. The belief in God as a national deity gradually developed into the belief in God as the only god, the creator and ruler of all people. This concept of one God is central to Judaic, Christian, and Islamic tradition.

Furthermore, the concept of God as a source of power is part of the same tradition. In the Old Testament, for example, the prophet Micah defiantly shouted, "I am filled with power, with the Spirit of the Lord."[16] In the New Testament, Paul the Apostle wrote the Corinthians, "Do you know that you are God's temple and that God's Spirit dwells within you?"[17] Traditionally this spirit was thought to inspire charismatic figures such as saints, prophets, teachers, and healers.

According to the Old Testament, the spirit was sent by God in the act of creation to maintain human life. Wisdom, discernment, and prophecy were the three most common expressions of God's spirit at work. The leadership of God's people was also said to be a demonstration of God's spirit.

In the New Testament, Jesus was said to be baptized by God's spirit, guided by God's spirit, and enabled to do his work by God's spirit. This same spirit was thought to show itself in the early Church in the form of glossolalia, or "speaking in tongues." Rituals such as the laying on of hands are still believed to be sacramental signs of the presence of the Holy Spirit and a transference of healing powers or spiritual authority. The Holy Spirit is also experienced by many in moments of worship, prayer, inspiration, and sudden insight.

Most frequently, the phrase *"Holy Spirit" refers to "the spirit of God," which can be present and active in the spiritual lives of people.* Theologian Paul Tillich believed this to be a spiritual presence that surrounds us like the air we breathe and is always present, though not always noticed.[18]

This spirit is called by many names. Some call it God; others

Responding to the spirit

JOHN JAMES

*In touch with
the Cosmic Spirit*

DAVID B. REED

*Reaching for
the Holy Spirit*

JANE SCHERR

*Connecting with
the human spirit*

Behold the human spirit

JANE SCHERR

The defiant power
of the human spirit

DAVID M. ALLEN

The human spirit
released

DAVID M. ALLEN

Spirited at any age

say Tao, Christ, Brahman, Wakan-Tanka, Atman, Buddha, Jehovah, the Great Spirit, or the World-Spirit. Still others use phrases such as a Higher Power, the Ultimate Reality, Life Energy, Cosmic Consciousness, the Creator, the Godhead, the Supreme Self, or the Ground of Being. The richness of names for the spirit led psychiatrist Carl Jung to conclude toward the end of his life that the names we use mean little, for "they are only the changing leaves and blossoms on the stem of the eternal tree."[19]

Whatever words we use, there is an almost universal belief in the cosmic and holy spirits as sources of power. They nurture our lives with hope and strength. As astronaut James Irwin marveled as he returned from space:

THE EARTH REMINDED US OF A CHRISTMAS TREE ORNAMENT HANGING IN THE BLACKNESS OF SPACE. . . . THAT BEAUTIFUL, WARM, LIVING OBJECT LOOKED SO FRAGILE, SO DELICATE, THAT IF YOU TOUCHED IT WITH A FINGER IT WOULD CRUMBLE AND FALL APART. SEEING THIS HAS TO CHANGE A MAN, HAS TO MAKE A MAN APPRECIATE THE CREATION OF GOD AND THE LOVE OF GOD.[20]

OUT OF TOUCH WITH THE SPIRIT

Increasing numbers of people are becoming aware of how they have ignored, denied, or been out of touch with the spiritual part of themselves and other sources of power available to them. They have lost the sense of curiosity and wonder about the spiritual dimension of life. It's almost as if they were standing on the shore of a crystal-clear stream, thirsty yet not knowing how or where to quench their thirst. There are five reasons this happens so often.

First, some people are out of touch with this dimension because they have *never known its power*. They miss out on many possible transcendent moments and do not know what they're missing. Such people often live routine lives, working, watching TV, and not noticing the world outside. They are cloistered, living within narrow confines, often so tied to responsibilities that they do not search for something more. Or they may be active in the world but missing out on real living. Afraid to risk, they walk through life zombielike, following the path of least resistance.

Second, people can feel out of touch with the spirit because at one time they *were involved in a spiritual search but gave it up.* They experienced a passion for life but, for some reason, later came to feel disappointed or alienated from it. Alienation often occurs when something happens that does not conform to our expectations, and we discover we cannot control people or events. Alienation also occurs when once meaningful people, beliefs, or traditions lose their importance or truth.

Third, people also feel out of touch with the spirit because, although they may believe a spiritual part of themselves, they *do not believe spiritual power is available to them personally.* Because of real or imagined guilt, they may believe that they have been abandoned, cast out because of unforgivable sins. Or they may believe that spiritual power is unpredictable and they can't count on it.

Fourth, people can feel out of touch with the spiritual part of themselves because they have *taken a wrong path.* They have gone down a path without heart that has dulled their senses. Abusing food, alcohol, or drugs, discarding friends, living a dishonest life, and avoiding responsible participation in a community are all symptoms that a person's spirit has become dulled and numb. Negative habits and life-styles inhibit the healthy power within.

Fifth, people can feel out of touch with the spirit because they are involved in or surrounded by *dehumanizing conditions.* Being homeless or living in substandard housing, being jobless or working on a job that is degrading or run unethically, feeling locked into a relationship that is overly draining or blocks personal growth—all can distract or deter us from appreciating the wonders and potentials of the human spirit.

Yet as long as we are alive, the spirit is there. As Eric Berne maintained, "If no radio is heard in someone's house, that does not mean he lacks one; he may have a good one, but it needs to be turned on and warmed up before it can be heard clearly."[21] Even when the volume of the spirit is low and we are not paying attention to it, we may still hear inner conversations raising questions about life and what it means to be human. To turn up the volume, we need to call upon defiant power within us.

THE DEFIANT POWER OF THE HUMAN SPIRIT

When people are constrained, intimidated, or abused—whether at home, at work, or on the streets—they often express a spirit of

defiance in fighting for their freedom. They do the same when they
fight against authoritarian structures that do not allow freedom of
speech or other basic human rights. The cry, "I will be free," comes
from the depths of the human spirit.

Viktor Frankl, a Viennese psychiatrist who lived through the
horrors of the Nazi concentration camps of World War II, observed
fellow prisoners in the camps and noticed that some kept fighting
to survive while others gave up. Those who fought to survive had
a defiant spirit that they held on to, even when confronted by the
probability of death.[22] Frankl coined the phrase, "the defiant power
of the human spirit," to describe the tenacious determination that
we can call upon to deal with life's challenges. People fight for
breath when suffocating, fight for food when starving, fight for
health when sick, fight for love when lonely. Defiantly they take a
stand. It is this defiant power of the human spirit that can enable
us to hold fast to a value or a relationship we believe in and take
a stand in the face of adversity.

This defiant power is not merely going against someone or
something. It is not merely resisting, attacking, or stubbornly op-
posing others. The defiant power of the human spirit is expressed
when people take a stand *for* something. When fighting for
causes—whether in the public arena or in private circles, in large
cities or small communities, in corporations or government organizations—people mobilize this defiant power to build strategic
alliances, create power blocks, and rally public support.

Wanting to live, and to live in freedom, is so universal that
it permeates our existence. The human spirit is indeed mightier
than the sword and can break out to enliven and enhance our lives.

MERGING OF THE SPIRITS

Occasionally we experience transcendent moments when there is
a merging of the cosmic, holy, and human spirits. Everything seems
united. These are mystical experiences in which, for the moment,
we forget ourselves and feel at one with all that is. There are no
boundaries, no distinctions of time and space.

Transcendent moments such as these, when everything
seems to be one, can happen at any time, in any place—perhaps
when we stand in awe of the magnificence of ocean waves, the
wind blowing patterns across a wheat field, the first snows of

winter, or the first blossoms of spring—perhaps when gazing over the rim of the Grand Canyon, or when sitting on a park bench watching a flight of birds overhead. At times like these, we may awaken to the sense that we are merging with some form of spirit beyond ourselves, a cosmic spirit.

Similar moments may happen when we sense the majesty of what we, as humans, have created. When listening to Vivaldi's *Four Seasons*, we may suddenly hear the music of the universe. When watching the sun going down behind the Golden Gate Bridge, we may get caught up in the beauty of its design. When catching a whiff of freshly baked bread, we may suddenly appreciate the little things in life that make life worth living. At moments like these the music of a composer, the design of an architect, or the smell from a baker's oven may transport us to another level of existence, and we may thank God for the moment.

A sense of oneness can also happen when we witness the birth of a baby or are touched by gentle hands of love. When a pet welcomes us home, when plants respond to our care, when the sun shines and the birds sing, we may also know the wonders of the cosmos and its holiness.

Transcendent moments may happen when we open our hearts in prayer or meditation. Or they may happen unexpectedly. When we read something that inspires us, such as the biblical eighth Psalm, our spirits may be touched to the core. This is evidently what happened to the psalmist, when, after being awestruck by a starry night, he saw the connection of the cosmic, the holy, and the human spirits and wrote:

> WHEN I LOOK AT THY HEAVENS,
>   THE WORK OF THY FINGERS,
>   THE MOON AND THE STARS WHICH THOU HAST ESTABLISHED;
> WHAT IS MAN THAT THOU ART MINDFUL OF HIM,
>   AND THE SON OF MAN THAT THOU DOST CARE FOR HIM?
> YET THOU HAST MADE HIM LITTLE LESS THAN GOD,
>   AND DOST CROWN HIM WITH GLORY AND HONOR.

Whenever moments such as these occur and we merge with a greater power, we do not forget it easily. The moments remind us of what we value and how we want to live. They remind us to search for similar moments when we can experience the oneness of all and the wonder of the human spirit.

❦ RECOGNIZING YOUR INNER SPIRIT————————————————

Following are some optional exercises to help you get in touch with spiritual dimensions of your life.

❦ START WITH CONTEMPLATION. Take a few minutes to reflect on what each of the following quotes might mean to you.

> CHALLENGING THE MEANING OF LIFE IS THE TRUEST EXPRESSION OF THE STATE OF BEING HUMAN.
>
> VIKTOR FRANKL[23]

> WE CAN SPEAK WITHOUT VOICE TO THE TREES AND THE CLOUDS AND THE WAVES OF THE SEA. WITHOUT WORDS THEY RESPOND THROUGH THE RUSTLING OF LEAVES AND THE MOVING OF CLOUDS AND THE MURMURING OF THE SEA.
>
> PAUL TILLICH[24]

> THE SEA DOES NOT REWARD THOSE WHO ARE TOO ANXIOUS, TOO GREEDY, OR TOO IMPATIENT. ONE SHOULD LIE EMPTY, OPEN, CHOICELESS AS A BEACH——WAITING FOR A GIFT FROM THE SEA.
>
> ANNE LINDBERGH[25]

> I SAID TO THE ALMOND TREE, "FRIEND, SPEAK TO ME OF GOD," AND THE ALMOND TREE BLOSSOMED.
>
> NIKOS KAZANTZAKIS[26]

> DON'T YOU EVER, YOU UP IN THE SKY,
> DON'T YOU EVER GET TIRED
> OF HAVING THE CLOUDS BETWEEN YOU AND US?
>
> ANCIENT NOOTKA INDIAN[27]

IMPART AS MUCH AS YOU CAN OF YOUR SPIRITUAL BEING TO THOSE
WHO ARE ON THE ROAD WITH YOU, AND ACCEPT AS SOMETHING
PRECIOUS WHAT COMES BACK TO YOU FROM THEM.
ALBERT SCHWEITZER[28]

❦ PERSONAL BELIEFS. Many people struggle with various ideas and
concepts of God. Other people are very clear about what they
believe. How about you? How would you fill in the following?
God is:

God is not:
What are your personal beliefs about the cosmic spirit?
The cosmic spirit is:

The cosmic spirit is not:
What do you believe is true about the human spirit?
The human spirit is:

The human spirit is not:

❦ YOUR HUMAN SPIRIT. Now turn your direction toward your own
human spirit. Are you approving of it? Curious? Critical? Indifferent?
Or what? Why is that?

❦ THE COSMIC AND THE HOLY. Experiences with the cosmic spirit,
holy spirit, and human spirit sometimes seem separate, sometimes
merged. Recall moments when you felt caught up in a sense of
awe with the cosmic or holy spirit. What memories come to mind
that led to such transcendent moments?

❦ DEFIANCE IN YOUR LIFE. Defiance can either mean stubborn op-
position, as in being *against* someone or something, or taking a
positive stand *in favor* of someone or something. Defiance can be
wise or foolish. Think of a situation when you used your defiant
power and answer the following questions:
A situation in which I used my defiant power:
How I expressed it:
How the situation turned out:

❦ WHEN YOU WISH UPON A STAR. A custom in many cultures is wishing on a star as it shoots across the night sky. For this exercise, visualize a shooting star, then make a wish. Try it two more times, making two more wishes.

After you have done this, consider how these wishes are related to your spirit. Then try to figure out which ego states seemed to be most involved in each wish.

3

PASSIONS OF THE SOUL

BY THE TASTE OF CLEAR WATER,
FOLLOW THE BROOK TO ITS SOURCE.
—THOMAS MERTON[1]

❦

AN EVER-PRESENT CHALLENGE

Like the urge of plants toward sun and water, there is always an irresistible urge within us for growth. Whether the plants live in lush grasslands of open fields, in dry and barren deserts, or on wild and windy mountain peaks, they always strive to grow.

In a way we are like plants as we too are challenged to grow, regardless of who we are or where we live. Living in lush surroundings, we can be seduced with comfort, or we can give up some of our comforts to rise to the challenge to grow. Living in a dry and arid emotional environment that is like living in a desert, we can either wither or choose to look for nourishment at a deeper level. Living in a violent situation, where storms whirl around our heads, we can be uprooted or we can choose to send down new roots in more hospitable locations.

We are challenged to grow in crowded city apartments where walls may be paper thin and privacy is hard to come by or is maintained with polite and distant greetings. We are challenged to grow while living in gracious homes surrounded by well-maintained gardens, or in the spread-out buildings of a farm, or in the almost lookalike houses that line the streets in suburbia, or in the small, humble buildings on the outskirts of town.

The challenge to grow is threefold: to get in touch with the urges that come from our inner core, to set goals that are compatible with the growth of the human spirit, and to develop the personal qualities that are needed to reach those goals. To meet this challenge, we need to become aware of how our urges get blocked, drained, or restricted and to learn what is needed to release these energies so that we have strength for the spiritual search.

URGES OF THE HUMAN SPIRIT

At any moment irresistible stirrings from within, like small inner voices, can nudge us, saying, "Use me," or "Set me free." These voices can build until they become so strong they demand our attention. When this happens, we feel we have to do something right now.

These irresistible stirrings to do something are due to universal urges that come from the depths of the spiritual self. They reveal the functions of the human spirit and seek to be released in the direction of meaningful goals. Although they cannot be precisely measured, they can be known, experienced, and observed.

With the capacity to generate power and passion, the urges are energy sources. Like coals of a fire, they may burn brightly and motivate us to take action or die down if our spirits are low. Yet their potential energy is always there and can be reignited.[2]

When we are in touch with these urges, they prod us to develop our potential and meet challenges. When we are out of touch with these urges, we become passive; life seems mundane and boring. These urges are so powerful that, even if blocked or repressed and in spite of our passivity, they eventually push from within to be expressed.

Although capable of being distorted and used in destructive ways, the universal urges of the human spirit are basically positive and life-enhancing. They stir us to begin a spiritual search for meaning. They constantly encourage us to grow, to live more authentically, to be aware of what is important, and to increase our commitments to a life of meaning.

We are born with seven basic urges: to live, to be free, to understand, to enjoy, to create, to connect, and to transcend.

The urge to live is the most basic urge that all healthy persons experience. It is the desire not just to survive but to be as healthy as possible—to have a heart that beats and a brain that works, to be able to do things and be in control of our personal environments.

When we become unhealthy or when life loses its meaning, we often feel lethargic or hopeless. Then, if we find new reasons to live, we may experience a new sense of hope. With hope, the urge to live floods back, creating energy to live a life full of vitality, passion, and wholeness.

Jill Kinmont was eighteen years old, a beautiful and modest skier competing for the American Olympic team, who, just before the Olympic tryouts, crashed in a slalom race. Her neck was broken, and she was permanently paralyzed from her shoulders down. Specially designed implements for eating and extensive psychotherapy helped Jill regain minimal use of one hand, but she not only had to give up skiing, she also had to give up self-care and depend on others. These incredible hardships did not destroy her urge to live but strengthened her spiritual search for meaning in her life. Her hope that she could be useful to others someday sustained her through her agony. To teach children with learning disabilities and other handicaps, she went to college, got her teaching credentials, started working with children in exclusive Beverly Hills, and then went to a Paiute reservation to teach Indian children. Jill is a moving example of the resilience of the urge to live and the power of hope.[3]

The urge to be free—physically, emotionally, and intellectually—is another basic force within the human spirit. This urge for physical freedom starts with the first gasp for breath at birth and continues throughout life. The search for emotional and intellectual freedom comes at anytime and is expressed in such words as, "I want to decide for myself!" When freedom is restricted or denied from outside sources or suppressed from within by fear or anxiety, we may give up and give in or become restless and rebellious.

With courage, the urge to be free becomes a passionate motivating force. The need for courage is apparent at all times and in all cultures. On a worldwide basis, cruel and inhuman punishment is often meted out, at home or in penal or mental institutions. It is a blot on the human race. Any form of forced servitude or restriction can kill the body, mind, and spirit, but does not always succeed.

Because he advocated human rights, Jacobo Timerman, a newspaper publisher in Buenos Aires, was kidnapped by the military in 1977, tortured for three months, and kept imprisoned for two more years—even though his release had been ordered by Argentina's supreme court. These were years in which ten thousand people were killed without trial by Argentina's military dictatorship and when another fifteen thousand mysteriously "disappeared." Tortured by recurrent use of electric shocks, beatings, and fourteen-hour-long interrogations, blindfolded and isolated in a cell without windows, tied so he was unable to stand up, not allowed to wash for months, and without access to anyone, not even the voices of others, Timerman survived. Supported by international outrage, he was finally released and exiled, although all of his assets were confiscated. Because of his spiritual urge for freedom, he still fights courageously for human rights, especially the freedom of speech, the freedom from torture, and the right to a fair trial.[4]

The urge to understand is another universal aspect of the spiritual self. This urge leads us to search for knowledge so we can be well informed and make intelligent decisions instead of being ruled by others or by circumstances. When we don't know what's going on or when we don't understand why things are happening, we often feel frustrated, confused, or even angry. We may pretend to understand, or resign ourselves to not understanding. However, the challenge to grow is so compelling that curiosity inevitably leads us to search for more knowledge, regardless of our age.

Mitsu Fujisawa decided at the age of 112 to get her first formal education by enrolling in Japan's Open University. As a child, she had been a street peddler with no chance to study. In 1988, however, after listening to a professor speak on longevity, she signed up for his class on health and physical education. Behold the human spirit and the urge to understand at any age.[5]

The urge to create activates our unique ways of thinking, being, and doing with goals that show we are capable of originality. It also energizes us to seek vocations and avocations in which we can release this urge. Without outlets for the creative-productive urge, we become angry, indifferent, listless, or despairing. When the urge is free-flowing, we create something new, and this builds self-esteem. Imagination is the quality we need to develop to express the urge to create.

The American artist affectionately called "Grandma Moses" did not take up painting until she was in her late seventies when arthritis interfered with her farming chores. Her only education was a few summer months of school when she was a young girl, yet she painted over two thousand pictures and became known for her clear use of color and small details of everyday life. She gave her paintings away or sold them for almost nothing until she was finally "discovered" by an art collector. Now they are exhibited in the most prestigious art galleries. It was her urge to be creative and the passionate use of her imagination that enabled her to paint something original.[6]

The urge to enjoy is a natural urge of young children, as natural as the urge to live. It remains with us throughout life and pushes us to search for happiness unless it is blocked by training that "nothing is funny" or interfered with by ongoing fatigue, criticism, disillusionment, or tragedy.

Yet even in such trying circumstances, if given the slightest chance, the human spirit again searches for ways to enjoy. Enthusiasm for life is the key that changes monochromatic events into rich, Technicolor experiences.

Of course, enjoyment takes many forms. We can enjoy being with others or enjoy being alone. One of us may prefer going to a sports event, another prefer curling up with a good book or walking the dog in the park. Different people have different ways of enjoying life. Some joyful times are brief, as when we go to a wonderful concert or a party that is fun. Other enjoyments, such as having a good friend, last for years.

Actor Bill Cosby is an example of someone with a playful spirit, one who enjoys life and brings laughter to others. Those who know him say he is this way all the time, often telling funny stories and playing practical jokes, even when he is offstage. Cosby's naturally playful spirit was encouraged in childhood by his grandfather, who served as a role model by clowning around and telling funny stories that had a moral point. As a child, Cosby was a comedian who loved mimicry and would rather clown around than study. Now Cosby designs his own material, never stooping to include off-color or ethnic jokes, and focuses instead on the normal family events that can be seen as hilarious expressions of the human spirit.[7]

The urge to connect propels us to search for love in authentic relationships that are open and honest rather than manipulative or superficial. Authentic relationships can develop between any two people or in groups. Some relationships become so significant that people are willing to live for, fight for, and die for them, if necessary. Although mistreatment or being ignored often numbs this urge, genuine caring restores it. When we care, we reach out to connect with people, plants, animals, or a higher power.

Carl Rogers, the father of humanistic psychology, focused on how to encourage autonomy, self-worth, and love. He originated the nondirective, client-centered approach to psychotherapy as an expression of his own spiritual search for love and caring.

During his childhood, Rogers had been taught not to trust or care for people who were not part of his family. His theory, however, stressed just the opposite. He developed it while working with emotionally disturbed children who were unable to love because they had not received caring from trustworthy people.

With "unconditional positive regard," Rogers showed how all clients are helped by being in a caring connection. This kind of connection was developed by listening carefully and caringly to what a client had to say, by acknowledging and restating their spoken concerns, and by encouraging them to decide for themselves on the direction, speed, and length of their treatment.[8] His approach was an important contribution to psychotherapy and is widely taught to professionals who want to help others.

The urge to transcend is defined as the ability to pass beyond a human limit, to reach up as well as out, to let go as well as hold on, to be open to the unknown as well as the known. When we move beyond what we think of as human limits, we often transcend the everyday into an oceanic feeling of oneness. Fear, skepticism, or just being too busy frequently block this urge. However, it can flood back when we decide to be open to life's opportunities, to get involved with other people, or to get out and listen to the music of the spheres. Then boundaries fade into nothingness and a sense of unity and oneness with nature, the universe, or God is experienced.

Born in France, theologian Thomas Merton studied Protestant and Eastern religious traditions. As a young adult he became a Trappist monk, dedicated to austerity, hard work, and prayer. He was a conscientious objector during World War II and later extended his support to those working for racial justice and world peace. Temporarily silenced for independent thinking by his order, he wrote under various pseudonyms.

As a deeply committed Catholic, Merton was honored by both Pope John XXIII and Pope Paul, yet put his trust in a wider perspective—in the oneness of all—and believed that Christians should not delude themselves with the idea that the grace of God is monopolized by any particular structure of belief. "God doesn't obey the traffic lights of any religious system and a Catholic," he said, "would do well to keep an ear open for the activity of the Holy Spirit which 'blows where it will.' "[9]

The holy spirit as well as the cosmic spirit may blow at will, but the human spirit with its seven urges moves in understandable ways. The following chart illustrates how the urges of the human spirit motivate us to start out on spiritual searches of various kinds and delineates the personal qualities we need to achieve our goals.

The wonders of the human spirit motivate us to reach out toward specific goals, and to reach those goals, specific inner resources are needed. We need hope to live, courage to be free, curiosity to understand, enthusiasm to enjoy, imagination to create, caring to be able to make connections, and trust so we can transcend human limitations.

Urges of the Human Spirit	Goals of the Search	Powers Needed for the Search
to live	meaning	hope
to be free	self-determination	courage
to understand	knowledge	curiosity
to create	originality	imagination
to enjoy	happiness	enthusiasm
to connect	love	caring
to transcend	unity	openness

EXPRESSION OF THE URGES

Each urge is inherently good and seeks to be expressed in positive ways. At the inner core of our being, we all want to live and be free, we all want to understand and create, to enjoy and connect. We want to transcend routine and rise to new heights that enhance life. Although the basic direction of an urge is for positive goals, each urge can also be expressed in nonproductive or destructive ways. All of us have the freedom of choice in expressing our urges in a range from:

destructive   non-productive   productive

-                        0   +

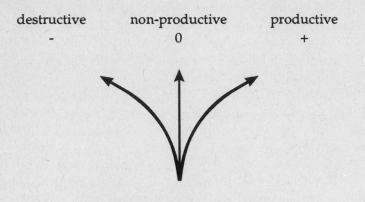

WAYS TO EXPRESS AN URGE

Destructive expressions of the urges are all too frequent. An extreme case is the infamous Jim Jones, a religious fanatic who brainwashed hundreds of people to give him all their financial resources and move to Guyana with him. Then, in 1978, when his dishonesty was discovered, he demanded that they show their loyalty and commit suicide with him by taking poison.

Child molestation is another destructive expression of a seriously misdirected urge for contact, just as drug abuse is a misdirected expression of the urge for enjoyment. Other common destructive expressions of urges include telling lies or sexist jokes, limiting the freedom of others while demanding one's own by supporting segregation, or becoming so immersed in one's own religion that one denies the validity of others'.

The most common nonproductive expressions of urges are procrastination, isolation, and indifference. We may ignore the wonders of the world or the wonders of ourselves. We may procrastinate and prevaricate, make excuses and exaggerations while saying to ourselves, "It doesn't matter," or "Nobody will know." We may be indifferent to other people's suffering, or we may go against our own better judgment and go along with the company or crowd so as not to make waves.

Other people might work too much and miss out on experiences that could make their lives meaningful. They may be so creative they become scattered and nondirected. They may become so hungry for love they act in a desperate manner and push others away. Or they may get so angry their resentments overshadow their love. These are nonproductive distortions of the spirit within us.

At any moment, each one of us can stop and shift our weight toward constructive, nonproductive, or destructive uses of our inner urges. We can ignore the spiritual self or we can pay attention to it. We can meet the challenge of growth. This choice, made deep in the privacy of our own inner spirit, gives life a sense of meaning.

IN HARMONY OR IN CONFLICT

The basic urges of the human spirit can function in harmony or can be in conflict. Whenever two or more urges are active and in harmony, they propel us to act with strength and determination. The urge to live, for example, is often linked to the urge for freedom because, for many, life without freedom isn't worth living, so they simultaneously fight for both. People may find the strength to escape from a war-torn country or to overcome poverty with its lack of opportunities. In life-threatening or spirit-threatening situations, the urges to live and to be free become passionate collaborators.

At a different level, the urge to connect with another person, intimately and with love, is often combined with the urge to create a child and enjoy a family or some other kind of long-term partnership. There are also times when the urge to understand is so high that the excitement of a new idea or insight can spark a transcendent moment.

However, inner urges are not always in harmony; they are often in conflict when one part of us wants to do one thing, and another part of us wants to do something different. If these desires are high and somewhat equal in force, inner turmoil and indecision result. Sylvia Morales, an architect for an engineering firm, was

Urges of the human spirit

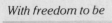

With freedom to be

DAVID M. ALLEN

JEAN-CLAUDE DERNIS

In search of knowledge

Determined to live

Created beauty

LEFT: Enjoying life
RIGHT: Connecting with love

Transcending disabilities

one of the firm's most productive employees. She was working on a time-consuming project that was very interesting to her and so did not pay attention to the signals her body was sending her. When she discovered she needed major surgery that would keep her in bed for weeks, Sylvia ignored her conflict between work and health and delayed her decision until she finally had to be admitted to the hospital as an emergency case.

Any of us can feel conflict by having a long-held goal that interferes with other important desires. As one mother explained, "I want to go to school and complete my degree, but I also want to spend more time with my children. How can I decide?" In situations such as this, although family and friends may offer advice, ultimately the choice belongs to each one of us.

The uncertainties and vicissitudes of life are such that, at times, we are forced to give one urge more attention than another. Achieving freedom and self-determination may be the priority at one time; at another time it can be superseded by the urge to connect with someone who can give and receive love.

The priority we assign to an urge often changes as circumstances change. Secretary-general of the United Nations U Thant had two major priorities: his spiritual practices and his political responsibilities. He was a Buddhist and Burmese who believed that it was necessary to pursue each of these two priorities daily so that he could put his thoughts, words, and deeds into the right perspective for the day ahead. U Thant wrote:

WHEN I ENTER MY OFFICE IN MANHATTAN, YOU WILL UNDERSTAND THAT I MUST FORGET THAT I AM A BURMESE AND A BUDDHIST. ONE OF MY DUTIES IS TO RECEIVE MANY PEOPLE . . . IN ORDER TO RECEIVE AND FULLY UNDERSTAND WHAT MY HUMAN BROTHER HAS TO SAY TO ME, I OPEN MYSELF TO HIM, I MUST EMPTY MYSELF OF MYSELF.[10]

It is often difficult to switch gears from one set of values to another. What is important at one moment may be less important the next. In being committed to people, U Thant expressed the passion of the human spirit to meet challenges and grow in the process.

WHEN THE URGES ARE BLOCKED

The natural tendency is for urges from the inner core to seek expression, but they can be blocked by oppressive laws and traditions. Laws that prohibit the freedom of speech, assembly, or religion, or laws that limit opportunities block the energies of the human spirit.

To experience what it's like when an urge is blocked, imagine a fast-moving river where the energy of the flow is blocked by a dam. One of the most common ways that the expression of an urge is blocked is when we are discriminated against. We may be judged negatively for being disabled though able to work, for being overweight though willing to work, or for being socially awkward though polite and competent. Being judged by race, sex, age, religion, or ethnic background inhibits people from expressing their natural potentials.

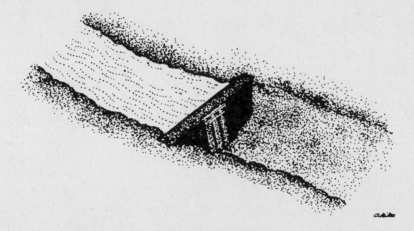

Societal laws that enforce inequality are like dams across the rivers of peoples' energies. So are discrimination and restrictive customs based on race, religion, sex, or ethnic background. They hold back the spiritual energy of both the oppressed and the oppressors. The "have-nots" feel held down while the "haves" feel threatened as they try to maintain control.

Day-to-day realities can also block the expression of our inner urges. Someone who wants to go back to school and can't afford to will find the urge to learn and understand blocked. Someone who has to work long hours and does not have enough time to spend with friends will find the urges to connect and to enjoy life both blocked.

When energy is blocked by other people's criticism, ridicule, or judgments, destructive reactions often surface. We may become increasingly defensive and self-protective; we may feel guilty, anxious, fearful, self-doubting, or lonely. Consequently we tend to act angry, controlling, perfectionistic, and closed to new ideas. We may disregard others and exhibit attitudes of inferiority or superiority.

Even when the urges of the spirit are blocked by laws and tradition, criticism, or ridicule, they may still push to be expressed in some way. Dissidents will protest, people will march, and others will long for something better.

The fight to be free from internal and external blocks such as these is a lifelong challenge. Sometimes our desire for breaking free is dulled because we feel so drained of energy.

WHEN ENERGIES ARE DRAINED

Energy is *drained* by physically exhausting jobs, continuous demands by children or creditors, or constant compliance to others. People who always comply may say, "I'm running around trying to please everyone and feel like a chicken with its head cut off" or "I have five more things to do and no time to do them" or "The phone rang all day and I'm too exhausted to do anything tonight."

Commuting in heavy traffic, living in an unsafe neighborhood, being faced with financial problems, or having poor health drain off needed energy. Crowds, noise, criticism, isolation, poor food, unpleasant surroundings, exhausting life-styles, dirt, disorder, and pollution also add up to exhaustion. Being a parent or a stepparent, or being the spouse of someone who needs constant care drains energy. When energies are drained, we lose our enthusiasm for life.

Drained energy can be understood by visualizing a river where the water is drained off by too many irrigation ditches or canals. In time the river runs dry; the reservoir becomes empty. The same applies to people. Too many demands or requests by others drain people dry. This often happens to people who are very nice to others yet do not take good care of themselves; they say "yes" when they need to say "no" to others.

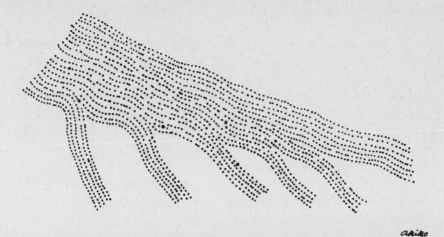

akiko

Single parents who work, take care of a house, shop, cook, care for the children, and still try to eke out some time to be with friends or lovers are drained of energy. Then there are people who are in demanding jobs, such as public school teachers, hospital nurses, and clergy who feel so committed to their students, patients, or parishioners that they feel they can't say "no." In a precarious job market, managers and supervisors may have to say too many yeses to their bosses and even complete their subordinates' work because if they don't, they might lose their own jobs. And many people have such large financial obligations—helping their children through college or caring for elderly parents—that they have to work excessively long hours or hold a second job just to make ends meet.

Some of the common internal responses made when energy is drained are preoccupation with mistakes, lowered self-esteem, guilt, anger, confusion, fear, worry, obsessive thinking, and depression. We may even become physically ill or accident-prone. In this state, we are too tired or too preoccupied to notice the beauty of life, to try something new, or to respond to others in loving ways.

WHEN THE SPIRIT IS RESTRICTED

Energy is usually *restricted* by negative feelings such as fear, guilt, and anxiety. Some people do not trust themselves, others, or any sort of higher power. When people feel this way, their self-criticism increases, their self-esteem decreases, and they end up feeling anxious.

Anxiety is caused by disapproval either of oneself or by others. The disapproval may not actually occur; anxiety can occur even with the anticipation of disapproval. Anxiety also happens when people believe it is impossible to do what they believe they must do. This belief causes anxiousness, which can lead to apathy, procrastination, or worse. "When I'm anxious, I feel frozen," is a common response to any kind of threat. In such cases, spiritual urges can be severely restricted.

The Latin word for anxiety is *angustin,* meaning narrowness. Picture a river that has been narrowed or restricted by boulders or logjams in the water. The flow of the river becomes turbulent, and the river may become dangerous to travel.

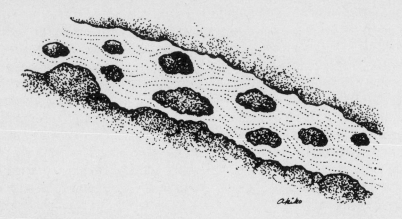

What happens to the river's flow is similar to what happens to people who feel so restricted by anxiety that they hold back from facing the challenge to grow by developing their potential and making decisions. Holding back increases anxiety even more and restricts power for the spiritual search.

The internal dialogue of such people is often self-critical, "I never do anything right," or despairing, "No one will ever forgive me." These negative thoughts are like heavy boulders interfering with their energy. Unforeseen accidents or slight criticisms from others may also add "debris" that interferes with open channels of energy.

One of the first signs of anxiety is that people tighten up.

They pull in their shoulders as if to ward off a blow. Emotionally they begin to use various psychological defense mechanisms such as denial, projection, and rationalization, and their fears and feelings take over. When anxiety builds, the freedom to be oneself and to set one's own goals and directions may seem to be a pie-in-the-sky dream rather than a possibility, and people tend to isolate themselves from others.

When our inner core urges are blocked, drained, or restricted, we are out of touch with the spiritual self and feel half dead. Then, with a crisis or even a warm compliment, we may wake up and suddenly draw upon long-ignored sources of high energy and passionately respond to the challenge to live a full life.

FILLED WITH PASSION

People with high energy often lead us to wonder, How did they get that way? How do they stay that way? Where do they get their energy and passion for life? What is passion all about, anyway?

Passion is an intensified urge that is directed toward a specific goal. It is a state of psychological intensity with a strong commitment to be or do something. The word *passion* originally came from the Latin *passio* meaning suffering. Currently it is more often used to refer to any strong emotion—love or lust, joy or devotion. In everyday parlance it is used more casually. People sometimes speak of having a passion for music, for exercise, even for ice cream. With so many different uses for the word, it seems necessary to clarify how it is being used in reference to the inner urges of the human spirit. *Passion for life is the intense desire, interest, and willingness to release the inner urges of the soul.*

To engage in a spiritual search requires passion. Having an urge is not enough, and good intentions are insufficient. We need to be passionately involved in life and need to find ways to express our passions on a path with heart.

When we do not express an urge, it is more often because we have not allowed the urge to grow into a passion. Instead, we have become passive. To be passive is to do nothing about something that we need to do something about. Of course, passivity can be life-saving. It is not always wise to fight against certain situations or people. However, when we do not respond with the power that comes from our inner urges, it is often an unhealthy passivity.

Naturally, the amount of passion we devote to any search can change as our moods or our circumstances change. Regardless of our moods and circumstances, we can draw on incredible resources. Imagine a reservoir that is always full because streams continually flow into it from snow-capped mountains and hidden natural springs. From the reservoir often flows a river of water that is clear, inviting, and free-flowing.

People filled with passion are like clear, life-giving rivers. Their cups runneth over with energy as they share their joie de vivre with others. Because they focus their energies on what is important, the world becomes a better place. With vitality, they search for deeper understanding and new avenues for creativity. In addition, they are responsive to the inner spiritual resources that help them survive in hard times. And with a deep respect for others, they attract respect in return.

As long as we recognize that the wondrous urges of the human spirit are intended to be free-flowing, we can risk ourselves and fall in love with life. When we decide upon goals that have meaning and release our spiritual urges to become passions, a path with heart becomes obvious and beckons us to move on.

MOVING BEYOND OURSELVES

At first, the desire to express the urges of the inner core is aimed at goals that have personal meaning and bring some kind of personal satisfaction. This process begins when we become aware of feeling restricted and unable to express all our energies. "I wish" and "I want" are frequent statements at this stage and reflect a hunger for change. Ruminating on the desire for change can spark the fires of self-determination and move us to take some kind of action.

As our desire gains more intensity, a wish may grow into a decision, expressed as "I will." Deciding to do something new may sound easy, but taking action may be hard. For example, if a particular urge has been held back for years, it is not easy to release it, even when we want to. But if the path has heart and meaning for us, action will seem more natural and success be more likely.

Yet most people's vision of life extends beyond the horizons of concern only for themselves. Like concentric ripples formed by a pebble thrown into a pond, the urge to express the human spirit is a movement that begins with oneself and moves out toward others.

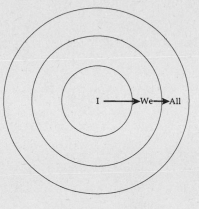

MOVING OUT TO OTHERS

Most of us want to move beyond our self-centeredness to join others so that they, too, can release the passions of their souls. United, we can do more than I could do on my own. The "we" can be a family struggling to escape the tyranny or terror of war, "we" can be neighbors who band together to rid the neighborhood of drugs, or "we" can be teachers and parents joining together to improve local schools.

Becoming even more committed to life, liberty, and the pursuit of happiness, we may recognize that if we focus only on ourselves, our family, and friends, we are not doing enough. Everyone has needs. Sometimes when we get a glimpse of others' needs, they seem so overwhelming that we look the other way and give up. Other times an inner passion grows to do something about others' problems. We may decide to fight for others' health and freedom, or we may work so others can have opportunities to get an education and be creative. We may discover that we want the whole world to shine and no one to be shadowed or diminished by anyone else.

The more we are able to release our own urges and focus them with passionate concern for others, the more likely we are to be caught up in a spiritual quest. As mythologist Joseph Campbell explains, "The ultimate aim of the quest must be neither release nor ecstasy for oneself, but the wisdom and the power to serve others."[11]

❦ RECOGNIZING YOUR INNER URGES————————————

Following are some exercises to help you begin to recognize your urges so that you can release the power and passion that is inherent in them.

❦ CONTEMPLATION ON THE HUMAN SPIRIT. Focus your attention. The following quotes may open doors to deeper understanding of your passion for life.

> BY BELIEVING PASSIONATELY IN SOMETHING THAT STILL DOES NOT EXIST, WE CREATE IT. THE NONEXISTENT IS WHATEVER WE HAVE NOT SUFFICIENTLY DESIRED.
> —NIKOS KAZANTZAKIS[12]

> I KNOW THE JOY OF FISHES IN THE RIVER THROUGH MY OWN JOY, AS I GO WALKING ALONG THE SAME RIVER.
> —CHUANG TZU[13]

> IF WE HAVE THE COURAGE AND TENACITY OF OUR FOREBEARS, WHO STOOD FIRMLY LIKE A ROCK AGAINST THE LASH OF SLAVERY, WE SHALL FIND A WAY TO DO FOR OUR DAY WHAT THEY DID FOR THEIRS.
> —MARY MCLEOD BETHUNE[14]

> LIFE CAN BE PULLED BY GOALS JUST AS SURELY AS IT CAN BE PUSHED BY DRIVES.
> —VIKTOR FRANKL[15]

❦ THE FLOW OF YOUR ENERGY. Energies from inner core urges are not always active. They can be blocked by laws or traditions; they can be drained by overwork or fatigue; they can be restricted by anger or anxiety; they can be ignored because of skepticism or ignorance.

Visualize yourself by a river, that represents the flow of your energies. See the river with a dam across it so your energies are held back. Is there anything in your life currently blocking your inner energy from flowing freely?

Visualize the same river being drained or diverted by irrigation ditches so that its flow loses power. What in your life is draining your energy?

Look at the river again and imagine it full of rocks and boulders, problems that create anxiety and make your energy flow unpredictably like rapids. What boulders are making you anxious?

Imagine walking along the riverbank, lost in thought about some task and not really noticing the river at all. Why is that happening?

Finally, visualize the river flowing freely. Stay with this picture for a few moments. What message do you receive?

🐛 A FRUSTRATED URGE. Think about an important problem you have been trying to solve. What did you feel, think, and do about the problem? Now, fill in the following:

The problem I have is:

The urge I am not expressing enough is:

I am not expressing it because:

If I released that urge, I could:

If I did this, my life would change in these ways:

My Urges	High, Medium, or Low Energy?	Reasons

live

be free

understand

create

enjoy

connect

transcend

❦ URGES AND ENERGY. Consider the past week and rate the energy that you experienced coming from each of your urges.

What are the patterns of your energy? Is there any urge you need to pay more attention to?

❦ GOALS FOR THE FUTURE. Make a list of some of your goals for the future. Then indicate which of the basic urges will be most needed to reach your goals.

❦ PAUSE AND REFLECT. Before going on to the next chapter, you may want to write down some questions you have about the basic urges, especially as they relate to your own life.

4

THE URGE TO LIVE

WHEN THE WINTER IS SEVERE
THE PINE TREES IN THIS ANCIENT LAND
STAY GREEN THROUGHOUT THE YEAR.
IS IT BECAUSE THE EARTH IS WARM AND FRIENDLY?
NO, IT IS BECAUSE THE PINE TREE HAS WITHIN ITSELF
A LIFE-RESTORING POWER.

—OLD CHINESE PROVERB[1]

❧

TO LIFE!

From time to time, in the privacy of our own thoughts or in conversations with others, most of us wonder about life and death, We may ask, "Why is it that sometimes I feel so full of life and energy and other times I don't?" "Why can't I feel positive and energetic all the time?" "Why does my energy fluctuate so that sometimes I feel like a cup overflowing with love and power, and other times like an old empty cup with no refills available?"

In a more pensive mood, we may even wonder, "Is my life determined by genes or the environment, by destiny, by God, or purely by luck?" "Does life have a purpose? If so, what is it?" "Is there something more important I should be doing with my life?" We wonder why we sometimes want to close the door, hide under the blankets, and turn off the whole world. We also wonder about the many other times when we feel like opening the door and shouting out a toast for the whole world to hear: "Here's to Life!"

The toast, "Here's to Life!" implies an excitement about life and to what life may bring us. Most of us know what it is like to feel fully alive and also what it is to feel numb, or half dead.

Naturally we want to experience and express our aliveness more fully.

THE URGE TO LIVE

The urge to live is rooted in an all-pervading energy of life. Central to Chinese tradition is the understanding and harmonic use of this life energy, which is called *chi.* Chi is the broad general term for the vital force of the universe. There are many kinds of chi; two especially important ones are Tai Chi and Zheng Chi.[2] Tai chi is the cosmic energy of the universe, an energy that permeates everything. Mist, wind, and air all contain tai chi, and we know it through cosmic rhythms such as changes in seasons and weather that can increase or sap our energy. A fresh wind after a period of high humidity is invigorating, as is sunshine after days of gray skies. In contrast, a sandstorm can decrease energy and send us into fits of coughing. The first snow of the season is stimulating and exciting, except to those who are cold and homeless.

Zheng chi is the personal life energy that flows within the human body and which, when freely flowing, provides a person with vibrancy and vitality. Zheng chi follows natural patterns of energy flow and blood circulation, pulsing along pathways or channels called *meridians.* One of the primary aims of acupuncture and meditation is to focus and strengthen this vital chi energy to encourage health.

This life energy is influenced by genetic components we have inherited. For example, a person may inherit a potential for health and long life or a potential for a specific disease.

The urge to live is expressed in striving to survive, in looking for ways to be comfortable, and in searching for meaning or purpose. These are expressions of an important continuum of life from survival to comfort to meaning.

Survival ----➤ Comfort ----➤ Meaning

THE URGE TO LIVE

We do many things each day to ensure our physical survival, such as eating, sleeping, and balancing our body heat by adding or removing clothes. Unless we are helplessly ill or severely depressed, our determination to survive endures lifelong. We may generally be honest people yet become thieves for a crust of bread or a swallow of water if starving or seriously dehydrated. We may be generous and give money to the poor and homeless yet manipulate the system to get a donated organ that is difficult to get and may save our life.

The drive to survive keeps people alive and hopeful, even when faced with desperate conditions, as was the case for sailor William Buie. One night in a storm, when Buie's ship was pitching wildly, he became seasick and fell overboard. It was dark, the water was cold, and no one saw him fall or heard him yell. His ship sailed blithely on, yet his urge to live remained high because he believed someone would find him eventually. He took off his shoes and pants and knotted his pantlegs to trap air in them and use them to help stay afloat. Then, for two hours, to strengthen his hope, he kept on singing the only song he knew, *The Tennessee Waltz*. Incredibly, he was heard by a sharp-eared sailor on another ship and rescued.[3]

The movements of an unborn child who is struggling to be born reflect this survival urge. Then, after we take our first gasp of air, we seek to survive with comfort. We like our many comforts, whether they are the physical comfort of a warm bed at night, the psychological comfort of a good friend with whom to talk, or the spiritual comfort of a deep faith.

The word *comfort* comes from the Latin *comfortare* meaning to strengthen. Bread and milk provide *physical* comfort; having someone to talk with provides us with *psychological* comfort; experiencing forgiveness, acceptance, and love provides us with *spiritual* comfort. In fact, the Greek name for the holy spirit is *parakletos* meaning comforter.

Each of us seeks to establish personal "comfort zones," which are areas in which we feel safer and more confident. A comforting place might be the home, which shields us from the harsh elements of daily life. It can be a psychotherapist's office where we go to seek ways of solving problems and learn of our worth. A comfort zone may also be a sanctuary where we go to pray. One person may find comfort at work, another by sitting on top of a mountain.

Comfort zones can also be states of mind. When people feel loved, they often feel more self-confident; when recognized for their efforts, more committed; when working toward meaningful goals and life dreams, more happy; and when feeling a oneness with all life, they often feel a sense of inner peace.

Sometimes our comfort zones are invaded by others. Anyone whose house has been burglarized knows what it is like to have a comfort zone invaded. We can also dissipate our comfort zones when we slip into negative states of mind. This is usually a sign that the spiritual self is aching to be reexperienced and expressed in more positive ways.

The urge to live is not only sustained by cosmic and biological energy, it is also mobilized when the power of the spiritual self is directed in a positive search for meaning. Even when bodily energy is low, people can get in touch with other forms of energy than can sustain them. Psychiatrist Viktor Frankl tells of prisoners in concentration camps during World War II who, with a purpose for living, were more likely to survive than those who had lost hope and purpose, even though all suffered similar physical deprivations. Frankl relates an incident of a group of physicians who, recognizing the need for intellectual stimulation to avoid becoming deadened, met secretly and shared medical information with each other. Their intellectual and spiritual energies sustained them when their physical energy and vitality were almost nonexistent.[4]

THE SEARCH FOR MEANING

Although enjoying personal comfort is better than fighting for survival, in many ways comfort is not enough. There is a natural hunger for meaning that yearns to be satisfied. The urge to live and the ways it is expressed can be thought of as ranging on a continuum from our most basic biological needs to our highest goals, whether centered around oneself or directed toward others.

Even when survival and comfort are uncertain or not possible, people may seek for deeper meaning to life. Charlie Wedemeyer has difficulty surviving and his life is very uncomfortable, yet he finds meaning in being a high school football coach. Since 1977 he has suffered from amyotrophic lateral sclerosis or ALS (often called Lou Gehrig's disease). In this disease, all nerves and muscles below the face eventually deteriorate. Although his life expectancy when ALS was diagnosed was only three years, he has kept on coaching for more than twelve years.

Now a quadriplegic who cannot move or speak, his spirit is still robust. He speaks to community groups through his wife, Lucy, who reads his lips and interprets what he wants to say to the audience. With her help, he also continues to coach a team that did so well that it made it to the state championships in 1985. When people ask how he is able to maintain his positive spirit and zest for life, Charlie responds, "There is one answer. I wouldn't be here today if it wasn't for God." Lucy, who was his high school sweetheart, echoes this. "We both feel as if it's okay if it's over at any time, because we've had such a joyful life."[5]

The urge to live is most intense when we find meaning in our positive experiences. Everyday common experiences—seeing a flower open, watching a fish flicker through the water, viewing a sunrise after a week of fog, catching an unexpected smile from a stranger—can bring meaning to our lives and can sometimes be enough to keep us going during tough times. Life can suddenly seem very desirable when we just look around and recognize that we are part of the universe.

The search for meaning can also come through the spiritual practices of religious groups. Religion, says Ashley Montagu, is "the grammar of the human soul." The urge to live can grow during the quietness of a Quaker meeting or a Buddhist temple. Even an empty chapel may provide peace to a weary soul. Mantras such as Om repeated in unison with others or the sound of a Gregorian chant or the use of prayer are powerful ways to bring peace to the restless spirit and help it find new meaning and hope for life.

Yet sometimes we want more than just "being." We want to be doing something, because "doing" also brings meaning to life. Even with a tight commuting schedule we may stop to give a friend a ride, or take the time to comfort a small child in a grocery store who is crying because she can't find her mother. Small kindnesses add meaning when we give them or when we receive them.

In addition, we often want to do something on a larger scale. We may want a job where we can use our gifts and talents. We may look for meaning in being creative, in searching for knowledge, in loving and being loved, in working for a cause, or in service to God or to other people. Each of us has our goals, our tasks, our missions, to which we long to say yes. These can be like spiritual imperatives.

It is not unusual for terminally ill patients who are hospitalized to keep themselves alive until particular persons they love come to visit. It is as if there are some things they want to share before they die. Many people also seem to prolong their lives by working up to the time of their death. Their work has so much meaning that their passion to live continues until their projects are accomplished.

THE NEED FOR HOPE

The urge to live and its motivating power to search for meaning increases when a person feels hopeful. *Hope is a belief that certain wishes are obtainable.* With hope, the thirsty person sees the glass of water as being half full instead of half empty. In fact, hope includes seeing the possibility of a full glass. Yet hope is not the same as optimism. Optimism is waiting for things to turn out well without putting in the effort that is necessary for making changes. Hope is intrinsically active, not passive.

Hope continually motivates us to do something to achieve our important and even our not-so-important goals. When we cook a meal, we hope it will be tasty. When we go to a party, we hope to enjoy ourselves. When we start a book, we hope to finish it. When we feel good, we hope to stay that way, and when we don't, we hope to recover. Hope pervades our lives and sustains us through thick and thin. Hope is looking to the future with confidence.

We all have many hopes. Sometimes we hope for health or prosperity, sometimes for friends or fame, sometimes for oneness with others or with the cosmic or holy spirit. The passion to live and to find meaning in life rests on hope.

Urge of the Human Spirit	Goal of the Search	Power Needed for the Search
to Live	Meaning	Hope

Psychiatrist Erik Erikson believed that basic hope develops in early infancy,[6] when infants make preverbal decisions about whether it is safe to trust people to take care of their physical and emotional needs. Children who are neglected or brutalized often decide it is not safe to trust others and become suspicious of any form of friendliness. Or they turn off their feelings and become overly independent with the attitude, "I don't need anyone, I'll do it all myself." Still others become deeply afraid. They panic if criticized and withdraw from or comply with any demand to reduce the panic. Children who are ignored or harshly treated, who grow up underloved and overworked, often give up hope.

On the other hand, children who are well treated by having their basic physical and emotional needs met are naturally hopeful. If encouraged to have friends, taught how to act around adults, and supported in their efforts to do well in school, they usually feel self-confident and have positive expectations.

Throughout life, the sense of hope fluctuates for most of us. When school projects and jobs succeed, when friendships, love, and marriage go well, we naturally feel strong and hopeful that good things will continue to happen. When love doesn't work out or when school or jobs disappoint us, we may feel discouraged, even hopeless.

Feelings of hopelessness arise when the body and mind do not have enough of what they need to be healthy. Anyone whose physical survival is threatened can become hopeless. Hope also decreases with emotional problems, family crises, exhausting responsibilities, or life changes that are too many or too drastic. If the burdens become overwhelming, people can break down physically, emotionally, and spiritually.

Hopelessness also results from being addicted to an impossible life-long dream. A single parent with three children to support who has a life dream of going to medical school is likely to feel hopeless in the face of insurmountable financial obstacles. A person with a life dream of staying married "till death do us part" may also feel hopeless if a spouse demands a divorce.

We may also feel hopelessness when life has little or no meaning. A promotion at work may mean nothing if the job itself is uninteresting or if a love relationship has just collapsed. When life loses its meaning, people lose hope and numb themselves, mistreat themselves, or sink into depression.

When feeling hopeless, people are unable to cope with unhappy memories of the past, with the way life is in the present, and with how it might be in the future. Telling them to "cheer up" and to "look on the bright side" often has little or no effect; doing things with them and accepting their mood is more helpful in easing their despair.

It takes a strong passion to live to fight against hopelessness in desperate circumstances, yet when hope is maintained, it can summon a powerful inner strength in us. Furthermore, hope is good medicine, an essential ingredient for a meaningful life. With hope, depression fades and enthusiasm for life reappears. Enjoying life, in spite of handicaps and setbacks, becomes a goal once again. Hope helps pull things together and integrate what was, what is, and what can be.

WHOLISTIC HEALTH

Vitality and an eagerness to live are best observed in people who are healthy. The word *health* comes from the Anglo Saxon root *hal,* which means both whole and holy. The word *holistic,* sometimes spelled *wholistic,* was first used in the 1930s by Jan Christiaan Smuts, former premier of South Africa. Today it has become increasingly popular in the fields of medicine and psychology. A healthy approach to life emphasizes the wholeness and health of body, mind, and spirit.

Around the world, people are becoming better informed about anatomy and disease. Medical programs on TV, articles about exercise and nutrition in popular magazines, and self-care health books all provide information that is being eagerly sought and used by people who are taking more responsibility for their bodily health.

For the body, relaxation, proper nutrition, and exercise are essential. When John F. Kennedy was president of United States, he initiated an active campaign to encourage people to get in better physical shape by exercising. Before his time, it was rare to see people running for exercise, something commonly seen today. As we adopted new values and structured our time to include more exercise, life expectancy has risen—so has life satisfaction.

Exercise demands that we get out of the comfort zone of a favorite chair and do something. Working out provides significant benefits in addition to improving our physical condition. The worries of the day may be forgotten while we are immersed in strenuous physical activity and, at the same time, the mind may become free to wonder and daydream about what life's all about.

The search for meaning through physical efforts is most clearly seen in athletes who deliberately work to improve their health and performance. Peak performers often develop a winning attitude by using visualization techniques in which, in their mind's eye, they see themselves as healthy and performing well. Former basketball star and coach Bill Russell of the Boston Celtics explains how he used this technique by sitting with his eyes closed, watching plays in his head. "I was in my own private basketball laboratory, making mental blueprints for myself."[7] Tennis champion Chris Evert also uses this technique, as does golfer Jack Nicklaus, who calls it "going to the movies."[8] Positive visualization is an important aid to improving physical health and performance.

Rest and relaxation are as important as exercise for many people. Vacations and weekends off provide temporary freedom from physical and emotional stress and exhaustion and are among the oldest and most effective forms of self-care and healing. Taking time off at home, turning off the phone and saying no to demands of others or those we impose on ourselves can also be life saving and provide an oasis where we can think about life and the search for meaning.

The search for physical and emotional health can also be aided by psychotherapy and counseling. Many theories and techniques can be used to help people discover meaning in their lives. The modern disciplines of psychotherapy, based on age-old principles of listening empathetically and exploring alternatives, are all based on trust and cooperation between client and therapist. In a trusting situation, we can clarify our problems, reduce stress, and improve our lives.

In Transactional Analysis, for example, a person may learn how each part of their personality can be involved in a search for meaning. The Child, rooted in the body, will usually be concerned with staying alive, being comfortable, and enjoying sensory experiences. The Adult might decide to find meaning in other ways and, for example, study psychology, sociology, and philosophy to understand why people do what they do. The Parent, if directed toward positive goals, will often find meaning in taking on altruistic responsibilities, in some kind of helping, advising, or directing role.

Physical activity and psychotherapy are not the only roads to health; friendship is also healing. A good friend or family member may call it to our attention that we are showing symptoms of stress and suggest that we need to take some time to sit down and have a heart-to-heart talk about what's going wrong. Or a friend may suggest we go off and do something fun to break the routine and boredom. Good friends and family members who love us stick with us through thick and thin and often add incredible meaning to our lives.

Richard Leakey, anthropologist and director of Kenya's National Museum, had become dangerously ill with kidney failure and flew to London for treatment. Dialysis three times a week was painful, costly, and would prevent his returning to his previous activities. A kidney transplant was the only satisfactory solution, yet there was only a 1 in 20,000 chance of finding a compatible donor. His brother Philip's tissue was compatible, but because of a serious disagreement, they had not spoken to each other for ten years. Richard was reluctant and embarrassed to accept such a gift, especially when he knew it would lower Philip's chances for survival if he ever had kidney problems. Yet Philip was willing to give his kidney, and the surgery was performed. Personal survival and comfort were not Philip's highest priority when his brother's life was at risk.[9]

Having some time alone is important for most people's sense of well-being as well as health. Meditation is a tool that has been used since the dawn of history to reduce emotional turmoil and even control illnesses such as high blood pressure or ulcers. Through meditation a sense of direction can be recovered and life gains new meaning. There are many ways to meditate but the essential feature of all ways is to quiet the mind so that even the soft chirp of a single bird can be heard. The chirp can bring a moment of wholeness to the self.

OUT OF BALANCE

Many times the urge to live is seriously weakened because we are out of balance with ourselves. Like a three-legged stool with one leg too short, we can feel lopsided from being too busy, too worried, too bored, too isolated, or from the loss of a love relationship or a life-long dream. We can get out of balance by driving ourselves to overwork, going on and on until we get a splitting headache, a nagging back pain, an ulcer, or something else that forces us to quit what we're doing, at least temporarily. Or we can drive ourselves, trying to please someone who is hard to please, until we feel worn out and withdraw in protest. Then we may feel "justified" in taking time out to repair ourselves and restore our balance.

We can get out of balance with all kinds of experiences. Even a minor cold can interfere with our comfort. Losing a job because of a cutback, merger, or being fired can be a shock and a threat to self-esteem that puts us so much out of balance that we give up in depression or resignation. Very few people are fortunate enough to have a continuous supply of natural energy so that they are always in balance.

The ability to live in balance is disturbed whenever circumstances threaten our survival, comfort, and hope for life. The demands of life may seem too tough, and it may seem impossible to find a free hour to rest or get some exercise. Unfortunately many of us make up excuses to avoid doing what we need to do if we want to stay balanced. The excuse may be, "I've got too much to do to take time out to rest," or "It takes too much energy to get on my bike."

In more severe circumstances, such as when facing a serious illness such as cancer, some people become severely depressed and give up their will to live. Others, after hearing the bad news, go through the initial shock, then diligently seek medical assistance. Still others turn to prayer to find spiritual strength that might assist them in regaining their health. If health is not possible, they strive to develop attitudes that help them cope with their illness from a position of emotional and spiritual strength.

Instead of developing a sense of emotional and spiritual health, some people use some form of denial to cope with the pressures of life. Denial can take many forms. People can deny a problem exists: "Everyone drinks! It's no problem for me." We can deny the importance of the problem: "Sure, I drink a lot, but I always get to work." We can deny the solvability of the problem: "At lunch, I have to have a drink or two with my clients or I'll lose their business." We can deny our own ability to solve the problem: "Yes, I drink too much, but I just can't help it. I'm under so much pressure." Last, we can deny other people's ability to help us: "There's no one who cares enough to help me."[10]

The same denial process is used by those who minimize their high blood pressure, eating disorders, substance abuse, or psychosomatic problems. When we use any form of denial, we are giving in to negative attitudes instead of mobilizing the positive powers of the human spirit.

When the urge to live is seriously out of balance for an extended period of time, complaints grow more serious: "There's nothing to live for," "I can't face another day with this pain," "I haven't the courage to go on." People may think of suicide when they find they cannot solve their problems.

HOPING FOR A MIRACLE

When nothing seems to work, many people begin to hope for miracles. This hope seems to be a natural response of the human spirit in the face of overwhelming or seemingly insoluble problems. Believing in miracles is one way people try to overcome hopelessness.

Some people do not believe in miracles. They claim that so-called miracles are only mixtures of superstition, self-suggestion, and excuses that people invent to comfort themselves and cure their hysterical, psychosomatic symptoms. An equally skeptical view is that miracles are fortuitous events of nature. A sudden cloudburst that puts out a fire, or an earthquake or tidal wave that does no damage, is often said to be due to Lady Luck. Luck is given the credit when something hoped for, yet unpredictable, happens.

The word *miracle* is often used in more casual ways: "Wow, it was a miracle I got to school on time!" It's also used to refer to exceptional skills or efforts: "It's a miracle the way he performs surgery." Traditionally, the word is used to refer to an extraordinary or astonishing event caused by the intervention of God or gods: "I didn't think I was going to live until I prayed about it and suddenly knew God would help." An important step in the very successful worldwide program of Alcoholics Anonymous and other twelve-step programs based on AA is admitting the need for God or some higher power. Admitting this need can be a humbling experience that builds a foundation for finding new meaning in life and seems like a miracle to all concerned.

Many religious groups believe in miracles, even though religious leaders do not agree on the concept. Muhammad said that only the Qur'an was miraculous. Buddha said that the only miracles were revelations of the inner self. And Confucius taught that there were no miracles.[11] In spite of what they said, each of these three was credited by their followers with having performed miracles.

In Judeo-Christian tradition, there are many stories of people with miraculous powers. In the Bible, *miracle* means work of power. While some people think of biblical miracles as historical events that actually occurred as recorded, others think of them more as metaphors that shed light on important human concerns.

In Roman Catholic tradition, miracles are believed to happen by the direct intervention of God, often working through a saint, and occur in response to faith and prayers. For a cure to be officially labeled a miracle by the Church, there must be proof that the cure was sudden, the illness was so serious that the person would not get better with conventional treatment, and the symptoms remain absent for at least a year after the healing occurs.[12]

A belief in miracles is often based on faith, and faith healing is a widely known phenomenon. Studies of faith healing at the Shrine of Our Lady at Lourdes have long been a source of scientific interest. Nobel prize–winning biologist, sociologist, and surgeon Alexis Carrel, who developed a method for suturing blood vessels in the early 1900s, investigated healings he had witnessed there and found many to be true.

Similar research was conducted by Dr. Bernard Grad of McGill University on the effects of the laying on of hands. This is an ancient faith healing ritual that is still widely practiced and is based on the belief in the transference of healing energy. Some say the energy comes from God; others say the healing energies come from the person who is laying on his hands. By 1974, Dr. Grad had concluded that most of us have the power to channel some kind of cosmic life force for the purpose of healing.[13] In his

The urge to live

*The energy
for life*

*The search
for meaning*

IAN JAMES

FRANK JARRETT

DAVID M. ALLEN

Getting in shape

Celebrating life

The need for hope   *An everyday comfort*

research, Dr. Grad found that people who are skeptical of this process can interfere with normal healing, and that people who believe in its potential and have a strong urge to live can often stimulate their own healing. Recently the laying on of hands, or what is now called "therapeutic touch," is being taught in some nursing schools because evidence shows that the miracle of loving touch helps patients to heal.[14]

Another view of miracles is that people create their own by developing positive mental attitudes. Dr. Carl Simonton's studies on cancer show that people who believe in "mind over matter" and use visualization techniques to help cure a cancer are more likely to be cured than those who are skeptical of cure.[15] Similarly, Dr. Bernie Siegel, a surgeon and professor at Yale University who has studied exceptional cures of cancer patients, believes that those who develop cancer have often felt despair about their lives for many months or even years. His research shows that cancer patients have a better chance of getting well if they express their feelings of depression, anxiety, and hostility. When negative feelings are expressed and worked through, instead of being harbored, hope often returns, which confirms Bernie Seigel's belief that "In the face of uncertainty, there is nothing wrong with hope."[16]

After being diagnosed as having lung or throat cancer, a person with hope may decide to stop smoking. After discovering high blood pressure, a person with hope may make major life-style changes that reduce the amount of stress in his or her life. After having a heart attack, a person with hope may decide to eat differently and exercise regularly. People do these things because they want to survive and be comfortable and, beyond that, to live a life that has more meaning. In this way, they help to create their own miracles and works of power.

We have all heard stories that show this power, such as that of a ninety-two-pound mother who "miraculously" uses superhuman strength and lifts a two-thousand-pound car off her trapped child who has been run over. She doesn't stop to use self-hypnosis to avoid the pain as a person on the way to having an uncomfortable dental or medical procedure might, nor does she use visualization as she might if she were preparing to perform at a higher level. She just acts from the basis of her hope and her love.

One of the hoped-for medical miracles today is that a discovery will be made on how to prevent and cure AIDS.

There is reason for hope. Other serious diseases have been conquered. The discovery of vaccination, for example, led to the control of many diseases. In 1796, Edward Jenner, a British country physician, took a major step in disease control with the discovery of a vaccination against smallpox. When a farm girl with an infection came to Jenner, he suspected smallpox. The girl told him she couldn't have smallpox because she had already had cowpox. Jenner decided to scientifically test the folklore that cowpox was a protection against smallpox. He injected cowpox from the skin lesions of cows into humans and discovered the cowpox did indeed protect them from smallpox. This discovery was called *vaccination* because it was derived from the word *vacca,* meaning cow.

However, it took 200 years before enough interest, information, and vaccine was available to conquer the disease worldwide. In 1967, there were between 10 to 15 million cases of smallpox, with 2 million deaths in a single year. Then, the U.N. World Health Organization campaigned against smallpox, and by 1979, there were no cases of smallpox reported anywhere in the world. The miracle of medicine's ability to save lives had won.

Those concerned with AIDS have high hopes that something similar will be discovered for AIDS treatment and will be inexpensively available on a worldwide basis.

Although the urge to live and the passion to experience a full life are universal, the possibility of death raises questions about what happens next? Is there an afterlife, and if so, what is it like?

BODY AND SOUL

The goal of a long life is nearly universal and, as our years are limited, it is not surprising that the concept of an afterlife is appealing. As Bismarck, the great German chancellor, expressed it, "Without the hope of an afterlife, this life is not even worth the effort of getting dressed in the morning."[17] Yet because a belief in life after death is common, there is no scientific proof either for or against it.

Belief in life after death is based on the belief in a soul, for it is the soul that is thought to live on. Theologians tend to use "soul" and "spirit" interchangeably and define them as the part of us that shares divinity and does not die but continues on beyond physical death.

Philosophers disagree on the nature of the soul. Plato claimed that nothing could destroy the soul, that it was "the most divinest part" of us, and that although the soul is within the body, it is also independent of the body. Aristotle, his student, said that the body and soul are one and therefore, when the body dies, the soul also dies. Only "reason" is eternal.

The debate has followed similar lines through the ages since then. Avicenna, a famous eleventh-century Muslim physician and philosopher, agreed with Plato that the soul was indeed immortal. In contrast, Averroes, his contemporary who integrated Greek with Islamic thought, agreed with Aristotle that only reason is eternal.

The ancient Egyptians and Chinese believed in a dual soul. To the Egyptians, the *ka* soul survived death but stayed near the body, so the body had to be maintained by embalming. The *ba* soul did not remain with the body but went off to the land of the dead. The ancient Chinese believed there was a sensory soul that lived in the body and disappeared at death and a more rational soul, called the *hun,* did not die and was the object of ancestor worship.

If there is a soul, then where is it during life? The ancient Egyptians thought the soul was in the heart or bowels. The Sumerians and Assyrians said it was in the liver. Plato said it was in the head, but Aristotle was sure it was in the heart because the heart pumps the blood that sustains life.

A major breakthrough occurred when Leonardo da Vinci dissected the brain and, not finding the soul there, pioneered a new approach to the controversy. Building on his work 150 years later, René Descartes declared the body was only a machine and that the brain was entirely distinct from the mystical domain of the soul. This theory became known as dualism, the belief that body and soul are separate. With this, the question came up again: Where is the soul located if it is distinct from the body? Descartes said that although they are separate, the body and soul constantly interact and the soul, itself, is in the pineal gland.

It is interesting to know that just beneath the pineal gland is a bit of the brain stem that generates the alertness necessary for consciousness. Because there is some reflex movement even after the brain dies, in the early nineteenth century there was a widespread argument that there was a "spinal cord soul."

There have also been debates on whether or not the soul can leave the body and wander about temporarily. In support of this, "out-of-body experiences" have been reported by many people who have been declared clinically dead then returned to life. They claim to have experienced themselves as being outside their bodies and able to observe themselves somewhat objectively. The same claim has been made by some children who have been seriously abused and some adults who have been tortured.

Research about whether or not the soul or human spirit exists and, if it does, whether it leaves the body is being conducted on many fronts, including medicine and quantum physics. Raymond Moody, a physician working in acute-care hospitals, has interviewed hundreds of people who have died and been resuscitated. Their stories are remarkably similar—they experience themselves as separate from their bodies, floating above their bodies and looking down at themselves in wonder.[18] Psychiatrist Elisabeth Kübler-Ross's research indicates that children who are dying often know it and see themselves "going toward the light."[19]

The study of death and dying is called thanatology, from the Greek *thanatos,* meaning death. This study is becoming increasingly important as more and more decisions are being made about organ transplants, life support systems, euthanasia, and physician assisted suicides. Even the definitions of life and death are being reexamined.

The various beliefs regarding the body and soul have generated different beliefs in life after death. Today there are four common beliefs about the body and soul and life after death. One of the oldest is reincarnation, the belief held by Hindus and many Buddhists that the soul continues on after death and returns in another body until a soul's "karma" is worked out. Karma is the sum of the negative deeds or actions a person has committed in a lifetime that need to be corrected in subsequent lives to achieve Nirvana, which is the state of bliss achieved when death and rebirth are no longer necessary. People who believe in reincarnation think that there are lessons to be learned in solving problems in this life and that it is better to learn them now than repeat the problems in another life. With this belief, the urge to live is directed toward solving interpersonal problems and living a life that has meaning because it is ethical.

In contrast, traditional Christians and Muslims believe in the immortality of the soul. They maintain that at death people either go to be with God (Allah), who may be loving and merciful or judgmental and wrathful, or they go to purgatory or hell to be without God. With such a belief, they often strive to live according to what they believe is God's will and accept death as a step toward their desired salvation.

The existential point of view is concerned with responsible action in this life without much concern for an afterlife. Classical Judaism has this focus; that the meaning of life is to live according to ethical principles and religious practices. Other people with a nontheological point of view agree that human beings have a unique capacity to design their lives through ethical and loving decisions and actions. They may live by a creed proposed by Etienne de Grellet: "I shall pass through this world but once. If therefore, there be any kindness I can show, or any good thing I can do, let me do it now . . . for I shall not pass this way again."[20]

A fourth perspective, often called the "scientific" point of view, is held by many who decide to remain undecided because there is no scientific proof about what happens after death. By suspending judgment, they are able to live with the unknown and also express a high urge to live.

Whether or not the soul or spirit leaves the body during lifetime or after death cannot be scientifically proven, but growing evidence points to the hope for answers to these and other questions about immortality and the meaning of life.

CELEBRATING LIFE

Dag Hammarksjold was a great leader of the United Nations who handled many critical international incidents with diplomacy and was often able to find peaceful solutions to difficult conflicts. However, his search for meaning and purpose in his own life was not easy. For many years, he was despairing, self-accusatory, and even suicidal. The many important political and financial tasks he performed for his native Sweden did little to lift him out of his despair.

Unexpectedly in 1953, he was elected Secretary-General of the United Nations. For him, this was a turning point, a decisive moment. He had wanted to find something to live for that would also be great enough to die for—and world peace was this to him. He wrote in his diary, "God has a use for you, even though what he asks doesn't happen to suit you at the moment."[21]

Dag Hammarskjold had at last discovered his life's purpose in working for the United Nations. He was awarded the Nobel Peace Prize in 1961, and shortly before he died in a plane crash that same year, he wrote one of many prayers,

> FOR ALL THAT HAS BEEN—THANKS!
> TO ALL THAT SHALL BE—YES![22]

If we review our own lives from a similar perspective, perhaps we can also give thanks for what has been, what is, and what might be. For it is in from the depths of our spirits that we are called to be both whole and holy. Reaching out for life and purpose, we are engaged in a spiritual search. Like the astronauts who first landed on the moon, we can also take a giant step for humanity by living with hope and celebrating. "Here's to Life!"

❦ RELEASING YOUR URGE TO LIVE————————

The following optional exercises will assist you in releasing your urge to live.

❦ FOR CONTEMPLATION ON LIVING. Take some time and get into a quiet situation in which you will not be interrupted for a while. Consider what meaning these quotes might have for you.

> WHAT IS LIFE? IT IS THE FLASH OF A FIREFLY IN THE NIGHT. IT IS THE BREATH OF A BUFFALO IN THE WINTER TIME. IT IS THE LITTLE SHADOW WHICH RUNS ACROSS THE GRASS AND LOSES ITSELF IN THE SUNSET.
> —CHIEF CROWFOOT[23]

> I CANNOT MAKE THE UNIVERSE OBEY ME. I CANNOT MAKE OTHER PEOPLE CONFORM TO MY OWN WHIMS AND FANCIES. I CANNOT MAKE EVEN MY OWN BODY OBEY ME.
> —THOMAS MERTON[24]

THE LUST FOR COMFORT, THAT STEALTHY THING THAT ENTERS THE
HOUSE AS A GUEST, AND THEN BECOMES A HOST, AND THEN A
MASTER.

—KAHLIL GIBRAN[25]

MANY PEOPLE TREAT THEIR BODIES AS IF THEY WERE RENTED FROM
HERTZ—SOMETHING THEY ARE USING TO GET AROUND IN BUT
NOTHING THEY GENUINELY CARE ABOUT UNDERSTANDING.

—CHUNGLIANG AL HUANG[26]

WHEN I STAND BEFORE THEE AT THE DAY'S END, THOU SHALT SEE
MY SCARS AND KNOW THAT I HAD MY WOUNDS AND ALSO MY
HEALING.

—RABINDRANATH TAGORE[27]

LIVE AS IF YOU WERE LIVING A SECOND TIME, AND AS THOUGH YOU
HAD ACTED WRONGLY THE FIRST TIME.

—VIKTOR FRANKL[28]

🍒 FLUCTUATIONS IN YOUR URGE TO LIVE. Probably your urge to live
has been higher at some periods in your life than at others. Recall
some times in childhood and adolescence, as a young adult and
more recently, when your urge to live was high and also when it
was low.

Times of High Urge to Live

In childhood

In adolescence

As a young adult

Recently

Times of Low Urge to Live

In childhood

In adolescence

As a young adult

Recently

❦ HIGHS AND LOWS OF HOPE. In the past, how have you acted when your hope was high? When it was low?

Nowadays, how do you act when your hope is high? When it is low?

Do you see a relationship between your urge to live and your feelings of hope?

❦ DENYING YOUR POWER. In this exercise, consider the four ways you might deny the reality of a physical problem or condition that lowers your physical energies. Then fill in the following statements.
My unsolved problem is:

I deny I have a problem or a negative condition by:

I deny the importance of my problem or condition by:

I deny the solvability of my problem or condition by:

I deny my ability to solve my problem or improve my condition by:

I deny anyone's ability to help me by:

Now imagine that you have solved your problem or improved your condition. How would your life be different?

❦   YOUR SELF-CARE PLAN. Consider your physical condition and how you care for your body in regard to diet, exercise, relaxation, sleep, alcohol, and so on. Do you want to take any first steps toward changing your condition in any way? What are you willing to do to bring this about? Write out your plan.

❦   YOUR SEARCH FOR MIRACLES. How do you define the word miracle? Have you ever hoped for a miracle? For example, think of some time in your life when you, or someone you loved, was very sick and got well. Did you think of it as a miracle of some kind? If you did, to what or to whom did you give the credit?

THE URGE FOR FREEDOM

❦

THE TORCH OF FREEDOM

Feeling free is one of the greatest sensations in life. When we feel free, the sky seems bluer, the trees greener, and the air fresher. When we feel free, we feel more energy and enthusiasm. People are more interesting, and we are willing to get more involved with them. Life is more challenging, and we welcome the challenge. At times like this, we may become more active in searching for significant goals and more aware of our cosmic connections.

Yet most of us experience innumerable situations in which we do not feel free. We feel trapped externally in oppressive or depressing situations, or trapped internally in our inner worlds of anxiety, fear, and confusion.

When we feel trapped, it is natural for us to wonder how we became trapped and how we might get free. We may ask ourselves, "What can I do to get out of this mess?" "What would it take to break free and really become the person I want to be?"

Possibly the most famous symbol of freedom is the Statue of Liberty holding her lighted torch of freedom at the entrance of New York harbor. The statue is known throughout the world, especially to the millions of immigrants who passed through Ellis Island into the United States in search of freedom. When the statue was unveiled in 1886, inscribed on its base were words written for the occasion by Emma Lazarus:

KEEP, ANCIENT LANDS, YOUR STORIED POMP! CRIES SHE WITH SILENT LIPS. GIVE ME YOUR TIRED, YOUR POOR, YOUR HUDDLED MASSES YEARNING TO BREATHE FREE . . .

The yearning to breathe free is the soul trying to express itself, and the Statue of Liberty reminds us of this universal yearning.

Charlie De Leo, who has been the caretaker of Miss Liberty's torch for many years, claims that the torch represents the holy spirit as well as the spirit of freedom. When he goes on his daily rounds, high in the statue to clean the torch, he kneels and prays for continuing freedom.[2]

THE URGE TO BE FREE

Instinctively and intellectually we know that freedom is a basic right and seeking it is a natural expression of the human spirit. The universal urge for freedom arises from each person's inner core and creates energy to break out of the actual or imagined prisons of body, mind, or spirit. As individuals, we want to feel free to think our own thoughts and to do what we want to do, at least within reason. As groups, we want to be free to associate with whom we choose and express what we think.

To be free is to have the opportunity to choose. Psychologist Rollo May puts it more eloquently in explaining that freedom is the "capacity to pause between stimulus and response and, in that pause, to choose the one response toward which we wish to throw our weight."[3] With each act, we choose one possibility over another.

Some of these choices may be relatively unimportant such as choosing to go to a movie instead of staying home to watch TV or choosing to eat one meal instead of another or wear one style of clothes instead of another. These kinds of choices have little to do with survival or ultimate purposes. They are more choices of comfort or preference.

The choices we make when freedom is at stake are much

more important. We can choose how to use our time, energies, and resources, and our choices inevitably affect others. Therefore what we do with our freedom is a crucial matter.

We all want many kinds of freedom. One of the most important is *physical freedom.* Physical freedom is being able to come and go, to do and not do, according to our own choice. None of us enjoys being tied up or locked up in any kind of cell or room, in a hospital bed or wheelchair. We want to escape from prisons of stone and steel, or from prisons of our bodies if we are trapped by age, pain, or disease. We also fight for physical freedom when trapped by a natural catastrophe. If caught in a fire, we fight for air. In the case of an avalanche, we fight to get free of the snow. In the case of an earthquake, we fight to get out from under falling debris. There is a natural biological response to get free from a dangerous situation.

In addition to physical freedom, we want *emotional freedom,* to be unencumbered by negative feelings of confusion, low self-esteem, and mistrust. People with a strong urge for emotional freedom usually work hard trying to understand themselves and others. They read books that might be useful, listen to self-help tapes, and take classes or attend workshops directed toward understanding personality and making changes. They may also seek psychotherapy to help in the process.

When we are able to live with less fear and anxiety we often increase our *intellectual freedom.* We think with more clarity and are able to solve many problems that seem unsolvable when we feel emotionally trapped. Thinking more autonomously, instead of automatically agreeing with others, we prefer the kind of work that permits independent thinking. Educators and parents who believe in intellectual freedom frequently feel called to teach others how to achieve it.

The urge for freedom also includes the desire for *religious freedom.* Some religious systems demand full obedience to particular dogmas and rituals; the Satanic cults are the most obvious and abhorrent. Throughout the world there are other religious groups who feel justified in persecuting or annihilating those with different beliefs. In such cases, they are not free but chained to their own way of thinking, believing it to be superior to all others. An increasing number of people do not agree with self-righteous and discriminatory religious groups. They study their own religious faith in depth and also study other religious traditions for the enlightenment they can bring.

In addition, many religious groups are freely joining together rather than pushing apart. For example, spiritual leaders from all over the world and from all major religious traditions now gather together yearly for the World Day of Prayer for Peace. They respect each other's differences while uniting in a shared commitment.

There are many people who do not belong to any organized religious groups but search for *spiritual freedom*. They seek to understand the meaning of life, to live ethically, recognize universal truths, find wisdom, feel a sense of harmony with all, and sometimes feel close to God. These people often find a spiritual meaning in nature, in art, or in connections with other people.

Freedom has many faces. If we accept the free choice of others as valid expressions of the human spirit on various paths with heart, then we increase our own freedom and support the universal desire for self-determination.

THE SEARCH FOR SELF-DETERMINATION

When the urge for freedom is felt strongly, it leads to the search for self-determination. All people want to be self-determined unless the chains of brutality and neglect have been so dehumanizing that a person becomes an obedient robot or a drugged captive animal. We all try to break out of situations that confine us— clothes that are too tight, rooms that are too small, jobs and schools, cultures, and relationships that are too restrictive. "I want my freedom!" is a personal cry that can turn into a group demand, "We want our freedom!"

Once we achieve freedom from something or someone, our challenge then becomes what to do with our freedom. Theologian Abraham Heschel claims: "To be or not to be is not the question. The vital question is: how to be and how not to be."[4]

We want to be free because we want to be in charge of our own lives. We want to be self-determining. *Self-determination is having the freedom to choose our own fate or course of action without being compelled to do so by others.* It is acting on the basis of decisions we freely, and sometimes courageously, make rather than being controlled by the whims or demands of others. Self-determination is also acting deliberately, not unthinkingly on the basis of habit, conditioning, or internal psychological pre-disposition.

When the goal of self-determination becomes a passion, people are willing to go to great lengths to achieve it. Sathaya Tor, a Cambodian, was, at age seven, taken from his family by Khmer Rouge soldiers and put into a child labor camp in the notorious killing fields of Cambodia. There he had to work twelve hours a day on only two scoops of rice. His urges to live and be free were so strong that he survived the hard reality: "I knew that when I was really starving, no one would take care of me. I had to take care of myself."[5] To do this at age seven was an incredible task.

At age fourteen, he was finally set free. His self-determination then led him to immigrate to the United States and later become a student at Stanford University where he continued to expand his horizons of choice and his vision of a better life.

The search for self-determination is often motivated by a vision of a better life. When people make a move—from one part of the country to another, from one country to another, from one job to another—they have a vision that life will be better in the "promised land," their new environment. This is how it is for many of us; we imagine life will be better once we are free of something or someone.

In spite of a deep desire to be self-determining, we may find it difficult to make the decisions necessary to fulfill our visions. Freedom may seem too difficult to achieve, so we procrastinate indefinitely or defer to others for decisions. We may act eager to please, hungry for approval, and fearful of making mistakes. When our only priority is to make others happy, then we give up our own freedom.

It is not unusual for people to avoid self-determination as the result of having been punished and repeatedly criticized for making poor decisions. They are fearful of being blamed once more. To them, there is less danger in doing nothing than in risking further punishment.

All of us, however, are usually decisive in some areas of our lives even if not in others. We feel free to pursue certain self-determined goals while avoiding others. We can be decisive at work yet act meek with friends or indecisive about getting into a committed relationship. In situations such as these, our indecision may be due to the fear of making a mistake or losing out on something better. By committing to a lifetime relationship, we may fear giving up the freedom to be romantically involved with many others. By committing oneself to a social cause, we may be called upon to give up comfort and safety.

With freedom, we make wise decisions and foolish ones. We develop a passion to break free and be self-determining or we sit back in passive comfort or hide out of fear. Achieving freedom is not easy, and we may long for more courage to break free and stay free.

THE NEED FOR COURAGE

The urge for freedom and the search for self-determination requires courage to make decisions and act on them. *Courage—the willingness to act positively in spite of fear*—has the same root as the French word *cœur,* which means heart. Courage comes from the heart, the inner core of the spiritual self, which can pump energy and courage through our psychological and physical selves in much the same way that heart pumps blood through a body. The more we feel the urge for freedom, the more we want to be self-determining. As our desire to be self-determining grows, we need to become more courageous. This process can be diagrammed:

Urge of the Human Spirit	Goal of the Search	Needed for the Search
Freedom	Self-determination	Courage

Most of us want more courage because we doubt we have enough. However, if we are passionately involved in the search for freedom, we can decide to *act* courageously even when we don't *feel* that way.

Courage is like taking a step into the unknown with the hope that it will turn out all right. In 1969, the whole world watched TV with excitement when Neil Armstrong took the first step on the moon. It was a courageous step. Hope was high, but no one was certain that it could be done until it was actually accomplished.

Courage is easily recognizable when someone performs a daring rescue or a valorous act against all odds. It is also present in the person who fights to live with integrity while afflicted by an incurable disease. This requires the courage to affirm life, in spite of its pain, finiteness, and ambiguities. It takes courage to endure the agonies of chemotherapy or the aches and pains of aging.

Courage can be observed in other ways. We see courage in the person who remains cheerful when facing the unpleasant consequences of an accident or mistake. We see it in the actions of someone who is poor yet living with pride and dignity. We see it in the parent who cares for a child with severe problems and in the stranger who takes food to others who are hungry. Returning to school after years of not going also requires courage. So does moving to a new country or taking a stand in an unpopular cause. We see courage in many ways.

Courage is most observable when it is expressed physically. Soldiers who brave death to protect their comrades show physical courage. So do political prisoners who are willing to endure torture for the sake of their beliefs or their comrades.

Darwin Carlisle was a courageous girl who refused to die. She had been abandoned by her mother at the age of nine and left alone in an unheated attic for several days. When she was found, Darwin was so badly frostbitten that her legs had to be amputated.

Artificial legs were designed for her, and on these new legs she gained some freedom by learning to walk. Astoundingly, she also learned to roller skate and ride a bicycle within only two months! This happened after her *great*-grandmother, who was awarded custody of Darwin by the court, encouraged her to seek physical freedom in spite of being handicapped.[6]

Less dramatic expressions of courage show when a person who is frightened of speaking in public does so in spite of the fear, or when someone who is depressed decides to get up each morning and face the day regardless of feeling unhappy. It also takes courage to face criticism without being defensive or overwhelmed. Psychological courage is often needed when changing careers or moving from one location to another or revising a lifestyle.

Betty Ford was the wife of the president of the United States when she courageously "went public" and told the people of the United States about her mastectomy and thus encouraged other women to take more positive attitudes toward themselves if they needed similar surgery. She later admitted to her addictions to alcohol and drugs and how she broke free of them.[7] This encouraged others to do likewise. Next she founded a center where people could go to break their addictions. When Betty Ford responded to

the powerful urge to be free and live a healthy life, without de-
fending herself with denial or secrecy, she helped others to
freedom.

Courage is sometimes bolstered by religious faith. It was
this kind of faith that Lech Walesa held throughout the years of
struggle for freedom in Poland. As one of the founders of the
Solidarity movement in 1980, Walesa had what he believed to be
a God-given mission—to help his people transcend restrictions
imposed by an unpopular government and restore social justice
and the chance to work under the flag of freedom. For organizing
workers in protest of unfair conditions, he was put in detention
for one year and then kept under continual police surveillance for
several more years. During these hard times, what sustained him
was the discovery that "deep religious belief, deep faith, eliminates
fear" and that "all I do, I do because I have faith."[8]

To take a stand and to let others know what we believe in
often takes physical, psychological, and spiritual courage. Doing
what needs to be done, whether in our own behalf or in service
to others, requires courage. As philosopher Martin Buber explains,
"Life lived in freedom is personal responsibility or it is a pathetic
farce."[9]

THE CHALLENGE OF FREEDOM

To live a life of freedom often poses some difficult realities. Freedom sometimes feels scary. We may be free to change careers yet
stay enslaved to a particular job out of the fear of making the wrong
choice. We may be free to start a project yet hesitate and procrastinate out of fear of failure. We may be free to protest against some
social inequity yet remain silent because we fear retaliation.

Freedom can be also be confusing. Doing things to please
other people or to get others' respect or admiration is natural, yet
some people go too far and design their whole lives to gain others'
approval. Like chameleons, they do and say what they think other
people want to hear or expect of them. When it comes time to
express their own inner desires, they are confused about what they
want. "I don't know what to do. I'm so used to doing things for
other people, I haven't the foggiest idea of what *I* want." To those
who constantly seek approval, personal freedom can seem debilitating.

Freedom can also be overwhelming. Children who are given too much freedom, for example, and are allowed to do anything they want may become fearful because no one is sufficiently involved to give them parental direction. They often withdraw into loneliness or establish very dependent relationships. Some feel a compulsion to go along with the crowd and do what others are doing, while others marry early as a way to avoid facing the fear of freedom. Others with too much freedom "act out" so that parents and teachers are forced to pay them more attention and exert some control. This kind of freedom leads children to feel as if they are cast out to sea without knowing where to go or how to get there. The same is true for adults who go through divorce or lose a job or retire and find they have too much time on their hands. They may feel displaced and disoriented, at a loss about what to do next, or they may even feel defeated and go into a long-term depression.

The challenge of freedom can be unwelcome for many reasons so people often choose to avoid it. Instead of making courageous, autonomous, healthy choices, they limit themselves by responding in unfree ways and develop habitual patterns of conforming, controlling, rebelling, withdrawing, or being indifferent.

Conforming to the expectations of others, when we do not agree with them, is a self-imposed loss of freedom. People who continually do this do so at the expense of their own identities. They ignore their own preferences, take away their own freedom, and give up the search to be self-determined.

Controlling others to prevent them from acting independently is another pattern some people use. They want to be fully in charge of their total environment and, like children who manipulate to get their way, they apply pressures to relationships to try to stay in charge of other people's freedom.

Rebellion is another way people limit their freedom. By fighting for one thing, they push against another. In fighting against hypocrisy, they may become staunchly independent, even stubborn, and be highly critical of others. Or in resisting being told what to do, they may not listen to others and end up isolating themselves from other people.

Being indifferent to others develops from being mistreated or ignored over long periods of time. People who have become indifferent cannot trust others, so relationships lose their importance. These people are not concerned over others' freedom. They simply don't care.

Withdrawal into depression is a tragic response to the challenges of freedom. In this condition, people isolate themselves, diminish their chances for enjoying others, ignore the powerful urges of the inner core, and give up hope that anyone cares enough to come to their rescue. They give up their passion for life. When this happens, the spiritual search comes to a stop.

The cry of freedom is often used to justify licentious behavior. Freedom is not a license to do just anything. It is license to do certain things responsibly. A driver's license grants permission to drive, not permission to drive recklessly; a parent may give permission to a child to go out for the evening, but that is not a license to stay out all night. We are all licensed in many ways— by tradition and laws, by government agencies and parents, even by ourselves. If we misuse our freedom we may do great harm to ourselves or others.

Many people misuse freedom. They take advantage of other people's weakness. Whenever we look around, read the newspapers, or turn on TV, we cannot help but see situations in which people act malevolently. They may molest children, sell drugs to teenagers, use other adults for selfish ends, or bilk the elderly out of their life savings. Or they may misuse their freedom against themselves. They may abuse alcohol or drugs or indulge in some other compulsive behavior of one sort or another or give up on life in some other way. Obviously, these abuses of freedom do not lead to that sense of opportunity that makes freedom so valuable.

Some people blame evil spirits when they do wrong, saying, "The devil made me do it." The current rise of Satanic cults and the worship of the devil is clear indication that this phrase is sometimes used as justification for sadistic acts.

Currently, most major religions minimize the concept of evil spirits. Like the theologian Paul Tillich, they are more likely to speak of the demonic instead of demons. Demonic in this sense refers to any force that creates division and chaos, whatever its origin.

Whether or not we believe in external demons, we can recognize the demonic within ourselves. It may emerge unexpectedly when we sometimes act in vengeful or malevolent ways, or have the potential for doing so. Or the "demon" may arise when we give in to an addiction that takes away our freedom.

In such a situation, we need to take the first step to change, by becoming aware of our potential for evil as well as for good, and by admitting that we need to change. When we do this, we are beginning to break free and search for a path with more heart.

MIND-SETS OF FREEDOM

The urge for freedom is universal, yet people respond to it differently based on the mind-sets they live by. *Mind-sets are firmly held beliefs, opinions, and expectations that govern the way we view ourselves, other people, and the world.* They are built up through experience and become habitual ways of thinking and feeling that affect our actions. Mind-sets are sometimes referred to as attitudes, scripts, or frames of reference.

People have mind-sets about almost everything in life. Their minds are made up about what they like to watch on TV, how to handle money, whether or not education is important, what is proper behavior, what they like or dislike in a spouse, even what they want to do with their spare time. The most important mind-sets deal with a person's opinions as to who's in charge of one's life and whether people or situations can be changed for the better.

When mind-sets are positive and realistic, they make life easier and guide our efforts in successful directions. When they are inaccurate or negative, they can blind us to other positive realities and block the natural expression of our urge for freedom and self-determination. Phrases such as "I can't" or "What's the use?" all reflect a sense of doubt and discouragement. Phrases such as "I will" or "I can" show an inner confidence and sense of determination.

A sense of inner freedom and self-confidence can arise from questioning mind-sets of those around us. This was true for psychologist Carl Jung. His school years were extremely difficult; mathematics, drawing, and gymnastics classes were so terrifying that he had a series of psychosomatic fainting spells. When he overheard his father explaining to someone that he might have epilepsy, Jung taught himself not to faint.

Jung questioned many things, and this so annoyed teachers

The urge for freedom

*Invitation
to freedom*

*Barrier
to freedom*

IAN JAMES

KAREN WARD

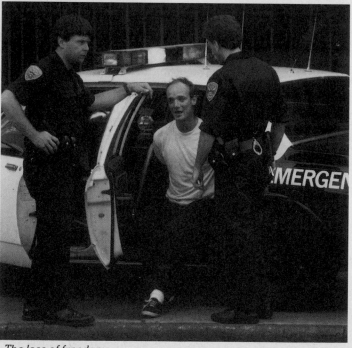

IAN JAMES

The loss of freedom

On the march

The courage to protest

Free to be

and peers that he decided to be silent about what was most important to him—"God's world." As a child, Jung became very critical of the church. He had expected his first communion to be a transcendent moment, but nothing special happened, so he never went to communion again. Yet he struggled to try to understand what God's will might be for him. His belief in God, and his perception of himself as gifted, gave Jung the freedom to be self-determining. He threw off the shackles of childhood mind-sets and created an important psychological theory that includes respect for the spiritual dimension of life.[10]

Obviously, childhood experiences and beliefs are not the only determinant of adult decisions. Mind-sets can change whenever something happens that is so important that we question our beliefs. The unexpected loss of a job when jobs are scarce can be a severe blow to a person's self-worth and lead to giving up a previously held sense of confidence and self-determination. Breaking free of an addiction can change self-deprecating mind-sets to those that are more freeing and self-appreciating. Good friendships can also have a positive influence on mind-sets. And the influence of a spouse over the years can have a major impact, either positive or negative, on a person's mind-sets. But, because of our basic urge to be free, mind-sets can be changed at any time.

CULTURAL MIND-SETS

The mind-sets we hold are always influenced by the cultures we live in. Every culture or group has its own mind-sets—whether the group is a nation, a work team, a school, or a family. *Cultural mind-sets are the spoken and unspoken beliefs and assumptions held by specific groups of people within a society or group.*

Cultural mind-sets include what is expected of those who are outsiders as well as what is expected of "in-group" members. These expectations dictate what is considered acceptable or good behavior and what is considered out of place or bad. These dictates exert enormous pressure on individuals to conform to group values and to limit their own opportunities to become self-determining. Every culture and subculture has group prejudices that are mind-sets similar to those held by individuals but even stronger, since they are constantly being reinforced by more people—by the culture. Like the Berlin wall, mind-sets are hard to overcome. But even the Berlin wall came down.

Until the sudden appearance of *glasnost,* freedom of information, assembly, speech, and religion were restricted in the Soviet Union for many years. The openness of glasnost changed mind-sets within the U.S.S.R. It has also changed the attitudes of people who were outside the country and looking in. As freedoms within the country became more permissible, many people's mind-sets became more open.

When people change cultures, their old mind-sets are challenged as new ones are formed. Immigrants and refugees who seek freedom by settling in a new country usually experience a period of confusion when the new country and culture's mind-sets are quite different from those they are accustomed to. In unfamiliar surroundings, they may decide to try to blend in and become assimilated, or to retain their own cultural identity, language, and customs. The culture that suddenly receives many immigrants and refugees may also become confused. Suddenly there are people who look different, talk differently, and act differently. These differences change the racial, ethnic, or religious balance of the society and can affect the cultural mind-sets.

Cultural mind-sets can also change because of strong influences within the culture. The change can be a very slow evolutionary process, as was the case for the beliefs that slaves should be free and that women should have rights equal to men's. Because people are not always willing to wait indefinitely for social change, they rebel. When cultural mind-sets have been too oppressive for too many, peasants have revolted against kings, slaves against masters, the poor against the rich, one political or religious group against another. All kinds of people who cherish freedom have banded together and stormed castles, put fire to government buildings, and killed political leaders who have blocked their freedom.

Revolution is usually preceded by a long period of dissatisfaction and unrest in which some attempt is made to change the oppressive cultural mind-set. Unplanned riots, full-scale revolutions, or war may follow. Many countries have emerged out of revolutions and wars resulting from differences in cultural mind-sets, and in the past 3,421 years, the world has been free of war for only 268 years, according to historian Will Durant.[11]

Fortunately, many cultural mind-sets are changed in less violent ways. The nonviolent protests of Mohandas K. Gandhi are remembered for their long-range impact on India and the entire world. In the early 1900s, Gandhi was a leader in resisting institutional racial prejudice in South Africa. Later his efforts shifted to the struggle for independence of India. Gandhi believed so deeply in nonviolence that several times when his own people reacted violently against the British, Gandhi fasted until the fighting stopped. It is not surprising that his spiritual search for freedom, with the goal of self-determination, led to his being given the title, *Mahatma,* which means great soul.[12]

Another effective leader in forcing cultural change with the use of nonviolence was Martin Luther King, Jr. In the 1960s, the mind-set in most of the United States was that black people should be prevented from voting, riding public buses with white people, and attending integrated schools. Yet so many were against this serious form of discrimination that King was able to mobilize their energies in the struggle for freedom.

Courageous enough to confront an entire culture, his demonstrations, sit-ins, marches, and speeches, inspired a lot of soul-searching in America. Thousands joined him, marching peacefully for civil rights while singing "We Shall Overcome." King's passion for black Americans to be self-determined influenced Presidents Kennedy and Johnson to propose the Civil Rights Act of 1964 that finally guaranteed all citizens the right to vote.[13]

With similar commitment, university students throughout the world have changed cultural mind-sets as they marched to demonstrate their concern for peace and freedom, in spite of the possible loss of life or liberty.

WOMEN ON THE MARCH

Women have often marched beside men in the universal struggle for freedom. In ancient times, the Roman historian Tacitus wrote of the German women and children who marched with the warriors and whose cries urged them on. Plutarch wrote about the barbarian women soldiers who not only went with men into battle, but also fought with swords and axes. Viking and Celtic women were also known as warriors and were greatly feared.

One of the women warriors known by name was Joan of Arc (1412–1431), a native of France. Although she was burned at the stake for her audacity, Joan is the only person, either male or female, to have command of the armies of an entire nation at age seventeen.

Christian Ross (1667–1739) was another powerful woman who was denied her right to be self-determining. Thought to be a man, she marched as a British trooper for ten years. When it was discovered that she was a woman, Christian Ross was reassigned to a "woman's role" as army cook and, thereafter, was called "Mother Ross."[14]

Women have also used nonviolent techniques in their long march for freedom. In 195 B.C. in Rome there was the Oppian Law, which prevented women from owning gold, forced them to dress in drab colors, and restricted their movement to their immediate home environment. Women organized themselves and marched against this law. Crowds of women came in from country towns and villages. In an organized fashion they waylaid men on their way to the Roman forum, urging that women should be allowed to adorn themselves and move as freely as they had formerly done. After much debate in the Senate, this law, which had been in effect for twenty years, was repealed because of the revolutionary march.

Between the years A.D. 1640 and 1647, working class women in England marched three times: once for protection against religious persecution, once for reasonable working conditions, and once again when 5,000 women marched against the House of Commons to end the civil war then in progress.[15]

Theroyne de Mericourt (1762–1817), formerly a courtesan and an opera singer, was among the first to storm the French Bastille in the struggle for freedom and equality. She later led a women's march to Versailles, where working women protested to the king and his luxurious court about the unfairness of the high price of bread. Many women fainted with hunger during the march. As a result, the National Assembly created new legislation providing for the more equal distribution of grain. However, because of the power of this march, women's organizations were no longer allowed to meet.[16]

Many women have been so passionately concerned with freedom that they have been willing to take strong action to get it. In a letter dated March 31, 1776, Abigail Adams warned her husband, the politically influential John Adams, who was at the Continental Congress trying to free the colonies from English rule:

IF PARTICULAR CARE AND ATTENTION IS NOT PAID TO THE LADIES WE ARE DETERMINED TO FOMENT A REBELLION, AND WILL NOT HOLD OURSELVES BOUND BY ANY LAWS IN WHICH WE HAVE NO VOICE OR REPRESENTATION.[17]

One of the first women's marches in America was in 1872, when Susan B. Anthony led a group of women to the polls in Rochester, New York. These women marched to test their right to vote under the fourteenth Amendment, which guarantees that right to every U.S. citizen. Some were arrested. At one of the trials a judge ruled that the fourteenth Amendment did not apply in the case of women![18]

In spite of being ignored or mocked, women have struggled for their lives and for their right to live according to their own self-determined values. However, even after they won the right to vote, other rights were denied them.[19]

As recently as 1964, women were ridiculed in Congress while it was establishing Title VII of the Civil Rights Act. This very controversial act gave people the right to equal job opportunities and pay, regardless of their race.

Some congressmen, who did not want the bill to pass, added amendments designed to undermine it. One such amendment was that there could be no discrimination on the basis of sex. When the word "sex" was added to the amendments, the House of Representatives collapsed in laughter, and the ridicule of women began to build. It became so extreme that it turned the situation around and raised consciousness *in favor* of women having equal job opportunities with men. When the amendment was finally put to a vote, 168 were in favor and 133 opposed. A woman's voice from the House gallery was heard to cry out, "We made it! God Bless America!" She was promptly removed by the guards.[20]

The march toward freedom and self-determination continues. Neither chains nor ridicule will hold back people of
courage who have a strong belief that sooner or later justice will
prevail.

MODELS, MENTORS, AND SPIRITUAL GUIDES ─────────────

The major purpose of seeing-eye dogs is to help blind persons
move around safely. Most of us have eyes that can see yet we are
also blind in some ways. To find our way to freedom often requires
a guide, much like a seeing-eye dog, who will help us discern
which way to go and what to avoid.

Anne Frank and Hermann Buhl had imaginary friends that
served this purpose. When fourteen-year-old Anne was hiding from
the Nazis, her guiding spirit was an imaginary friend, Kitty. In her
diary she poured out her feelings to Kitty to find courage and hope
for freedom. In a similar way, mountain climber Buhl, who reached
the summit of the Himalayas, claims to have had a "partner" with
him on the last stage of the climb, an imaginary guide who cared
and strengthened him during the long hours of tension, fatigue,
and loneliness.[21]

There are many kinds of guides. Parents guide families,
politicians guide countries. When the guidance is well done, we
feel secure and confident, willing to risk what is necessary for self-
determination. When guidance is poorly given or absent, we long
for something more. We believe that if we had better guidance, we
would have a passion for life and find a path with heart that leads
to freedom.

In the search for competent and caring guides, many people
turn to experts or authorities, counselors or consultants, educators
or religious leaders to help them develop their inner strength. In
this day and age, many of us want some help to make it through,
so it's natural to turn to others who understand the journey and
can show us the way.

Children often turn to a favorite parent or relative, a special
friend, an idealized character from a novel, even a movie hero or
television heroine who can serve as a model of courage. Teenagers
emulate teachers or coaches who have been inspiring. Adults
may look to business leaders, national heroes, or political figures

as examples worth following. The memory of historical leaders are often called to mind when leadership and courage are needed.

Mentors also have a strong influence on the development of a person's courage to be self-determining. A mentor is usually an expert in a particular field who gives personalized attention to individuals. The master and apprentice relationship is one form of this type of attention. Another form is common in schools and universities, where teachers or professors guide students on a one-to-one basis. On a job, a professional colleague or boss may take the same role. If mentors believe in freedom of thought and action, they inevitably help others become self-determining.

The most powerful quality about most models and mentors is not so much what they teach, as the passion with which they teach it. When this passion comes from the heart and is generated by experience and wisdom, these people touch the spirit of others and thus become spiritual guides.

The concept of spiritual guides is common in all cultures. One widespread belief is that the spirits of family members who die can remain active, giving spiritual guidance and support to their descendants in some unexplainable way. Ancestor veneration is based on this belief and in many cultures people put food and water on shrines dedicated to their ancestors to show respect for the continuing spiritual connection. Similarly, native people of North America have often based their lives on spiritual illumination achieved during their spiritual searches or on vision quests through encounters with the spirits of animals, as well as with the spirits of elders.

Instead of turning to the spirits of their ancestors or elders, some people turn to saints as spiritual guides. Christian tradition considers all believers to belong to the "communion of saints" and Roman Catholics also believe specific people who have been canonized as saints have a special relationship with God. Believers often pray to them both for guidance and for intercession.

Others turn directly to God for guidance, usually through prayer in which they try to open themselves to the will of God. Saint Francis of Assisi is known for his prayer for spiritual guidance: "Lord, Make me an instrument of your peace. Where there is hatred, let me sow love . . . Grant that I may not so much seek to be

consoled as to console . . . For it is by giving that we receive."
Similarly, members of Alcoholics Anonymous groups are invited
to turn to God or some higher power for the courage to break their
addiction.

Even in medicine, the concept of spirit guides is being used
today. Physician Carl Simonton, who treats patients with traditional
medicine, also trains patients to relax and visualize meeting an
inner guide who can help them get well as part of their treatment.[22]

However, even a strong belief in a spirit guide does not take
away all the elements of uncertainty in life. We hope for help and
protection, yet do not know if it will be enough for our needs.

EXPERIENCING INNER FREEDOM

There is something in us that does not like fences. Whether the
fences keep us in or keep us out, we don't like our freedoms
restricted. Signs reading KEEP OUT or NO TRESPASSING, can be irritating.
International border crossings, with gates, guards, and guns, let
us know even more emphatically that we are not fully free. Our
urge for freedom reminds us that we don't want to be fenced in.
We don't want to be limited by oppressive conditions or structures.
We want basic freedoms, including the freedom to worship as we
please, to be free of torture and other inhumane practices, to
have a homeland, a decent living situation with a job, and educational opportunities. We know that fighting for these freedoms
often requires great courage. Sometimes it also requires that we
band together to fight for a cause, other times we have to do it
alone.

Even if we are not physically free, we can remain free within ourselves. Liu Chi Kung, a pianist who placed second to Van
Cliburn in the 1958 Tchaikovsky Competition, was later imprisoned
for seven years during the Cultural Revolution in China. During his
imprisonment, he was unable to play the piano, yet he was not
crushed by this tremendous loss. In fact his skills seemed to improve. After his release he explained how this was possible, "Every
day I rehearsed every piece I had ever played, note by note, in my
mind." Rehearsing with his mind, Liu Chi Kung's spirit remained
free.[23]

Inner freedom, such as Liu Chi Kung's, comes from being able to ride the waves of uncertainty and not letting external circumstances overwhelm us. Most of us have a high need for predictability. We do not like the unexpected. When cars, children, or coworkers behave in unpredictable ways, we often become frustrated or puzzled. "Why is this happening to me?" we may wonder. "Why can't I count on things going the way they're supposed to go?"

Life does not always turn out according to our plans. Inner freedom comes from being able to live with limited freedom, uncertainty, and change. We need to be open to the challenges life brings. We need to be willing to "walk a narrow ridge of uncertainty." This is a term used by philosopher Martin Buber to describe a person of faith who moves out courageously in spite of uncertainty and risk.[24] Being on a narrow ridge is a bit like being a high-wire circus performer who, without a safety net, still moves forward with trust and courage.

There are few safety nets in life. We might take a wrong step and slip and fall or make a poor investment and lose it all. We could get into relationships that don't work out, or speak up and then find we have said the wrong thing. The potential for things not turning out as we hoped is everywhere whether we are consciously involved in a spiritual search or only in the regular routines of living.

Life has few certainties. Often we don't see the guideposts that could tell us where we are going. We struggle to find our way through the maze of life, calling out to each other with bits of advice or requests for information or help. As we make the journey along the narrow ridge of uncertainty, one of the few certainties is that we need each other.

❦ RELEASING YOUR URGE FOR FREEDOM————————

Following are optional exercises to help you release your urge for freedom physically, psychologically, and spiritually.

❦ START WITH CONTEMPLATION. Look over the following quotes and choose one that catches your interest. Then focus on it for a while and let its messages about freedom become clear to you.

BETTER TO DIE ON ONE'S FEET THAN TO LIVE ON ONE'S KNEES.
—DELORES IBARRURI[25]

EACH PERSON DESIGNS HIS OWN LIFE. FREEDOM GIVES HIM THE
POWER TO CARRY OUT HIS OWN DESIGNS, AND POWER GIVES THE
FREEDOM TO INTERFERE WITH THE DESIGNS OF OTHERS.
—ERIC BERNE[26]

EMANCIPATION FROM THE BONDAGE OF THE SOIL IS NO FREEDOM
FOR THE TREE.
—RABINDRANATH TAGORE[27]

IT IS QUITE POSSIBLE FOR SOMEONE TO CHOOSE INCORRECTLY OR
TO JUDGE BADLY; BUT FREEDOM MUST ALLOW SUCH MISTAKES.
—SANG KYU SHIN[28]

WHEN THE MORNING'S FRESHNESS HAS BEEN REPLACED BY THE
WEARINESS OF MIDDAY, WHEN THE LEG MUSCLES GIVE UNDER THE
STRAIN, THE CLIMB SEEMS ENDLESS, AND SUDDENLY NOTHING WILL
GO QUITE AS YOU WISH—IT IS THEN THAT YOU MUST NOT HESITATE.
—DAG HAMMARSKJOLD[29]

WE MUST BUILD DIKES OF COURAGE TO HOLD BACK THE FLOOD
OF FEAR.
—MARTIN LUTHER KING[30]

IF WE WANT A FREE AND PEACEFUL WORLD, IF WE WANT TO MAKE
THE DESERTS BLOOM AND MAN GROW TO GREATER DIGNITY AS A
HUMAN BEING—WE CAN DO IT.
—ELEANOR ROOSEVELT[31]

❦   FEELING TRAPPED IN THE PAST. Think back to several situations in the past in which you felt trapped. Then answer the following questions.

Situations in Which I Felt Trapped	What I Did About the Situation	What I Can Conclude from This

❦   THE NEED FOR SELF-DETERMINATION. This exercise is to help you recognize your ability to break free. Take a few moments to think about these questions.

How would you like to be more free and self-determining?

What self-imposed restrictions are you using to hold yourself back?

What kind of courage do you need to mobilize your inner strength to break free? The courage to be . . . ?

To feel and act more freely, what permission would you need to give yourself?

❦   RECOGNIZING YOUR MIND-SETS. Mind-sets can lead us to express the urge for freedom in positive ways, or they can enslave us in their rigid expectations.

Become aware of some of the beliefs that control your life, such as the importance of financial success, or your beliefs about the roles men and women "should" take, or your expectations of how children should act in specific situations.

How did you develop these mind-sets? Are they directed toward freedom, or do they restrict freedom? Do you want to hang on to them or change them in some way?

❦   MEMORIES OF COURAGE. For this exercise, take time to sit down and relax. Let yourself visualize times when you acted with courage on behalf of yourself or others. See yourself in those situations once more. Listen to your words or replay your thoughts and feelings. Re-experience the power you felt when you were courageous.

Now imagine a future situation in which you might not feel courageous and would rather run away but can't. When you have a clear picture of this situation, see yourself acting with courage and self-determination.

❦   MODELS, MENTORS, AND SPIRITUAL GUIDES. Think of guiding spirits in your past, either real or imaginary, living or dead, religious or secular, to whom you have turned for protection and advice. Then fill in the following.

Guiding Spirits
I Have Known:
_____

How They Were
Important to Me
_____

6

THE URGE TO UNDERSTAND

THE EXPANSION OF KNOWLEDGE MAKES FOR AN EXPANSION OF
FAITH, AND THE WIDENING OF THE HORIZONS OF THE MIND WID-
ENING OF BELIEF. MY REASON NOURISHES MY FAITH AND MY FAITH,
MY REASON.

—NORMAN COUSINS[1]

CONGRATULATIONS!

Graduation ceremonies are times of celebration and rites of passage. They symbolize the completion of one form of learning and the transition to another.

Getting robed, putting on a mortarboard, lining up and parading into an auditorium or theater are all part of the excitement. Next come inspirational and congratulatory speeches. Finally, the diplomas are awarded. Friends and family crane their necks to watch the one person whom they see as most important. Flash cameras record the memorable occasion, enthusiastic applause rings out, and the eyes of many fill with proud tears.

Ida Grosvald was sixty-nine years old when she entered college. At that time her husband had Alzheimer's disease and she had leukemia. During her first weeks in the university, she was so exhilarated she said, "I feel like a sponge, ready to take in the world." In spite of several setbacks along the way—when she had a car accident and had to have fifty stitches in her nose, when she had an appendectomy, and she fell and cracked several ribs—her urge to understand remained strong. She graduated in five years with a bachelor's degree in human development, and at the graduation, her daughter gave her a card on which she had written, "I can't understand it! There weren't any cards 'To Mom on her graduation.' I'll have to write Hallmark."[2]

In a sense, life is a series of graduations when something is completed and we begin to look to the future. We want to know what's around the next corner. We're curious about our next step in life and hope to understand its significance.

THE URGE TO UNDERSTAND

The urge to understand is a basic motivation in everyone. It is one of the seven urges of the human spirit that continually seeks to be expressed. *To understand is to comprehend the nature and significance of something.* When people understand something, they have a wider perspective of its place in the larger scheme of things. They comprehend its overall structure and grasp its underlying principles.

Understanding is like looking down from the window of a plane, seeing familiar landscapes below, and recognizing how everything is connected with everything else.

Understanding implies an ability to work successfully with something and use it in a variety of circumstances. In this way an understanding of mathematics is useful in figuring a food budget or computing gas mileage, in doing bookkeeping or building a bridge, in measuring cloth or charting the flight of a spaceship.

The urge to understand relates to the familiar questions of what, where, when, why, and how. They range from the casual, "What do you want to do tonight?" to the more significant ones, "Why isn't my child doing well in school?" "How can I pay my bills this month?"

Finally, we may ask much more profound questions that delve into the meaning of life. "Why do people and nations have so much difficulty living together in harmony?" "How was the universe created—by a big bang or by a supreme power?" "Is there a hidden reason for things happening, or does everything depend on random chance and personal choice?" "What is the meaning of right and wrong, of good and evil, of heaven and hell?"

The questions we ask and the answers we develop may be very important to us or may have only casual significance, or be somewhere in between. One of the difficulties of our fast-moving lives is finding the time to decide what is worth understanding and what is not worth putting energy into.

THE SEARCH FOR KNOWLEDGE

Knowledge is the key to understanding, yet knowing about something is not the same as understanding it. Knowing a person is not the same as understanding that person. Knowing how to work a computer is not the same as understanding its inner workings, as any self-taught computer hacker will admit. People can know they are physically sick and not understand why. They can know that they feel anxious and not understand why. They can also know they are spiritually hungry and not understand why. Yet knowing about something can provide the foundation for later understanding it. There are three basic kinds of knowledge we seek: facts and information, practical know-how, and spiritual wisdom.

Wanting to know *facts and information* and wanting to understand what they mean is a distinguishing human trait. We learn the alphabet so we can learn to read. We study numbers because they enable us to live in a society dependent on calculations, measurements, and mathematics.

In this computer age we live in, facts tend to be thought of as impersonal bits of data, but facts and information can be like toys that intrigue and delight. Philosopher Lin Yutang thought of facts in this way: "A fact is something crawling and alive, a little furry and cool to the touch, that crawls down the back of your neck."[3]

Looking for facts is what started Charles Darwin, that insatiable student of medicine, theology, and natural sciences, off on a historic five-year voyage on H.M.S. *Beagle.* By observing geological formations, fossils, and many forms of life that existed only in specific locations, such as the Galápagos Islands, he amassed a tremendous number of facts. Attempting to find patterns in the facts and reasons for the patterns, he arrived at his theory of evolution. When his theory was published as *On the Origin of Species by Natural Selection,* it proved very controversial. Theologians and others who believed that creation occurred in seven days were especially irate because they interpreted Darwin's theory to mean that human beings evolved from monkeys rather than by a specific creative act of God.[4] Years later, Darwin's conclusions formed much of the foundation of modern biology.

Sophia Germain, a French mathematician during the time of the French Revolution, studied mathematics as avidly as Darwin did natural history. Despite the fact that her parents would allow her neither light nor heat as they did not want to encourage her studies, her insatiable curiosity led her to study secretly. Wrapping herself in a blanket and reading by candlelight, she studied philosophy and mathematics and was especially interested in geometry. Because it was believed that women should not be educated, she entered scientific contests and corresponded with famous mathematicians using the male pseudonym "Le Blanc." Although the Eiffel tower was designed and constructed using her theory of elasticity of materials, her name was deliberately omitted from the list of seventy-two men whose knowledge contributed to its structural stability and beauty.[5]

We also search for *practical know-how*. When we have know-how, we can perform a task or accomplish something that requires skills and expertise that can be gained only through experience and experimentation.

Five thousand years ago, the women of Egypt were able to produce ice to cool their homes in spite of the heat. They did this by filling shallow clay trays with water and placing them on damp beds of straw. The damp trays, evaporation, and lowered temperatures at night allowed ice to form. The evaporating ice kept the houses cooler the following day. In India, grass mats were soaked with water and hung over the windows at night for the same effect. When the wind blew and evaporated the water, the temperature in the house could drop as much as thirty degrees.[6] This kind of knowledge was so valued it was passed from generation to generation.

Another kind of knowledge that is passed from generation to generation is found in China, where children learn at a very early age to use the abacus, an ancient device for calculations. Eventually, they become so proficient that they can calculate very complicated mathematical problems in their heads without an abacus or any other external aid. Contests with large celebrations for the winners are held for those who have learned this skill.

In our search for greater understanding, we are discovering that even animals have the capacity to increase their know-how. Carl Sagan, professor of astronomy and space sciences, tells of chimpanzees who have been taught sign language and have a working vocabulary of 200 words. They can also distinguish between grammatical patterns and syntax. One of these chimpanzees, Lana, has been called "gifted" and has a computer created just for her. With this she is able to carry on a conversation with humans as she types, monitors, and corrects her own mistakes.[7]

The third type of knowledge people seek is *spiritual wisdom. Spiritual wisdom is the ability to discern inner qualities and essential relationships, then to put one's faith in their positive aspects and integrate these insights into one's life.* Spiritual wisdom comes from knowing how to apply universally humane principles to everyday life.

A search for spiritual wisdom often leads us to search for the essence of things, their central nature, the vital elements that give something its character and ultimate value. As we seek to understand the essence of love, truth, equality, compassion, freedom, or similar values, and as we find ways to bring these qualities into our lives and the lives of others, we gain spiritual wisdom.

Some people search for spiritual wisdom by studying religious writings; most religious groups have books which they consider to be holy and inspired. The Qur'an of Islam, the Vedas and the Upanishads of the Hindus, the Popul Vu of the Maya, the Old Testament of Judaism, the New Testament of Christianity, and the Book of Mormon of the Latter-day Saints contain many different styles òf writing, stories, psalms, creeds and proclamations that may lead to spiritual wisdom.

Many others use meditation as a way to spiritual wisdom. Wisdom may emerge from deep meditation when the mind is totally still and at the same time has no limits. Suddenly there may be a moment of insight. For other people, insight may come in moments of prayer, contemplation, or worship. Spiritual disciplines, such as the spiritual exercises of Saint Ignatius or various yoga practices, are designed to facilitate their searching, finding, and understanding. Most frequently, the search for spiritual wisdom leads many people to ask questions about God.

CURIOSITY ABOUT GOD

People speak of God in many ways. They speak reverently with awe and devotion or doubtfully or with disdain. They argue for and against the existence of God. Their opinions often reflect the fact that God is described differently by various religious groups.

We may hear some attitudes toward God, or gods, or some higher power labeled Western or Eastern, or said to be coming from primitive or advanced cultures, or characterized as fundamentalist, charismatic, traditional, or "new age" beliefs. Whatever the label or source, when we talk about some form of a formless God, what are we talking about? Are we talking about a God that can't really be known? Or are we talking about a God that we believe we have personally known? Are the beliefs we hold reflections of childhood? Are we speaking of God as defined by others or as defined by ourselves?

Personal beliefs about some form of higher power are influenced by our experiences; for many they are shaped in the family or by the claims of religious authorities as to the nature of God. Our views can also include reflections of our parent figures. If we had parents who were kind, we may expect God to be likewise; if we had parents who were critical or distant, we may project the same attributes onto God or higher power.

Our views are often influenced by life experiences, such as childhood religious training or lack of it, or living where our religious traditions are accepted or rejected by others, or having a life-and-death encounter or transcendent moment. Studying theology or contemporary religions and experiencing the good and evil of existence also influence our views. So do conversations with priests and rabbis, yogis, and other spiritual leaders, and religious and nonreligious friends.

Our views of God also arise from our psychological needs. If we feel a need for power, then our view of God will reflect that in envisioning an all-powerful God. If we feel the need for perfection, then we may believe God is perfect. If we feel guilty, we may view God as punishing. If we need comfort, we may find this in God, too.

Yet God may be unknowable. In fact, many religions believe this and say that the reality of God can only be alluded to but not defined.[8] Words, definitions, functions, characterizations only reflect facets or faces of God, and the essence of God may be beyond all these.

Among philosophers, however, arguments about God usually lead to philosophical debates based on one of three positions—ontological, cosmological, and teleological.

The *ontological* argument is the study of being and was developed by Anselm of Canterbury in the eleventh century A.D. He claimed that God exists because the *idea* of a perfect God exists: because we are capable of having an idea of God's being, then it must be true that God exists.

Contrary to Anselm's thinking is the argument that having an idea of a God, especially a perfect God, does not mean that God exists. We have many ideas, such as of winged horses, that do not fit reality.

The second position is called the *cosmological* argument, which was first proposed by Aristotle, then later by Thomas Aquinas (A.D. 1225–1274). In this argument, everything in the cosmos has a beginning and God was the first cause of it all and that God created the cosmos and activated life on earth. Before God, there was nothing.

Those against the cosmological argument of God as pre-existent of the cosmos, say that if everything has a beginning and a cause, then the same must be true for God. Or, if the universe had no beginning or cause, then this could also be true for God. Furthermore, if there was a beginning, there is no reason to say that God originated it.

The *teleological* argument claims that the existence of God is proven because of the obvious order and design of nature. Order, they say, must have come from a divine mind that designed everything for a purpose. Scientists who believe in God say that evolution does not negate religious belief. Instead, they believe evolution is the working out of God's long-range plan.

Those who argue against this concept of God as a grand designer with specific purposes raise the issue of whether or not God is as powerful as claimed. If God is a master designer, then why doesn't God set aside natural laws and intervene more obviously in history? Or, if God is good, why do evil, destruction, and pain exist? If God is omnipotent and all-powerful, why doesn't God intervene on behalf of good?

Some people conclude that since they do not have scientific proof of the existence of God, they will not decide whether or in what form God exists. Still others believe that since God is not something they have experienced, God probably does not exist. People who feel this way seldom talk about God or seek to understand the various interpretations of God's existence. Other people simply disagree with the entire concept of God. They may have high moral standards, be deeply involved in the betterment of society, care for the environment, and, in addition, not believe in God or any deity.

A person's belief in whether or not God exists and, if so, what God is like, is a direct reflection of a natural curiosity and a search for knowledge.

THE NEED FOR CURIOSITY

The urge to understand and to search for knowledge is fueled by our innate curiosity to know more. We want more information, more know-how and more wisdom. As a captain in the Navy stationed at the Pentagon, Grace Murry Hopper developed COBOL (Common Business-Oriented Languages), the first major computer language. Hopper claims she did it because of her insatiable curiosity for solving problems. As a child she kept taking apart clocks to see how they worked and equated herself with a baby elephant who pokes a long nose into everything. On active duty until she was eighty, Hopper believes that with computers, people will have more time to do what they want to do, whether playing tennis or jogging or reading all the books they want to read.[9]

Curiosity is a desire to learn or know—a natural inquisitiveness. All children express curiosity. They ask questions, try things out, and experiment with new possibilities. Philosophy is rooted in the questions of a curious child who asks "Why?" or "How do you know?" Concepts of ethics start with praise for good behavior and punishment for what is considered bad. The knowledge of history begins when parents talk about their grandparents and the way it was when they were little. An appreciation of fine arts begins with the first originals a child scribbles for the gallery on the refrigerator. Vocational skills develop when a child is shown how to use a hammer and nails or how to bake a cake. The study of mathematics begins when cookies are counted or broken into fractions for sharing. The study of physiology begins with the exploration of one's own body. Curiosity about medicine and nursing often starts when family members get sick and need care.

Just outside the home is the world of nature where opportunities to learn are abundant. Curiosity about trees and flowers is the foundation for studying botany; interest in lizards and birds is the beginning of zoology. When specific stars are pointed out by a parent standing awestruck while watching shooting stars, a child may be developing an interest in astronomy. And so it goes. From the theoretical physicist working on a question, "Why does it do that?" to the anthropologist trying to discover "What happened back when . . . ?" It is the natural child-like curiosity that drives human learning.

We need the curiosity we had as children to last all our lives. With or without formal education, we need to continue to be curious so we will always question ourselves, how we live, what we know, and whether the authorities in our lives are trying to dominate, not lead us, propagandize, not educate us. If our curiosity is blocked for some reason, we do not search for knowledge that is new to us and are content with what we know or with what others tell us is true.

One of the problems we all face is that there is so much information available that it is hard to get agreement on what is true. In 1975 a committee of six prominent historians were asked to make a list of the most significant events in United States history. Out of 365 events they listed, they only agreed on five![10]

If our curiosity remains active, we will learn from what others say but in addition we will seek our own truth. The urge of the human spirit is to seek understanding in order to gain knowledge, and curiosity is the tool needed for the search. The process is shown below:

Urge of the Human Spirit	Goal of the Search	Power Needed for the Search
to Understand	Knowledge	Curiosity

When we are searching for facts and information, our curiosity may take us to the library, to more experienced colleagues, or to observation and experimentation on our own. Our curiosity about practical know-how may lead us down the same paths. We may ask someone how to do something, or read about it, or watch someone else do it before we try.

MULTIPLE INTELLIGENCES

Our capacity to ask and answer important questions is often thought to be related to our intelligence and measured with tests of mathematics, logic, and language skill. However Howard Gardner, of the Harvard Graduate School of Education, challenged this narrow concept of intelligence in a study of the human potential. On the basis of his research, Gardner proposed that instead of having only *one* intelligence that can be measured by an I.Q. test, people have multiple intelligences.[11]

Acknowledging that some forms of intelligence—especially those having to do with mathematics and music—are related to the luck of the genetic draw, he points to extensive evidence of historical and cultural factors, family environment, and social expectations, that are highly influential on the development of any form of intelligence.

Intelligence is *an intellectual competence that requires a set of skills for problem solving*, according to Gardner. This competence enables us to solve existing problems and create effective responses to them. In addition we also have the potential for discovering new problems, and this provides the groundwork for the acquisition of new knowledge.

Although the exact number and nature of our multiple intelligences have not yet been determined, several are clear. Each is relatively autonomous but works in harmony with other forms of intelligence and can be expressed in many creative ways.

As children learn to count and compare quantities in their early experiences with objects, *logical-mathematical intelligence* develops. First mathematical skill develops and this leads to the ability to follow chains of logical reasoning and abstractions. Gardner believes this form of intelligence has been overemphasized or applied erroneously to other forms. Whereas a scientist such as Newton needed this type of intelligence in his work to figure out the movement of the planets, a writer such as Carlos Fuentes or a painter such as Claude Monet did not in theirs.

Linguistic intelligence is quite different and is most easily recognized in great writers and poets. A person with high linguistic intelligence loves words, their meanings, and how their sounds can be used. The poet W.H. Auden exemplified this when he said, "I like hanging around words, listening to what they say." Linguistic intelligence can be recognized in politicians, trial attorneys, and public relations people who often get what they want because of their ability to use words convincingly.

The facility to recognize and create harmonies and melodies, rhythms and tones is *musical intelligence.* Some people are extremely creative in this way. Richard Wagner said he composed like a cow produces milk, and Camille Saint-Saëns likened his ability to compose music to an apple tree producing apples.

Composers constantly have melodies and rhythms going around in their heads; noncomposers may find themselves silently singing or humming a catchy tune. The difference between us is that a composer listens to inner music and knows how to put it into form for others to hear. Most of us just listen and improvise on a melody we have heard before. Both actions reflect musical intelligence, but one takes a much higher or more developed level of skill than the other.

Musical intelligence usually emerges in early childhood and is greatly assisted by competent instruction and family encouragement. Arthur Rubinstein came from such a supportive family. As a child, he enjoyed all kinds of sounds. Instead of speaking, he would sing. At the age of three, when his parents bought a piano because of the interest in music he already displayed, Rubinstein played tunes on it not only normally but even while standing backward.

Whereas musical intelligence relies on hearing; *spatial intelligence* involves seeing and "the capacities to perceive the visual world accurately, to perform transformations and modifications upon one's initial perceptions, and to be able to re-create aspects of one's visual experience, even in the absence of relevant physical stimuli."[12]

Architects need to have a high degree of spatial intelligence. In Japan, some of the world's loveliest architecture, such as the Katsura Palace, is oriented around vistas of rocks, trees, and water, revealing the wonder of this form of intelligence. Sculptors, photographers, and interior designers who work with composition, form, and balance to create their works also use spatial intelligence.

The architect Frank Lloyd Wright was encouraged to develop his spatial intelligence even before birth. His mother believed in prenatal influence. When she was pregnant, she simply decided that she *would* have a boy and that he *would* be an architect, so she decorated the walls of his room with full-page wood engravings of old English cathedrals. Although her son did not design cathedrals, he became an architect, known for his unique ways of using form and space.[13]

Some cultures seem to encourage more spatial intelligence than others. On one test for spatial ability, for example, over 60 percent of Eskimo children scored as high as the top 10 percent of Caucasian children on the same test. Eskimos have developed this kind of spatial intelligence, according to Gardner, so they would not get lost in their flat and relatively featureless world of ice and snow.

The ability to control body movements and handle objects skillfully is *bodily-kinesthetic intelligence.* Dancers and gymnasts, swimmers and ballplayers, actors and mimes all have highly developed bodily-kinesthetic abilities. Athletes such as gymnast Olga Korbut, soccer star Pele, basketball great Michael "Air" Jordan, and martial arts master Bruce Lee have captured the world's attention with their remarkable bodily-kinesthetic abilities. Blind people who can sense objects in their environment without touching them and people who balance on skyscrapers with death-defying coordination also rate high in this type of intelligence.

Personal intelligence, as Gardner uses the phrase, refers to two capacities. One is the capacity to be in touch with our emotions, to be able to discriminate between the various emotions, and to use this information to understand and guide our own behavior. The second aspect of personal intelligence is the capacity to be aware of other people's moods, motives, feelings, and intentions. Outstanding teachers and counselors usually are high in both forms of personal intelligence.

The problem is that many of us do not appreciate our unique combinations of intelligence and capabilities. If we're poor in math or spelling, we may think of ourselves as stupid. If we're not bodily or kinesthetically agile, we may think of ourselves as clumsy. Similarly, we may not be a creative painter and feel sad about that, rather than feel good that we are creative with words, ideas, or the ways we relate to other people. We may be critical of ourselves for not being more capable in other areas. Or we may discount our innate strengths saying, "They're not so special. A lot of people are that way." The challenge is to recognize the reality of all our intelligences and respect our unique ways of expressing them.

A principle central to Taoist tradition is to accept one's own nature and make the most of it rather than going against the grain by trying to be like someone else.[14] A Jewish saying echoes this belief: "In the world to come, you shall not be asked, 'Why were you not Moses?' You shall be asked, 'Why were you not yourself?' "[15]

To be oneself is to stop trying to imitate others or to compete with them. When we recognize and accept who we are and what intelligences we have to develop, then we can relax and let ourselves go with the flow of our natural capabilities.

THE BRAIN CONSTRAINED

At one time it was widely believed that intellect was directly related to the size of a person's brain. Because women's brains are usually smaller than men's, it was assumed that they were less intelligent. Then some interesting studies were done that compared the sizes of men's brains. Some brilliant people, such as Oliver Cromwell, Ivan Turgenev, and Lord Byron, had massive brains. Others, such as Albert Einstein, did not; Anatole France had a brain only half the size of Byron's. On the basis of cases such as these, scientists concluded that intelligence cannot be correlated to brain size.[16]

There has been a long-standing debate on whether or not men and women think differently. Although researchers have provided us with relatively indisputable information about how the value systems of men and women differ from each other, they have not been able to tell us why our thinking processes might differ. Do men and women have different values because of organic differences in their brains, or do their different values grow out of their environmental realities?

As with all problems that involve human nature and human behavior, we find experts on both sides of the controversy. On one side, we have those who think that women are naturally "right-brained," or intuitive, specializing in visual-spatial tasks; while men are "left-brained," or rational, specializing in analytical tasks. On the other hand are those who argue that all differences in the way men and women behave and in what they value are due to culturally imposed patterns. Clarifying these issues until there is wider agreement cannot be done until we have much more data from the fields of biochemistry, anatomy, and neuropsychology.[17]

In the meantime, there is ample evidence that in every literate culture throughout history, our abilities to think and reason are not constrained by brain size as much as they have been blocked by laws, tradition, and prejudice. Minority groups and women have been traditionally barred from many educational institutions. As one of many examples, in 1600, Juana Inez de la Cruz of Mexico City had to disguise herself as a boy to attend school. She became a mathematician, painter, composer, and theologian, had an enormous library, and could write in four languages, including Aztec. However, she was eventually required to give up her library and her academic pursuits at the insistence of the religious order to which she belonged.[18]

In major educational institutions, women have been the largest minority to be rebuffed. As recently as 1873 at Harvard University it was taught that, although the higher education of women might not endanger their minds, it would certainly lead to atrophy of the uterus and would adversely affect the mammary glands. This point of view was perpetuated in a Harvard course using a textbook written by a faculty member, titled *Sex in Education, or a Fair Chance for the Girls.* The book was so widely read that it was reprinted seventeen times in only a few years.[19]

In the United States, one way women continued to be treated as if they had small brains and were unable to think as well as men was in being restricted from medical schools or residency programs. Although in Salerno, Italy, they were admitted to such programs since the thirteenth century, in the United States women were only first admitted to medical schools about 100 years ago, and in very small numbers. Yet by 1934, according to Ruth Abrams's study of women doctors in America, less than half of the nation's hospitals had ever had a woman physician on the staff. And since that time, "old boy" networks have often prevented women from getting good positions in hospitals. Even in the 1990s, getting into a good residency program is very difficult for women.[20]

Women constitute the largest minority denied equal opportunities to gain knowledge and understanding through education, but they are certainly not the only minority discriminated against in this way. In the recent past, Native Americans were displaced and moved to reservations with inadequate or nonexistent schools, and African Americans have been discriminated

The urge to understand

Benefits of the search for knowledge

JANE SCHERR

IAN JAMES

IAN JAMES

Musical intelligence   *Spatial intelligence*

The value
of interpersonal skills

IAN JAMES

Education
for the future

IAN JAMES

Kinesthetic intelligence

DAVID M. ALLEN

against through the use of segregated—separate and far from equal—schools. Today, refugees and immigrants are often rebuffed in the classroom for speaking in their native languages.

Sometimes constraints to gaining understanding through learning occur because of a lack of caring, awareness, or understanding. In many schools and universities, buildings are not accessible for those in wheelchairs or who are disabled in some other way. Fortunately this is changing as television is being "close captioned" for the hearing impaired, computers are modified for the visually impaired, and some school districts and communities provide special buses for those who are disabled and are still searching for knowledge.

CONTINUING EDUCATION

The quest for knowledge is a lifelong journey. Just as this quest can be blocked by external conditions, it can also be hindered by internal processes. However, most of us have experienced times when something in our personality structure blocks our curiosity and interferes with our search for knowledge. We may feel stupid or confused or that we don't have enough time for the search.

Like the debris that circles the earth from our space experiments, we all carry some debris constantly floating around in our psyches. Some of it, such as erroneous ideas and exaggerated feelings, can be controlled or dissipated, while other debris can be brought into awareness and used positively.

Transactional Analysis can be used to understand the process of how this kind of debris accumulates and interferes with the passion of the soul to understand life. It can also be used to discard outmoded behavior and beliefs and to enhance our continuing education.

The Parent, Adult, and Child ego states are independent parts of our personalities that determine our feelings, thoughts, beliefs, and behavior. Energy can flow freely between these personality parts, or it can be restricted or blocked. Psychological energy can flow from one ego state to another as a spontaneous reaction to a stimulus or as a deliberate act of will. This flow is necessary for clear and effective thinking. and is diagrammed:

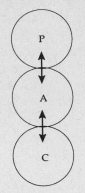

ENERGY BETWEEN EGO STATES

Understanding how to shift psychological energy increases our ability to understand. The inability to shift our internal energies is usually due to one of four basic ego state boundary problems.

In the most common ego state boundary problem, thinking is *contaminated* because the boundaries of the inner Adult are not strong enough to hold back our Parent opinions or Child feelings; they seep through into the Adult. Just as air that looks clear can be contaminated by invisible pollutants, when our Adult is contaminated, we may appear to be thinking clearly but actually be polluted by Parent opinions or Child feelings and adaptations. This problem is diagrammed:

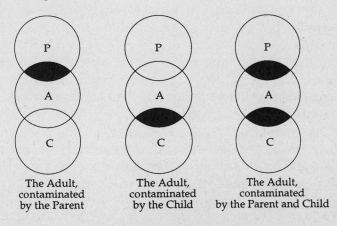

The Adult,
contaminated
by the Parent

The Adult,
contaminated
by the Child

The Adult,
contaminated
by the Parent and Child

CONTAMINATED THINKING

Beliefs that women are not as smart as men or that people of certain ethnic or racial backgrounds are stupid or lazy and incapable of excelling in school are contaminations of the Adult usually learned from parental prejudices. On the other hand, feelings of performance anxiety in academic situation are frequently contaminations of the Adult by the Child whose performance was harshly criticized in childhood. A double contamination is found in people who have been so harshly criticized by their parents in childhood that as grown-ups they continue the pattern of criticizing themselves and others when potential learning experiences are taking place.

To recognize the ongoing problem of contaminated thinking we must become more objective and ask ourselves, "What data am I using in making my decisions?" "Are my beliefs or feelings leftover from the past, or are they appropriate to the current situation?" A few of the many areas in which contamination is common are self-esteem, gender roles, finances, raising children, and seeking further knowledge. Getting information about any of these kinds of issues strengthens the Adult ego state boundaries so that we can think more effectively.

Severe confusion is the result of having *lax* or *collapsed* ego state boundaries. When this is the case, thoughts, feelings, and opinions are much more mixed up than when merely contaminated. It is as if the Adult is unable to regulate the flow of Parent opinions and Child feelings. Thinking and behavior become chaotic. A person with lax ego boundaries is unable to process information effectively and is often disruptive in the classroom or office.

At any time a person may experience lax ego boundaries. Extreme fatigue or crisis may bring it on. In a mild form, it is recognizable in statements such as, "I'm confused," "I don't know what's going on," or "I don't seem to be able to understand anything." In a more severe form, people may be unable to concentrate. They lose their healthy curiosity and sense of awe and may experience some kind of emotional breakdown. Lax ego boundaries can be diagrammed:

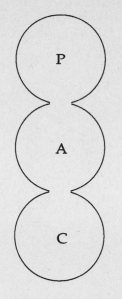

LAX EGO BOUNDARIES

There are many ways to develop firmer boundaries between our inner Parent, Adult, and Child. When feeling confused we can strengthen our Adult to build healthier ego state boundaries by asking ourselves, "How can I say what I want in a simple, clear, and concise way?" "If I continue to feel or act as I now do, what will happen next?"

Answering these kinds of questions makes us aware of our need to be more concise and focused. In many conversations, staying on one topic at a time is a big help in clearing up our confusion. Taking a course in logical thinking can also be useful.

In contrast to lax ego boundaries, some people have such *rigid* ego boundaries that they *exclude* one or another ego state. Rigidity is easily observed in the person who acts compulsively and lacks psychological flexibility. Rigid ego state boundaries can be a defense against awareness of psychological problems we have often caused by unresolved grief or fear. Rigid boundaries are also maintained by those who "can't tolerate" being wrong or out of control—the perfectionistic types. Rigid ego state boundaries may block curiosity or the integration of knowledge because they exclude or greatly restrict the normal use of all ego states: only one or two ego states are easily used, instead of all three. This is diagrammed:

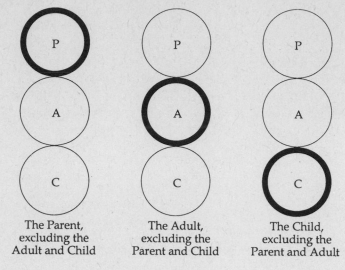

The Parent, excluding the Adult and Child	The Adult, excluding the Parent and Child	The Child, excluding the Parent and Adult

RIGID EGO BOUNDARIES

When we constantly use the Parent ego state, we exclude Child curiosity and Adult understanding and tend to value only traditional ways of doing things. At parties, persons who are always in the Parent ego state are not much fun and are not interested in hearing anything new or different that contradicts their personal beliefs.

Persons who constantly use a logical Adult usually concentrate only on facts and figures and ignore parental tradition and child feelings. At parties these people tend to talk business and will ignore others who are playful.

People who keep most of their energy in their Child ego state and exclude the Adult or Parent act like children in being self-centered and self-indulgent, or by sulking, weeping, procrastinating, or complaining. Typically they seek attention by being the life of the party or the brightest in the class or by always looking for a fight. They had too little or too much attention in childhood, or they got the wrong kind of attention and continue to look for that attention when grown up.

Rigid ego state boundaries can be relaxed if patterns of

overuse are recognized and other aspects of our ego states are expressed so that the natural flow of energy can be experienced throughout the entire personality.

People who overuse their Parent ego state need continuing education in how to relax and enjoy others. Those who keep their energy constantly in the Child ego state need to strengthen their abilities to think clearly and to develop consistent values. Those who are overly logical need to get in touch with feelings that they may not be aware of and give themselves permission to explore and express them in healthy ways.

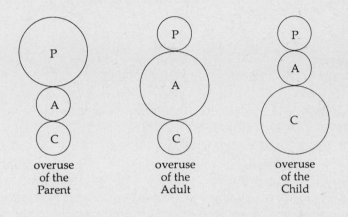

overuse
of the
Parent

overuse
of the
Adult

overuse
of the
Child

EGO STATE PORTRAITS

A fourth possible boundary problem is a *lesion* in the Child ego state. Lesions are unhealed emotional sore spots that, if irritated by some external stimuli, lead to an impulsive and irrational eruption of feelings or behavior. An unexpected explosion into rage or tears may indicate this condition exists.

Because the lesion never healed, the person who suffers it is overly sensitive to any stimulus similar to that which caused the original injury. For example, being ridiculed in school for making a mistake in front of the class or for being clumsy in sports may create such sore spots that a person may never feel comfortable speaking out in groups or trying athletic endeavors.

Vociferous explosions or emotional withdrawal when actions or spiritual beliefs are questioned by others are often due to lesions caused by severe criticism or ridicule in childhood.

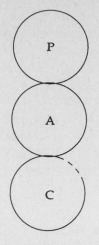

CHILD EGO STATE LESION

Emotional sore spots are injuries that can heal when we separate the present from the past. When lesions heal, the pain is gone though the scar may remain. We can heal by reminding ourselves that although the current situation is like something painful in the past, it is not the same event. The divorced adult has more choices than the abandoned child. Whereas it is normal to remember bad times, emotions can heal when we remind ourselves that many things are past history. Sometimes it helps, for the time being, to avoid situations that trigger the old feelings. Like having a broken finger that needs to be protected with a splint, temporary protection may be needed until healing occurs.

Ego state boundary problems frequently crop up in people's spiritual beliefs. People who have lax boundaries may be totally confused and not have any clarity or consistency to their beliefs. People with rigid boundaries tend to feel that their beliefs are right and that other people's beliefs are wrong. If they have a lesion, people may explode in tears or rage if a cherished belief is confronted. With contamination, Parent opinions or Child memories will taint their spiritual convictions.

The wide appeal of psychotherapy and counseling indicates that the urge to understand remains with us even if our thinking is impaired by psychological difficulties. In spite of these problems, we can have a vision that inspires us to find and follow a path with heart to reach our goals.

THE POWER OF A VISION —————————————————————

The search for knowledge often begins with a dream or vision of how the future could be "if only . . ." Sometimes a vision of the future is merely a daydream that is never realized. Other times it can be fully developed. The vision carries power to see into the future. Alfred Lord Tennyson wrote of this power:

I DIPPED INTO THE FUTURE, FAR AS HUMAN EYE COULD SEE;
SAW THE VISION OF THE WORLD, AND ALL THE WONDER
THAT COULD BE.[21]

Isaac Asimov has an ongoing vision of the world in which everyone can learn to understand science. He works to realize this vision through his teaching and writing. A biochemist and professor, he has authored almost 400 books in diverse fields. Although some of his works are on humor, history, and literature—in particular Shakespeare and the Bible—most of his books are on science and science fiction. Many are designed to make science understandable to the nonscientist. The vision of having everybody science-literate has also led him to write serious textbooks as well as one about satellites for eight-year-olds.

Another of his visions is a computer outlet in every home. Each of them would be hooked up to large libraries, so that we could ask any question and receive answers on whatever we want to know, "however silly it might seem to someone else."[22]

When we think about the urge to understand and the power of a vision, we may discover that a vision of what could be in the future has been an important beacon in our lives. This is true for Mary McLeod Bethune, one of seventeen children born to parents who were former slaves. At eight years old she began to visualize herself as learning to read. One day when playing with a doll that belonged to a white girl, she picked up a book and was told, "Put that down—you can't read." At that moment, she decided to learn how. Day and night she prayed for the opportunity. When picking cotton, she worked while she repeated over and over, "I'm going to read, I'm going to read."[23]

One day a teacher came to her parents' house and suggested

Mary be allowed to attend school. This was so important to Mary that she walked five miles to school and five miles back each day and then shared what she learned with her brothers and sisters. Scholarships for outstanding abilities enabled her to continue her education, begin teaching, and open a school for five girls, which rapidly grew and became a college. Over the entrance of the building, named Faith Hall, are the words, "Enter to Learn." On the inside of the door, to be seen when leaving, are the words, "Depart to Serve." This was Mary McLeod Bethune's philosophy for life. Understanding the importance of knowledge and putting it into service, she became official adviser to Franklin Roosevelt on minority affairs, founder of the National Council of Negro Women, as well as founder and president of Bethune-Cookman College in Daytona Beach, Florida. Her urge to understand and her search for knowledge emerged from the passion within her soul.

Today, the freedom to get an education is considered to be a human right. Universities are taking an active interest in recruiting minorities; many businesses, volunteer groups, and dedicated individuals are doing what they can to facilitate this process.[24] The vision of a world of educated people is a powerful one, and because of people like Mary McLeod Bethune, thousands have been able to don their mortarboards and gowns for graduation in the rite of passage into the future.

❦ RELEASING YOUR URGE TO UNDERSTAND——————

Now is your time to quietly explore your urge to understand, your search for knowledge, and the wonder and usefulness of your curiosity.

❦ FOR CONTEMPLATION. Here are a few thoughts that you might enjoy contemplating. Contemplation has a way of opening us up to understanding things at a deeper level than usual.

WHEN I LEARN SOMETHING NEW—AND IT HAPPENS EVERY DAY—
I FEEL A LITTLE MORE AT HOME IN THIS UNIVERSE, A LITTLE MORE
COMFORTABLE IN THE NEST.

—BILL MOYERS[25]

LIFE MUST BE LIVED AND CURIOSITY KEPT ALIVE. ONE MUST NEVER, FOR WHATEVER REASON, TURN HIS BACK ON LIFE.

—ELEANOR ROOSEVELT[26]

THERE IS TODAY—IN A TIME WHEN OLD BELIEFS ARE WITHERING— A KIND OF PHILOSOPHICAL HUNGER, A NEED TO KNOW WHO WE ARE AND HOW WE GOT HERE. IT IS AN ON-GOING SEARCH, OFTEN UNCONSCIOUS, FOR A COSMIC PERSPECTIVE FOR HUMANITY.

—CARL SAGAN[27]

I HOPE FOR THE DAY WHEN EVERYONE CAN SPEAK AGAIN OF GOD WITHOUT EMBARRASSMENT.

—PAUL TILLICH[28]

WE CLING TO OUR OWN POINT OF VIEW, AS THOUGH EVERYTHING DEPENDED ON IT. YET OUR OPINIONS HAVE NO PERMANENCE; LIKE AUTUMN AND WINTER, THEY GRADUALLY PASS AWAY.

—CHUANG TZU[29]

WHAT LAW, WHAT REASON CAN DENY THAT GIFT SO SWEET, SO NATURAL THAT GOD HAS GIVEN A STREAM, A FISH, A BEAST, A BIRD?

—PEDRO CALDERON DE LA BARCA[30]

HE WHO IS SLOW TO ANGER HAS GREAT UNDERSTANDING.

—PROVERBS 14:29

WISDOM IS BETTER THAN WEAPONS OF WAR.

—ECCLESIASTES 9:18B

❦ YOUR URGE TO UNDERSTAND. All children have the urge to understand many things. Let your memory drift back in time until you recall some of the things you puzzled over.

What used to puzzle me was:

What currently puzzles me is:

❦ CURIOSITY CAN BE PROGRAMMED. Many children are programmed against being curious with comments like, "What you don't know, won't hurt you," "Mind your own business." How was your curiosity programmed with words or actions when you were young? Were you encouraged or discouraged to be curious about your body? Your mind? Your spirit?

❦ INDEPENDENT THINKERS YOU HAVE KNOWN. Take a few minutes to recall some of the independent thinkers you have known or read about. How do you suppose they got to be that way? How have they intrigued you into thinking for yourself? Is there anything about them you could apply to your own life?

❦ YOUR MULTIPLE INTELLIGENCES. Each of us is intelligent in several ways. These abilities may or may not be developed. How developed are your creative capabilities? Rate yourself on a scale of 1 to 10, with 1 being undeveloped and 10 being highly developed:

Forms of Intelligence   Level of Development
Logical-mathematical

Linguistic

Musical

Spatial

Bodily-kinesthetic

Personal-Interpersonal

If you want to increase your level of development in one or more of these capacities, what do you need to do?

❦   UNDERSTANDING HOW YOU THINK: Everyone has difficulty thinking clearly sometimes, especially when worried, tired, sick, or in some kind of crisis. At times like these, boundary problems are apt to occur between ego states. Consider the following and fill in the blanks.

Lax boundaries—Situations when I tend to feel confused:

Contamination—Situations when my feelings or opinions seem to control my ability to think clearly:

Lesions—Situations when I tend to fall apart or explode irrationally:

Rigidity—Situations when I insist on being right and will not consider other points of view:

❦   A FRIENDLY DEBATE. Imagine you are sitting with some friends or colleagues and having a friendly debate about God. What point of view would you present? How might you present it? Do you think you would be understood and agreed with?

How about the others? What points of view and arguments might they present? Would you be curious and try to understand them, or not? What conclusions do you draw about yourself as a result of this imaginary debate?

❦   EDUCATION: A LIFELONG PROCESS. As you think of the future, what would you like to understand more fully? What kinds of knowledge do you need to search for?

Information I would like:

Practical know-how I would like:

Spiritual wisdom I would like:

What could you do to gain the knowledge and understanding you would like to have?

7

THE URGE TO CREATE

IMAGINATION IS MORE IMPORTANT THAN KNOWLEDGE.
—ALBERT EINSTEIN[1]

❦

CASTLES IN THE SAND

Sand castles built on beaches are usually simple creations erected for fun with small piles of sand surrounded by moats that only temporarily hold back the waves. However, some sand castles are carefully designed, elaborate structures. In Venice, California, and Coos Bay, Oregon, sand castle contests are held annually in which well-known castles are elaborately reproduced. Whether sand castles are simple or elaborate, there is something deeply satisfying about building them.

Fortunately many creative works are more permanent than sand castles. Anyone who sees the Taj Mahal in India finds this wonder of the world impossible to forget. Built by a Mughal emperor as a tomb for his beloved wife, it was created out of white marble in the 1640s. The great dome is inlaid with gemstones. In front of it lies a long shallow reflection pool lined with tall yew trees. To see all this in the moonlight, when the mausoleum and its four tall, slender minarets are reflected in the water, is to be awestruck by its beauty and by the creativity of the designer.

All of us are creative. Even if we don't build sand castles

or Taj Mahals, we wonder what we might create if given the opportunity. We ask ourselves why some people are so creative and others are not. Do I have some hidden creativity that I am not aware of? Could I invent something new if I tried? What holds me back from creating something I have always wanted to create? If I went ahead and created something new, would it turn out as I imagined? Would I be satisfied and would others appreciate it?

In a sense, the entire universe is basically creative. Each day is a new day, a day that has never happened before. Each of us is also a new creation as shown by our fingerprints and DNA structure. Day after day we think new thoughts, feel new feelings, try out new ways of doing things, get new insights. Each day we can experience the miracle of our own uniqueness together with the urge to create, which is impossible to destroy because it comes from deep within the inner core of the human spirit.

THE URGE TO CREATE

Everyone is born with the urge to create. It is part of the passion for life. Whether we are teachers creatively trying to encourage learning by piquing a student's curiosity or poets writing sonnets to express desire or scientists developing new antibiotics or office workers planning how to write an effective memo—we create.

The conversations we have with others are highly creative acts. When we put words and sentences together, we are often creating new ways to express ourselves. So, too, when we make phone calls and write letters, our words become creative ways of reaching out to each other. Even the oohs and ahs of babies are creative experiments with basic sounds and communication.

To create is to bring something new into being—a new solution to a problem, a new object or device, or a new idea or technique. Our creations may be eloquent or simple, of immediate use or with far-reaching implications.

The urge to be creative can be sparked by necessity, such as when we need to find creative ways to balance personal income with bills and spending habits. Whether living alone, as a family, or struggling through a divorce, the age-old challenge of needs being greater than income forces us all to be creative in handling our personal finances.

On the other hand, the urge to create can be sparked by a

deep fascination with an activity or a task. Artists, musicians, dancers, and actors often do what they do simply because they enjoy it. Their efforts may not lead to wealth, but the creative expression is worth the time. A similar pleasure in creating is also obvious when people are expressing themselves in their hobbies, whether gardening or woodworking, sewing or model railroading.

The desire for profit and personal gain is another motive for being creative. People start up new businesses or improve products and services with the hope of profiting from their creative efforts. The desire for a career and financial security leads many people to seek jobs with creative opportunities, such as chemists, cooks, carpenters, and computer programmers. Similarly, the desire to advance professionally, whether by promotion or skills development, often reflects a desire to use one's creative energies more.

Some people are motived to be creative not so much out of a desire for personal gain but more from a desire to please others. When one is shopping for a birthday present, preparing a special meal, or planning a family vacation, the underlying motive for such creative acts is often to make life more enjoyable for someone else. Volunteer activities, such as serving on the board of a community service group or caring for the aged or disabled, also entail a great deal of creativity. Good parenting requires it constantly!

The need to solve practical problems is another catalyst for being creative. Finding ways to manage work groups, market products, and respond to changes in the marketplace are creative challenges that often spur new research and development, start-ups, and mergers.

The urge to create can also be spurred by the desire to actualize values and ideals. People who work together for a cause—be it social, environmental, or political—often are exceptionally creative in their strategies for mobilizing action and engineering constructive change. This occurred when a group of statesmen got together in Philadelphia between 1774 and 1776 to serve the interests of thirteen colonies and emerged instead with the Declaration of Independence. Similar synergy can occur today when leaders of various sorts come together in "think tanks" to combine their efforts and wisdom to predict future trends and suggest strategies for change.

Whether motivated by necessity, idealism, pleasure, or personal gain, the urge to be creative lies beneath the surface of a great deal of what we do. Creativity does not depend on skills or intelligence, personality or opportunities, although each of these variables affects how we express it. Regardless of our level of capabilities, we can be creative with a particular goal in mind or just for the fun of it. Either way reveals the creative wonder of the human spirit.

Whereas all people are creative, some are more so than others. Many studies have been done on the relationship of intelligence to creativity. Some studies show that there is a high correlation between the two; others conclude that highly intelligent people are not necessarily creative and that many creative people do not have an unusually high IQ.

Occasionally there are people who are high in both intelligence and creativity. Their cognitive and analytical abilities range over a number of fields and their passion for life spurs an equally far-reaching creativity. Leonardo da Vinci is an example of this kind of person.

As an artist, Leonardo is best known for his *Mona Lisa* and *The Last Supper.* His sketches of birds, battles, and bodies also reflect the breadth of his artistic inspiration. As a writer, he covered many subjects—from medicine to mathematics, anatomy to astronomy, horses to hydraulics, philosophy to prophecy, fables to flying machines. Sometimes he wrote backward, using a form of mirror writing, and often put sketches related to the topic in the margins of his journals.

As a musician, Leonardo played an early version of the violin, invented a number of musical instruments, and made improvements on the organ. He wrote treatises on acoustics, on the human voice, and on the philosophy of music.

As an architect, Leonardo's interests included defensive engineering and military fortification, aqueducts and topography, helicopters, submarines, the underwater diving suit, and much more. He invented crossbows and matchlock rifles, machine guns and cannons.

His notebooks on inventions are said to read "like a modern mail-order catalogue that offers an ingenious tool or gadget for every conceivable purpose."[2] In fact, Leonardo designed and described all twenty-two of the basic elements of machines and mechanical tools (including gears, levers, valves, ball bearings, and flywheels), several of which were not even reinvented or redis-covered again until 400 years after his death!

Very few people are as farsighted or prolific as Leonardo, yet everyone is creative and expresses it in unique ways.

EXPRESSING THE CREATIVE URGE

The urge to create is not always put into the service of the good; it can be so distorted that it is consciously used for evil. Such diverse instruments as medieval torture racks or pornography de-signed to cultivate prurient interests clearly show that the imagi-nation of the human spirit may fall to the depths as well as rise to the heights.

In fact, any criminal activity that requires cunning is a dis-tortion of the urge to create. Drug smuggling is a particularly abhor-rent example. Devising computer viruses, mislabeling medicines to make an illegal profit, defrauding the public by selling substan-dard products to the government at excessively high prices, or taking advantage of the suffering of others by price gouging after a major flood or earthquake are creative yet destructive acts. Sadly, the list could go on and on.

At work, reinventing the wheel or doing unnecessary pa-perwork—while not evil—is a wasteful use of creative energy. Watching trite TV programs or reading trash novels are common ways to waste time that could otherwise be spent creatively.

More often, we use our creative energies for self-serving goals of comfort and pleasure. Thomas Edison, inventor of the lightbulb and 1,092 other patents, claimed his three highest prior-ities were to invent, to get money for his inventions, and acquire prestige for inventing them. Although in his youth, the excitement of inventing was his motivation, he later claimed, "Anything that won't sell, I don't want to invent."[3]

To be self-serving does not have to mean being crass and greedy. More positively, we may find creative ways to get work done while commuting to work or devise creative ways to avoid traffic on the way home, just as we may creatively plan a summer vacation. These activities are personally motivated and self-serving. They can also free time or energy for other things that interest us more.

For a creative activity to be part of a spiritual search, it needs to be passionately directed toward goals that are greater than self-satisfaction or self-expression. When this is done, the passion of the urge is not easy to deny or set aside. This must have been the case for Nikos Kazantzakis, a philosopher and writer well-known for his novel *Zorba the Greek,* about a poor man with a passionate love of life. Kazantzakis wrote of his own spiritual search in his autobiography: "All my life I struggled to stretch my mind to the breaking point, until it began to creak, in order to create a great thought which might be able to give a new meaning to life, a new meaning to death, and to console mankind."[4]

When one is involved in a spiritual search, the motivation for being creative may be directed toward reflecting the glory of God, as Michelangelo did with his painting and sculpting of religious themes. It may be directed toward inspiring a spiritual awakening, as statues of Buddha are meant to do. Rodin's statue *The Thinker* evokes our need for reflection. Or art can plead for peace as with Käthe Kollwitz's antiwar sculptures created in the very midst of Nazi Germany.[5] Or it can represent a deeply felt call to freedom, as did the statue of the lady of democracy erected in Tienanmen Square in Beijing.

Creativity that is a deliberate part of a spiritual search may be expressed not only in esthetics but in creative action. Great words—such as Shakespeare's—that force us to be introspective or speeches—such as Lincoln's—that rally us to confront social injustice usually come from the passionate soul of someone committed to creating a better world.

Whereas this kind of leadership is magnificent and often necessary, it is not the only way the creative passion of the soul is expressed. Creativity can also be seen in unexpected situations. Natural catastrophes such as hurricanes or earthquakes often bring out the best in people: they creatively search for ways to solve other people's homelessness, grief, and loss. Whether or not they do so because of religious orientation, they feel compassion for others and want to help in whatever practical and creative ways they can.

Seven-year-old Amanda Parham's compassionate solution to a serious problem won a national award. She invented a life-saving smoke alarm device for the deaf. Standard smoke alarms make noises or flash lights. However, if a deaf person is asleep, those kinds of alarms are no help. Amanda's smoke alarm triggers a mechanized arm that reaches out and "bops" the sleeper awake.[6] People of all ages can be inventively creative.

Artists express the creative urge in different ways. Some take a task-oriented approach, others a process-oriented one.

Michelangelo let his creative genius unfold during the creative process. He believed "every block of marble holds within itself designs more beautiful than the greatest artist can conceive."[7] He preferred what could be called a "process approach." He did not have a clear picture of his final project or goal; he trusted the form would emerge as he worked with the materials.

In contrast, Pablo Picasso was more goal-oriented. He completed his paintings much faster than Michelangelo, claiming that he saw the entire picture in his head before he started. Poet Robert Frost worked the same way. "Whenever I write a line," Frost claimed, "it is because that line has already been spoken clearly by a voice within my head, an audible voice."[8]

These two styles of creating—the task-oriented approach and the process-oriented approach—are very different, and both can be effective. In fact, they are both used in many kinds of creative activities, from theoretical thinking to day-to-day problem solving. If we develop our natural capacities and use an approach that works for us, we will express the creative powers of the human spirit.

THE SEARCH FOR ORIGINALITY

The urge to create is natural because it comes from the inner core of the human spirit and motivates us to use our creativity in original ways. To originate is to introduce or initiate something new or to make changes in something already established. It can also be to do something in our own fashion. When we are searching for originality, we search within ourselves to find innovative solutions to old problems, to invent new ideas or objects, to design new forms of beauty, to express ourselves in new ways.

Many people search to be innovative on paths of *aesthetic activities.* The choice of these activities arises from our inborn sensory preferences and results in the creation of works of art. When people are visually oriented, they may go into painting, sculpting, architecture, or graphic design. Those who are more auditory may search for ways to be original by composing or performing music. When people have sensitive palates, they are likely to produce exquisite meals or wines. Those who are intensely aware of odors may create perfumes or plant gardens of sweet-smelling flowers to express their creativity. All of these people express themselves aesthetically in ways linked to their sensory preferences.

We may also be attracted to the original creations of others. Ansel Adams's nature photography is an example of aesthetic creativity that draws the viewer into the wilderness in a way that seems to capture the sights, smells, and majestic feeling of the great Yosemite valley. His panoramic views of snow-capped mountain ranges, or close-up views of gnarled trees bent by age, draw the viewer into a spiritual contact with nature at its best.

The search for a way to express the urge to create is also seen in our *inventiveness*—in anything from kitchen gadgets to telescopes. This kind of self-expression is often found in those who tend to be mechanically minded. They see a need and try to meet it; they build bridges to cross previously inaccessible rivers and create rockets to go to Mars.

One doesn't have to be an engineer to be creative in inventive ways. Using something as simple as a coat hanger we may inventively clean out a stopped drain, open a car with its keys locked inside, replace a broken latch on a gate, or pull out a spool of thread that has rolled under a low piece of furniture. Much like monkeys that experiment with a stick to reach a banana, we creatively use simple objects to do what we want or need to do.

Josephine Cochran was inventive. She had servants and did not need to wash her own dishes, but they often broke her valuable china when cleaning up after her parties. The china was hard to replace, and the drain on her purse was exceeded only by the drain on her temper. Working in a woodshed, she began with a large boiler in which she constructed wire compartments for the plates. The boiler rested on a water wheel turned by a motor, and hot soapy water was squirted in. Josephine Cochran had created the first dishwasher. She patented her design in 1886 and the machine was successful in hotels and restaurants, though many people considered it to be frivolous for home use. It was not until the

1950s, when the germ-killing power of the dishwasher's scalding water was shown to be effective, that Josephine Cochran's invention became popular for home use.[9]

Wrestling with new ideas and experiments and creating new hypotheses and theories is a *theoretical* way to be innovative. It is common for people to create their own pet theories for how things happen. It is also interesting to note that theorists in one area are often thinkers in another. Newton, for example, who created the theories of differential and integral calculus, also speculated on God as the first cause of the universe.

People often develop new theories based on those originated by others who came before them. Jung, Adler, Horney, Berne and other psychologists, for example, have their theoretical roots in Freud's thinking, even though they disagreed with many of his concepts.

In addition to those who are theoretically-minded, there are also those—and that includes all of us—who express our creativity in *problem-solving activities*. A Sufi parable presents a lighthearted example:

A MONKEY THREW A COCONUT FROM A TREETOP AT A HUNGRY SUFI, AND IT HIT HIM ON THE LEG. HE PICKED IT UP, DRANK THE MILK, ATE THE FLESH, AND MADE A BOWL FROM THE SHELL.[10]

In everyday ways we are continually solving problems. If the car breaks down, we have to create a way to get to the office and may call a taxi or a friend or ride a bike. We are continually faced with everyday problems that force us to find our own solutions.

Gretchen Schulte, for example, recently found it necessary to use her creativity to solve a family problem: her children were taking her motherly services too much for granted. She cooked, cleaned, did laundry, sewed, and drove them to their activities. When she asked them to help her and they refused, she went on strike. To dramatize her action, she posted a very large sign outside her house that read, "Mom on Strike." Her desire to gain her children's cooperation led her to an original way to solve a common problem.[11]

The urge to be creative and the search to innovate is sparked by an expression of a natural, innate characteristic in us all—imagination.

THE NEED FOR IMAGINATION

To create something original requires the use of imagination. *Imagination is the ability to form a mental image or picture*. When we dream, we see moving pictures and hear voices that we imagine, at the time, to be real. Reading poetry, plays, and novels also evokes the imagination, and our worlds are expanded as we enter into the lives of others and read of them living out their passions and conflicts.

Albert Einstein had a visual mind. His theory of relativity was based on a sudden flash of insight he had when he visualized himself riding on a ray of light at the speed of light. This was the symbolic image that pointed him in the direction of his work on the theory of relativity.[12]

Although the capacity to visualize is important, imagination can also be understood in a broader sense. Composers and poets, for example, hear the notes and words instead of seeing them. Dancers and athletes feel their motions kinesthetically as well as visualizing them. A gourmet chef can smell what is cooking and imagine how it will taste. And magicians, who can pull a rabbit out of a hat, count on being able to manipulate the imagination of the viewer. More broadly, then, imagination refers to the ability to create a concept of something not actually present to the senses.

Some people see creative imagination as a unique quality of artists or scientists. However, it belongs to each of us as one of the basic wonders of the human spirit. We are creative by virtue of being human. Without imagination, there would be no creativity. Whether a child is creating a sand castle or an architect a multistory building, imagination is essential for creativity.

Urge of the Human Spirit	Goal of the Search	Power Needed for the Search
To Create	Originality	Imagination

Unfortunately there is no agreement on how or why imagination works. According to psychoanalyst Silvano Arieti, imagi-

The urge to create

Creating a family memory

*Expressing
the creative urge*

Creating the sounds of life

Needing a creative solution

Practical creativity

*Helping others express
their creativity*

nation works because the conscious mind creates words, ideas, and symbols. This often happens in the well-known process called "brainstorming," in which there is no deliberate effort to organize ideas and symbols at first, only to create them and throw them out for consideration.[13]

Harold Rugg of Columbia University poses another option. He believes that imagination occurs in the noncensored "transliminal mind," somewhere between the conscious and the unconscious. Sometimes called the "preconscious," the transliminal mind can be open and non-focused (as when daydreaming or letting your mind wander) or it can be in a relaxed and focused condition (as in meditation, trances, and hypnotic states). In either condition, there can be a creative flash of some sort when the imagination is able to integrate several seemingly diverse parts into a single whole, or to create a new idea out of familiar facts or unknown possibilities. A faculty group working on a new curriculum may go into a retreat setting and, because of being relaxed, may experience a creative flash that leads to an innovative plan.

Biologist and philosopher Edmund Sinnott believes that imagination is more likely to arise from the unconscious, often during dreams.[14] An example of this is the chemist Friedrich Kekule, puzzling over what possible structure for the benzene molecule could explain its particular behavior, then having a dream of a snake holding its tail in its mouth. This became a symbol for him that led to his development of a closed ring for the chemical structure of benzene and the understanding that some organic compounds are composed of not rows of atoms but rings of them.[15]

IMAGINATION AND DREAMS

Whether imagination works because of our conscious use of words and symbols or our insights when relaxed or meditating, there is no doubt that imagination is most active when we dream. Whether remembered or not, our dreams are expressions of the creative inner self. Like collages made of bits and pieces of colored paper, the collages of our dreams include symbolic expressions of many kinds: fragments of memories, the hopes and fears of our lives, expressions of urges and passions, of problems and creative problem-solving.

Sometimes it seems impossible to believe that we have created some of our dreams, especially when they are violent and terrifying. Yet we do. The unconscious and subconscious parts of ourselves keep on working even when we sleep. Although we may not remember most of our dreams, research shows we dream as many as five times a night and remember only the last one before waking.

There are many theories about dreams, what they mean, how to remember them, and how to put them to use. The Senoi tribe of the mountain jungles of Malaysia has an unusual way of recognizing the importance of dreams, a cultural approach. In this tribe, children are trained to dream in specific patterns; this includes turning nightmares into positive learning experiences. To the Senoi, dream life is more real than waking life. Each day, tribal members ask each other, "What was your dream last night?" After listening to each other, they discuss the dreams. The intent is to learn how to confront and conquer danger in dreams, and how to make them pleasurable with a positive outcome. Positive outcomes are achieved by demanding, or asking for, a gift from a dream lover or from any fearful image in the dream. By doing this, they believe there is always something positive that can be remembered and used when awake.[16]

In the psychological approach of Gestalt therapy, people are encouraged to reexperience their dreams as though they were watching them again on TV. They are instructed to describe the dream using the present tense, beginning with words such as "Now I see a big door in front of me. As I walk toward it I feel frightened. I'm afraid of what's on the other side of the door." At this point, a Gestalt therapist might say something like, "Start a dialogue with the door: 'Door, what are you doing in my dream?' " Or the therapist might say, "Be the door and put into words how you are feeling." The purpose of this approach is to "own" or accept the unknown parts of the self because, in Gestalt theory, each part of the dream is a part of the dreamer.[17]

In the Judeo-Christian tradition, dreams were often interpreted as messages from God; there are many such dreams from the Bible. One, from the Old Testament, is of the patriarch Jacob's ladder set on the ground and reaching to the sky with angels going up and down the ladder. In this dream God appears to Jacob and tells him that he will have children "as plentiful as the dust on the ground" and that God will protect Jacob and bring him back safely to his homeland.[18]

Tertullian, a second-century theologian, claimed, "Nearly everyone on earth knows that God reveals himself to people most often in dreams." Seventeen hundred years after Tertullian, Abraham Lincoln was searching in the Bible and counted fifteen chapters in the Old Testament and four in the New Testament that contained dreams. Lincoln concluded:

IF WE BELIEVE THE BIBLE, WE MUST ACCEPT THE FACT THAT, IN THE OLD DAYS, GOD AND HIS ANGELS CAME TO HUMANS IN THEIR SLEEP AND MADE THEMSELVES KNOWN IN DREAMS.[19]

More recently, psychiatrist Carl Jung disagreed with theologians and psychologists who would not admit the possibility that the voice of God might be perceived in a dream and, like Tertullian and Lincoln, Jung agreed with "the age-old fact that God speaks chiefly through dreams and visions."[20]

Daydreams also come from the imagination acting in our lives. They may be self-serving dreams of future glory, or revenge for real or imagined hurts. They may be about luxuries or heroism that enhance the quality of life. They may also be about doing something helpful that enhances the quality of life.

Like night dreams, our daydreams can be very original. Science fiction writers are noted for using daydreaming in their creative process. We may have as exciting an idea as they do but not develop it when in a nondream state, perhaps feeling that these ideas may be fun to think about but not worth the time and energy to work on. Something else might seem more important. On the other hand, what we create in our daydreams may be very important to us but be so far ahead of the times that the technology is not available for its development. For example, we might think of shipping nuclear wastes to the sun to be burnt up, but there is no way of doing it.

Sometimes the intellectual or social climate is not open to what we dream up, and our brilliant ideas may take generations before they are accepted by others. The typewriter was invented in 1714 but not widely accepted until Mark Twain found one in 1874 and used it. The Wright brothers' airplanes were also rejected as being of little practical use at first. And television was discounted by the *New York Times* in 1939 on the basis that "people must sit and keep their eyes glued to a screen: the average American family hasn't time for it."[21]

It often takes a courageous imagination to go against the status quo and risk rejection, yet this may be required if creative imagination is to bear fruit.

BLOCKS TO CREATIVITY

Each of us is born with the potential to create something innovative, yet our creative energies can be encouraged or inhibited, depending on the environment in which we are working.

Recent research by psychologist Teresa Amabile shows that writers and scientists engaged in creative work are both subject to the same kinds of creative blocks.[22] These blocks seem to result from a variety of causes.

The urge to be creative can diminish when our *choices are restricted*. This can be true for students who don't have reference books or computers they need, or to those whose assignment deadlines do not allow enough time for incubation of an idea.

Surveillance also blocks creativity. When people are being watched, they do not feel as free to express their originality as when they are working unobserved. For example, employees who are supervised in every detail of their work may feel so resentful of the watchful eye that they slow down, abandon their creative efforts, and act in passive-aggressive ways.

Fears of competition frequently inhibit creative expression. Those who feel as if they are in direct competition with others may be less creative than those who are not as concerned with such comparisons. Potential authors who compare their writing to other authors may feel discouraged and discount their own creative abilities. The same is true for people who are starting off in any other creative art and keep comparing themselves to others with more training, experience, or natural style. For example, Johannes Brahms destroyed a great deal of his own music because he felt it didn't measure up to Beethoven's.

People who think about all the *extrinsic or external reasons* for doing what they are doing—such as approval by peers—are less creative than those motivated by their own interests. People

who ask, "How am I doing?" or "What do you think?" are trying
to do things to please others rather than doing things that are
intrinsic expressions of their own creative selves. People like this
will often ask for others' opinions and advice rather than make the
most of their own.

Thoughts of potential reward can also block originality.
People are likely to be less creative when working primarily for a
reward than for other motives. Working simply for a paycheck may
not motivate employees as much as working on projects of personal
interest. When driven by more intrinsic motives, people create
because they enjoy it. They use their imaginative capacities to
create according to their own liking.

Another behavior that stifles creativity is fear of rejection by
others that leads to overconcern with perfection. In trying to do
things the right way, a person may miss the chance to do things
in a new way, or at least in a more personally satisfying way. The
parent who tries to be a "superparent" may create a fear of rejection
in their children by overemphasizing high achievement.

Most perfectionists fear rejection, but many people of talent
and genius have been rejected numerous times and continued to
be creative anyway. Mozart's opera, The Abduction from the Ser-
aglio, was rejected by Emperor Joseph II because it had "too many
notes." Beethoven's music was also rejected by a Boston music
critic who wrote that if his Seventh Symphony was not shortened,
it would "fall into disuse." Even artists may reject each other's
creations. Tchaikovsky detested the music of "that scoundrel
Brahms," whom he called "a giftless bastard."[23]

Sometimes rejection comes not from others, but from ourselves. We may imagine that we should be creative in specific ways
and criticize ourselves when we are not. We may believe we should
be more artistic or inventive, or that we should be good at one
thing when actually we are better at another. We may pressure
ourselves by thinking that we should be as good as or better than
someone else, or that we should be masters when we are still
apprentices. All of these shoulds inhibit us from appreciating our
uniqueness and making the most of who we really are.

Curiously, poor mental health is not necessarily a block to
creativity.[24] Painters Claude Monet and philosopher Jean-Jacques
Rousseau were emotionally unstable yet were able to control their
emotional states while doing their work, while Salvador Dali in-

corporated his emotional illness into his work. Philosopher Immanuel Kant and scientist Isaac Newton both suffered emotionally after they completed their great works, whereas biologist Charles Darwin recovered his health after he completed his theories. An even larger number, including Beethoven, Lord Byron, and Schopenhauer were on the border of mental illness but were not quite psychotic. However, using these examples to conclude that great creativity is linked to mental anguish would be wrong. Havelock Ellis studied 1,030 geniuses and discovered that only 4.2 percent were psychotic.[25] This shows that it is not necessary to be tormented to be creative. Furthermore, the urge to create is so basic that even when people are mentally or physically ill, they strive to express their passions for life in original ways.

Equally as remarkable are people with a high passion for life who either ignore or overcome blocks that might seem insurmountable to the rest of us. Marie Curie lived through many years of illness and great poverty. For much of her adult life, she had only three black dresses and lived with bare walls, a simple bed, table, and chairs, which she could use for sitting and working. Her scientific laboratory was in a damp, unheated greenhouse where the temperatures sometimes dropped near freezing. However, she never allowed her creative thinking to be blocked. Her commitment to science was her passion for life. With her husband, Pierre, she won a Nobel prize in Physics in 1903, and after his tragic death, went on to win a Nobel prize in Chemistry.

Madame Curie raised her daughter Irene to have a similar scientific interest. She took her to scientific meetings and when Irene was away at school, frequently wrote her affectionate notes that included mathematical problems to solve. When still in her teens, Irene worked with her mother in her laboratory and, together, they set up the first X-ray machines in the war zones of France during World War I. Later, Irene won a Nobel prize in Chemistry with her husband, much like her mother and father had done before her![26]

Barriers to creativity, even those as harsh as Marie Curie faced, can be overcome when we are in touch with our passion for life and the urge to create. The challenge we face is to keep attuned to these inner yearnings and to express them for the benefit of ourselves and others, creating a better world for future generations.

CREATIVE MYTHS WE LIVE BY —————————————

Myths are creative expressions of the imagination. Some we create ourselves; others are the works of creative people from ancient times. Myths are stories that reveal, in symbolic ways, something that is true—not scientifically—but true in the sense of its basic meaning and universality. The most common universal themes concern the creation of the world and the animals, plants, and people in it, how certain central activities started, the origin of good and evil, and how everything will turn out in the end.

Every culture has myths about creation, for example. In Africa, China, Greece, and Japan, creation symbolically breaks out of a fertile egg. In Hinduism, the beginning creation is the work of Brahman, the initial power that supports the universe. To do this Brahman merely opened his eyes and brought the world into being. In early Hebrew myth, God also creates the universe out of nothing. However, instead of doing it the Hindu way with an opening of eyes, the Hebrew God creates the universe with words. God "said" and it was done.

Other kinds of creation myths include those about people. In the Old Testament, for example, God shaped man out of clay, breathed spirit into him, and then created woman out of his rib. The Maori people of New Zealand and some tribes in Africa also have myths of mankind being created out of clay and of life being breathed into them. However, the Maori myth says the first thing they did on coming to life was to sneeze. And in a tribe of Togoland, West Africa, the first thing they did was to look at each other and laugh.

The serious study of mythology has been going on since the time of Plato and Aristotle, who claimed that myths were contrary to reason. This may be true if myths are taken literally. However, *myths are stories expressing the strivings of the human spirit dressed in symbolic language*. Taken metaphorically, they provide a path that can lead to understanding at a deeper level.

Knowingly or unknowingly we live as if in a mythic world. We live by the myths told to us by others about how we were created, about how we should live our lives, and about how our lives are going to turn out. We also create our own myths as a result of the experiences we have. When something good happens, we may believe it attests to our worth; when something bad happens, we may conclude we are responsible for it and are destined to experience similar pains in the future.

We live by myths that are like psychological scripts. The dramas and characters we play often resemble figures and themes from mythology. We may take the weight of the world onto our shoulders (like Atlas), or fear something will go wrong if things get too good (as did Damocles, who found himself under a sword held only by a horsehair). We may imagine we are entitled to control everyone around us (as Zeus, king of the gods, believed), or we may always be cleaning up other peoples' messes (as did Hercules in the stables of the gods). We may feel continually jealous (like Hera was of Zeus) or spend much of our lives thinking only of ourselves (as Narcissus was wont to do).[27] Similarly, we may strive to make it from rags to riches (like Horatio Alger) or fight for the rights of the poor (like Robin Hood). We may work to bring a little joy into someone's life (like Mary Poppins), relish adventure (like Tom Sawyer), or try to be good at all things (like Superman or Superwoman). It is our creative imaginations that stimulate us to live in this manner.

With similar creativity, we can also create the future. Many science fiction writers, from Jules Verne to Aldous Huxley and Isaac Asimov, have written about imaginative new worlds that could be created if, instead of our complaining about what is or is not, we focused our imagination to create what could be. Part of this task would be to find out how each of us could use our own energies to create a new world. It is this challenge that the words of Sri Aurobindo, found on the walls of an ashram in India, are calling us to respond to: "The world is preparing for a big change. Will you help?"[28]

CREATING A NEW WORLD

One person who did what he could to make the world a better place was R. Buckminster Fuller, who invented the geodesic dome, a structure made of interconnected tetrahedrons that form a grid of equilateral triangles and distribute weight evenly throughout.

Fuller was born cross-eyed and was unable to see small details—only large patterns and shapes—until he was four years old and got glasses. Then he fell in love with the universe and became fascinated by thinking about how to live in the universe and how to improve society by economical and careful use of the earth's resources.

He believed the universe was waiting to cooperate with us if we knew how to tune in to it properly and understand its laws. One of the laws of nature is the instinct to create a home. Mankind's first homes were domed caves, huts, and igloos that were quite practical in that they conserved heat effectively. Ancient domed buildings had survived for thousands of years after those built with parallel beams had collapsed. So Fuller concluded that domed buildings were the most natural and practical.

When Fuller's first geodesic dome was erected, the public's imagination caught fire. With incredible strength, lightness, and energy-saving capacities, geodesic domes now cover huge sporting arenas, pavilions, gardens, symphony halls, even factories and small homes.

An inspirational speaker who could hold an audience spellbound for many hours with his creative imagination, Fuller invited others to join him on the bridge between science and the humanities where there is "no toll to pay and a glorious view all the way."[29] His philosophy was expressed in the message that our creative intellect is God-given and that the "Great Designer" intends for us to be successful; if we are not, it will only be a minor setback because there are "trillions of other intellects working on billions of other planets toward His ultimate purpose."[30]

We may agree or disagree with his belief that creativity is God-given and intended for good. However, if we disagree, we may need to come up with our own original alternative and imaginative ways to create a new world.

❦ RELEASING YOUR URGE TO CREATE————————————

Following are optional exercises to assist you in your search for originality.

❦   FOR CONTEMPLATION ON CREATING. Look over the following quotes until one catches your interest. Then focus on it for a while and let its messages about creating become clear.

IN THE BEGINNING WAS THE WORD AND THE WORD WAS WITH GOD
AND THE WORD WAS GOD.

—GENESIS 1

'TIS GOD GIVES SKILL, BUT NOT WITHOUT MEN'S HAND: HE COULD
NOT MAKE ANTONIO STRADIVARIS'S VIOLINS WITHOUT ANTONIO.

—GEORGE ELIOT (MARY ANN EVANS)[31]

I AM ONE OF THOSE WHO THINK LIKE NOBEL, THAT HUMANITY WILL
DRAW MORE GOOD THAN EVIL FROM NEW DISCOVERIES.

—MARIE CURIE[32]

CREATIVITY REQUIRES THE COURAGE TO LET GO OF CERTAINTIES.

—ERICH FROMM[33]

NOW THERE IS ONE OUTSTANDING IMPORTANT FACT REGARDING
SPACESHIP EARTH, AND THAT IS THAT NO INSTRUCTION BOOK CAME
WITH IT.

—R. BUCKMINSTER FULLER[34]

❦ YOUR CREATIVITY. Everyone is naturally creative. We are motivated for different reasons, such as out of necessity, because of
fascination, for personal gain, to please others, to solve problems,
or to actualize values. Think of some of your creative efforts, then
complete the following:

What I created   My motivation for doing so
_____   _____

❦ WHAT HOLDS YOU BACK? What holds you back from expressing
your creative energies more than you currently do? Think of several
creative projects you are interested in. Then analyze if you are
holding yourself back, and if so, is it because of restrictive choices,
surveillance, expected evaluation, competition, extrinsic orientation, or fear of rejection?

❦   AN ACTIVE IMAGINATION. Your imagination is your most valuable tool in the creative process. The most active way imagination is expressed is in dreaming. Recall a recurring dream or a significant one that seemed important to you when you had it. If you were to experiment with a Senoi, Gestalt, or biblical approach to the dream, what do you imagine you might learn?

❦   YOUR NEW WORLD. Imagine what an ideal world might be like. Write a paragraph or two about it. Then jot down some creative ideas about what you could do to initiate the process of bringing it into being.

8

THE URGE TO ENJOY

IF YOU ARE NOT ALLOWED TO LAUGH IN HEAVEN, I DO NOT WANT
TO GO THERE.

—MARTIN LUTHER[1]

❧

FLYING HIGH

Balloons rising into the sky are beautiful to watch. They lift our
spirits and our imaginations. What if we could rise like multi-
colored balloons and soar weightless over the earth? The view
below would be breathtaking, to say the least. When astronaut
Edgar Mitchell first saw this view of our planet, he called it "a
glimpse of divinity."

Few of us ride in hot-air balloons, even fewer in space
shuttles. Yet we see pictures taken from these perspectives and
our imaginations soar. How exhilarating it must be to see this with
our own eyes!

Even though we may not fly high physically, we often fly
high emotionally. This is the natural high that comes when we
succeed at an important job or listen to a favorite piece of music
or experience a moment of sudden insight or deeply felt love. When
we feel high, many things suddenly seem possible. We feel eu-
phoric and may say, "What a wonderful day! I can hardly believe
it! I wish every day would be just like this."

The happiness of an emotional high shows in lightness and

smiles, in jokes and belly laughs. It can be seen when people shout for joy or dance with excitement. It is expressed at sporting events when a team is winning and fans jump out of their seats. We can even see it at airports when people hug loved ones as they arrive, at hospitals when good news is given, at birthday parties when presents are opened, and at weddings when couples say, "I do." Joy has many faces.

Yet because of the unpredictable nature of life, the capacity for enjoyment ebbs and flows with changes in external circumstances or changes in our moods, interests, or energies. Many of our days are not peak experiences. They are plateaus with nothing especially exciting going on, or they may even be "the pits" when everything seems to go wrong. Fatigued by too many pressures or a sudden crisis, we may wonder, "Why is life so hard?" or "What happened to the enthusiasm I used to feel?" Then, after some good news arrives or after a good night's sleep, we may once more bounce out of bed feeling more passion for life, more enthusiasm and optimism.

One of the biggest challenges we face is enjoying life one day at a time and over the long run. Another challenge is bringing joy and happiness to others—to those for whom we feel compassion, to those with whom we work, and, at a more personal level, to those we love.

THE URGE TO ENJOY

Regardless of the inevitable suffering and disappointments we encounter on the paths we follow, one of the universal energies of the human spirit is the urge to enjoy. Enjoyment is often thought of in terms of comfort, pleasure, and play, yet it is more than that. *The urge to enjoy is the desire of the human spirit to experience and express the delight of existence.*

This powerful urge to enjoy pushes from within to be satisfied—at the most basic levels and the highest. We yearn for the physical pleasure of a pleasant meal, a vigorous workout, or a sexual release. Beyond that, we may yearn for the psychological joy of being recognized at work or needed at home. We may want to go out and play, or stay in and get things done. We may yearn for the spiritual joy that can come from special moments in nature or deeply felt encounters with the sacred.

People have many different ways of enjoying themselves. Whereas some people like physical exercise, others prefer to sit and ponder. Some people like to go to the opera, others prefer rock concerts. Some like a solitary walk in the park, others like to socialize with friends. Still others enjoy a lazy day in bed or an active day at work. What is pleasurable to one may be boring or distasteful to another.

Poet W. H. Auden did not enjoy wearing shoes. Once asked what he would do if he became famous, he replied, "I believe that I would always wear my carpet slippers." When he later became famous, he was always seen in his slippers. He even wore them when going out to formal events.[2]

In spite of this deeply embedded urge to enjoy life, some people are afraid to because they expect that if they find enjoyment, something painful will happen next. A common example is those who have been disappointed in love relations and decide "I'll never run the risk again because if love fades or dies it's just too painful."

Others repress the urge to enjoy because they feel guilty or have low self-esteem and feel that they are not entitled to enjoyment. Instead, they may act overly competent as a way to hide their insecurities or try to please others and ignore their own needs. Still others say that even if they were to enjoy themselves, it wouldn't be enough to make up for some past tragedy or injustice. Then there are those who keep on postponing their desire to feel joyful until something important happens, such as when they get to be economically secure or when they finally get someone to understand them.

In spite of the internal brakes some people use to avoid being too happy, the urge to enjoy is a tenacious force within us. Boredom can numb us, tragedy can burden us, yet the urge to enjoy fights to be expressed. Even when times are bleak we hunger to be happy and enjoy life once again. Sitting in darkness looking out a window, we may feel overcome by challenges and unsure of what to do next. We may reach for a snack or a drink to deaden the pain, silence difficult questions, or give ourselves a pickup in some way. Or we may turn on the TV or go for a walk in order to feel better.

Even when times are bad, it is natural to want to feel good and be reassured that life is worthwhile and that adversity can be overcome. With this yearning in mind, we inevitably search for

happiness wherever we are—at home and at work, in our neighborhoods and in far-off places.

THE SEARCH FOR HAPPINESS

When we are happy we feel good. *Happiness is a feeling of pleasure and well-being that ranges from momentary contentment to
deep and abiding joy.* We all want happiness, yet it is often difficult
to find and even harder to hold on to. There are times when life
doesn't go well and the passion for life seems to be shadowed. At
moments like these, we are likely to ask ourselves, "What can I
do to feel better?" This question signals the beginning of a search—
a search for people or events or opportunities that we believe will
contribute to our feeling happy.

Happiness is a by-product of something else. It often
emerges from one of three sources: involvement in positive experiences of pleasure, involvement in activities that interest us, or
doing things at which we feel competent.

Through our senses we can experience innumerable moments that bring us simple pleasure. Taking a shower, embracing
a loved one after a long separation, sitting in the shade on a hot
day, tasting the first strawberries of spring, hearing the song of a
bird, and laughing with a friend are small moments of joy. Pleasures
such as these do not require any special effort. They come just
from savoring warm and happy moments and enjoying life as it
comes. The same joy can come from walking down a country road
in the moonlight, sitting in a sidewalk café eyeing people as they
pass, or lounging on a patio watching the clouds float by.

Involvement in activities that interest or challenge us is
another great source of joy. We can be fascinated when becoming
acquainted with a new job, a new friend, or a new hobby. Imagine
the pleasure of returning to school in midlife, catching up on
articles we have wanted to read but haven't had time for, joining
others in a march for peace, planting a flower or vegetable garden,
or experimenting with a new computer program.

Being able to do any of these things especially well brings
a heightened sense of enjoyment. But on the other hand, activities
in which we have no sensory pleasure or interest, or activities in
which we feel awkward or expect to be criticized are not much
fun. For example, trying to fix a leaky faucet can be a pain for

someone unskilled in plumbing; someone with those skills may find it easy to do and take pleasure in doing it fast and efficiently. Similarly, cooking can be enjoyable to someone who knows how to do it well; to the uninitiated, it can be a frustrating chore. And speaking in front of a crowd can be a nerve-wracking or an enjoyable experience, depending on one's confidence and capability. Competence can make a big difference in what we prefer to do to satisfy the urge to enjoy.

At a more significant level, there are three additional sources of happiness that Rabbi Harold Kushner highlights.[3] One is maintaining ongoing relationships with the same people over time. By continuing to relate to people who depend on us and whom we depend on, we build a sense of responsibility to and for these people. In doing so, we create relationships in which we can interact as whole persons, not merely as people playing roles.

Living for something greater than ourselves and knowing we are doing something that is making a difference is another ingredient of happiness. Whether helping a friend or a stranger, or joining with others in a shared project or cause, we often end up feeling happier because of our efforts.

Doing what Kushner calls "the right things" so we can live in harmony with life is another key element to being happy. Being responsible instead of overindulgent, friendly instead of distant, active instead of apathetic—all tend to bring happiness. Whenever we act ethically, we are guided by values that enhance life.

The directions that people choose in the search for happiness depends upon their needs at the moment. Psychologist Abraham Maslow, whose writings became the foundation for what is called humanistic psychology, believed that we all have a hierarchy of inner needs that influence our actions.[4] He arranged these needs in order of their importance on a triangle:

    It is natural to want to be on a path with heart that is
motivated by high values, yet the fact is our more basic needs often
rule us. We search for happiness at the level at which we are
experiencing a need. If starving, we are happy to get something to
eat. If our safety is threatened, we are happy if someone comes to
protect us. If we are lonely, a phone call from a friend may lead
to the happy feeling of belonging. When our self-esteem is low,
we may seek a compliment to raise our feelings of worth in order
to feel happier.

FROM PITS TO PEAKS

The happiness we experience varies from time to time. Feeling
happy is like standing on a high mountain peak unencumbered
by the mundane activities going on below. Feeling unhappy is like
being in a dark chasm without a ray of hope or a way to get out.
On a plateau we look around and wonder what to do or where to
go next.
    The levels of happiness and unhappiness between the pits
and the peaks are:

The Peak
elated and
ecstatic

happy and
enthusiastic

The Plateaus
contented or
restless and bored

dissatisfied
and
unhappy

The Pits
depressed
and hopeless

Being "in the pits" is a colloquial term for feeling terrible. The pits feel dark and dank, far from light and warmth, and, when we're there, we feel depressed and afraid, hopeless and despairing. This feeling can come because of poor health, failure, criticism, and rejection. It can come suddenly with the death of someone we love or the loss of a job and self-esteem. It may develop gradually with too many responsibilities on the job or at home.

Historically, being put into a pit has been one of the worst punishments ever inflicted because the sense of isolation and helplessness feels overpowering. Most of us have been in emotional pits from time to time and know that to remain there is physically, psychologically, and spiritually debilitating. We can't tolerate it. Some give up and die, others call out for help or desperately try to claw a way out.

Anxiety is one of the most common feelings that leads us to feel in the pits. Anxiety is an emotional state characterized by fear of impending danger and a sense of helplessness and sometimes panic. These feelings may be accompanied by physiological reactions such as increased heart rate, hyperventilation, perspiration, tension, nervousness, or agitation.

Anxiety arises, according to psychiatrist Harry Stack Sullivan, when someone experiences or anticipates disapproval from others. "Anxiety," he said, "is a signal of danger to self-respect, to one's standing in the eyes of significant persons, even if they are only ideal figures from childhood."[5] It occurs when thoughts, impulses, feelings, or inner conflicts that are unacceptable to one's own self-image begin to come into awareness. For example, people who consider themselves warm and loving may become anxious if they discover they only act loving for manipulative purposes, either to exploit others to get love for themselves, to avoid being rejected, or to protect against hostile or competitive feelings they deny having. Even a slight awareness of unacceptable aspects in oneself can create a feeling of anxiety.

Anxiety is also experienced when we imagine it is impossible to do what we believe we "should" do. This is often seen at universities toward the end of the semester. For some students, nothing less than an A is acceptable to their self-image. If they feel they can't meet this standard, they become anxious and may develop physical symptoms such as stomachaches or headaches or eating or sleeping problems that seriously interfere with achieving their goals. Later in life, similar anxiety may surface out of fear of evaluation.[6]

In addition to being blocked by anxiety, we can get into the pits by not believing that joy and happiness are possible. This attitude frequently develops during childhood. If we were often told to be quiet, we may repress our buoyancy; if we were often told we are stupid, we may repress our eagerness to learn something new. Or we can feel guilty for something we did or didn't do and conclude we are not entitled to enjoy life. Or we may feel so sad or mad about the past that we *refuse* to enjoy life. Any of these basic feelings can create so much anxiety that the natural urge to enjoy is blocked. We are stuck in the pits.

In contrast to the pits, plateaus are moments when life seems to level off and stabilize instead of going up or down. Plateaus are times to rest and recover, meditate and ruminate, know inner peace instead of turmoil. On plateaus, we may breathe a sigh of relief, look around, and take stock of ourselves and our situation. Or we may just sit back and comfortably relax. We turn to the simple things in life for enjoyment—a hot shower or clean sheets, a good meal or deep sleep, the familiarity of well-worn clothes or a favorite chair.

However, the negative side of life's plateaus is stagnation. We are creatures of change. When everything seems too static, we become bored and look for excitement. Children whine, "I'm bored." Teenagers complain, "There's nothing to do." Adults also grumble, "I'm not getting any fun out of life." Resentment may build and accusations fly: "It's boring staying home. You never want to do anything new." Or, "I'm bored going to the same old places, doing the same old things. Why don't we do something different for a change?"

Some people seek excitement by deliberately doing something dangerous—riding motorcycles too fast, rock climbing without ropes, scuba diving alone. Such people can become "excitement junkies," addicted to having drama in their lives. They may create havoc at work and derive a kind of perverse satisfaction from this. They may also provoke melodrama among their friends or family in going from one relationship to another, without stopping to develop deep commitments to anyone. The extreme cases are those who turn to the negative excitement of violence and crime, "just for the fun of it."

Other people find excitement in more positive ways. They may get excited over being involved in politics or going to a baseball or soccer game. They get excited over remodeling their homes or skiing down a mountain. At a more significant level, they may get excited in their search for meaning and for ways to be self-determined or get excited in a search for knowledge and how to create something original. Likewise, they may be excited in their search for God or for eternal truths.

High moments come when we feel great and things are going the way we'd like them to. Athletes often report feeling high after they catch their "second wind" and endorphins are released in the body, bringing about a sense of renewed strength and euphoria. Intellectuals also get a high. Archimedes, a scientist in the third century B.C., was sitting in the bathtub trying to figure out the principle of buoyancy. Suddenly, it became clear to him. He jumped out of the tub and ran down the streets of the city naked shouting, "Eureka," meaning "I've got it!"[7]

In a more everyday way, we may feel high when something special happens, such as when a child comes home with a good report card or a high school reunion reestablishes close and fond friendships or a difficult project turns out much better than expected. These happy moments give meaning to life and increase our passion for enjoying it more. There are also the high feelings that come with the "aha" experience of sudden insight, with the completion of a creative endeavor, or from hearing an inspiring speech.

Peak experiences are the most intense experiences of happiness. A peak experience is a state of emotion so intense that one may briefly be carried beyond thought or worry. Peak experiences feel like being outside of time and space, free-floating and not bound by routines. In peak experiences, we are caught up in a grander feeling of oneness and may not even be aware of ourselves as individuals.

Such moments may come during a profound encounter with a person, nature, or with art, music, or poetry in which we feel caught up and do not analyze or categorize the experience. Instead we feel deeply immersed in the moment. We transcend our lives in some brief yet mystical way and everything seems to be as it should. With body, mind, and spirit, we are able to experience life with a new sense of awe, wonder, and appreciation.

Similarly, we may experience a profoundly moving moment when we realize we have survived a near-fatal accident or when we are suddenly free of the tyranny or dangers of a repressive or war-torn country.

Religious ecstasy is another kind of peak experience. The ancient Greeks called it "a journey to heaven." The Jews said it was like being lifted up on eagles' wings. To Saint Paul, it was like being caught up into paradise and hearing things that must not and cannot be put into human language.[8] This is the transcendent moment that comes as a gift when the soul is open to experiencing the wonders of the cosmic, holy, and human spirit.

No one is able to have peak experiences on demand or as often as desired, yet people with a passion for life experience more peak moments than those who rein in the powers of their inner urges. Those who live fully are also able to endure plateaus or the pits and know that they will eventually move up to more positive feelings.

DYNAMICS OF SEX

An example of how life can be the pits, the peaks, or somewhere in between can be seen in sexual relationships. Whether a sexual encounter is deliberately planned or occurs on the spur of the moment, it can leave us satisfied or dissatisfied, elated or depressed. Real sexual communion is a celebration. Conversely, sex often feels like the pits when it occurs without real passion or emotion.

When a person's sexual life is on a plateau, it can be blessedly safe and physically satisfying, or it can become so predictable it is boring. When the spirit of playfulness and enthusiasm is missing, "having sex" just follows the same old routines. The body may respond but the mind may be elsewhere and the playful, sensual spirit asleep. In such cases, sexual performance may seem more like work than play. We may try harder and harder to enjoy it and perform all kinds of sexual gymnastics and still feel empty and lose hope of having a sexual relationship that has meaning.

Another sign that sex has reached a plateau is when it becomes a pastime based on the attitude, "There's nothing else to do tonight, so we might as well pass the time that way." In this situation, one or both partners eventually becomes disinterested and may seek out one-night stands or illicit affairs to break the monotony.

Sex is also the pits when it becomes entangled in psychological games. Flirting, teasing, inviting jealousy, or using sex as a means of reward or punishment leads to resentment. So does criticism of one's appearance, personality, or sexual performance. The fear of pregnancy or disease can also interfere with the joy of sex. Any time respect and consideration are absent and partners treat each other only as objects, sex is the pits.

In contrast, if sex for both partners includes tender caressing and genuine affection, then the occasion pleases not only the body but also the spirit. Physical, emotional, and spiritual intimacy such as this leads to deep feelings of happiness and a renewed enthusiasm for life.

THE NEED FOR ENTHUSIASM

The search for happiness requires enthusiasm. *Enthusiasm is the eagerness and excitement we feel when inspired and directing our energies into activities that we enjoy or to which we feel deeply committed.* Enthusiasm shows in fascination and intense absorption in what we are doing. It also shows in spirited and outward expressions of delight. Enthusiasm reflects an underlying positive attitude and expectation that arise naturally from the urge to enjoy. Enthusiasm is a powerful stimulant in the search for happiness that helps us move out of the pits and carries us across plateaus toward peaks of happiness. This dynamic process is:

Urge of the Human Spirit	Goal of the Search	Power Needed for the Search
to Enjoy	Happiness	Enthusiasm

Enthusiasm begins when someone or something sparks our interest. Its results can be obvious. For instance, when we are attracted to the great outdoors, we may go for long hikes, study biology and wildlife management, or take up nature photography.

Similarly, enthusiasm for a relationship leads couples to spend time together, building a future while enjoying each other. The plans they make, the gifts they give, the laughter they share, all reflect enthusiasm for each other.

Enthusiastic people are lively, animated, and exuberant. They tend to do things with intensity and gusto. Their passion for life is obvious. Furthermore, their enthusiasm is contagious, like a spark that catches fire and spreads to others. It can be seen at sporting events and political campaigns when people stand up and shout almost in one voice.

When people are enthusiastic about any aspect of life, their energy may lead them into meaningful, lifelong careers. Louis Pasteur was such a person. Pasteur, one of the founders of microbiology, was an artist in his youth and then became a chemist and a biologist. At age forty-six, he suffered a stroke that resulted in his left arm and leg being permanently paralyzed. He did not let this limit his passion for life or his enthusiasm for solving medical problems. He went on to prove the germ theory of disease, that microscopic organisms can contaminate other forms of life, that quarantine can prevent the spread of disease, and that antiseptics and sterilization in surgical situations cut the death rate radically. He also proved that vaccination could prevent rabies and developed the process of pasteurization, which is named for him and used to protect us from bacteria in milk products.

Pasteur's passion for life went beyond his laboratory. Not religious in the traditional sense, Pasteur calls our attention to the root meaning of the word *enthusiasm:*

THE GREEKS HAVE GIVEN US ONE OF THE MOST BEAUTIFUL WORDS OF OUR LANGUAGE, THE WORD 'ENTHUSIASM'—A GOD WITHIN. THE GRANDEUR OF THE ACTS OF MEN ARE MEASURED BY THE INSPIRATION FROM WHICH THEY SPRING. HAPPY IS HE WHO BEARS A GOD WITHIN.[9]

Enthusiasm, like other human qualities, can be used for good or evil. When people are highly enthusiastic, they may be called fanatics or zealots and may use their wild enthusiasm to inspire others to join them in their causes. Because the causes frequently promise change, people who are dissatisfied, bored, or depressed about life may be enticed by this approach. However, many positive political, social, and religious movements start with a highly enthusiastic and charismatic leader.

Furthermore, some kinds of jobs call for continuous enthusiasm, even when it is only an external façade. People in these jobs may say to themselves, "I have to go out there and act happy, even if I'm not." This kind of forced enthusiasm can be tolerable for brief moments but deadens one's spirit if it becomes a necessary habit. Nevertheless, the urge to enjoy motivates us from within to regain an authentic enthusiasm for life. We sometimes find this at work.

THE PLEASURE OF WORK

Work can be a major avenue through which the urge to enjoy can be expressed. Hans Selye, professor of experimental medicine at the University of Montreal and famous for his research on stress, affirms, "Work is a biological need of man. The question is not whether we should or should not work, but what kind of work suits each person."[10] An important aspect of the search for happiness is to find some kind of work about which we can feel enthusiastic. Our enthusiasm can arise from the experience of the job itself. Because of their enthusiasm and commitment, teachers enjoy helping students learn. Nurses enjoy helping others become well. Lawyers enjoy helping clients win cases. Religious leaders enjoy sharing their faith.

Beverly Sills, one of the world's best-known operatic sopranos, studied music as a child and by the time she was seven was on a weekly radio show singing selections from French and Italian operas. Encouraged by her mother, she had learned opera by listening to records of famous sopranos. By the time Beverly was thirty-seven, she was a famous opera star. After her retirement as a performer, she became director of the New York City Opera.

A celebratory performance, at age sixty-one, was a stupendous occasion. Many equally famous friends joined her onstage. As part of the evening, comedian Carol Burnett switched roles with Beverly. Carol sang opera and Beverly interrupted her with snatches from popular songs. Laughter broke out time and again, and tears of happiness flowed freely down the faces of all. The finale of the evening was the release of thousands of balloons in the theater.[11]

Even if the job is not particularly enjoyable, enthusiasm may

The urge to enjoy

*The joy
of excitement*

Natural pleasures

TAHOE DAILY TRIBUNE/IVOR MARKMAN

BRIAN DUFFY/FOCAL POINT

JANE SCHERR

Enjoying friends

The playful spirit

When work is play

Family play

be high because of the positive benefits it brings. A factory worker who constantly performs repetitive tasks may not mind the routine because the on-the-job relationships with others are enjoyable. An elderly janitor who constantly cleans up after others may work with pleasure to help a grandchild get through college. Some kinds of work are exhausting yet are steps to something better so are diligently sought out instead of avoided. A hospital intern may have to put in thirty-six-hour shifts, yet do so because of a deep commitment to the profession. A truck driver who has had only intermittent work or corporate executive who has been laid off may find great pleasure in the regular paycheck and health benefits of a new job, even if it is not exactly one they wanted.

However, being rushed, having too much to do and too little time to do it, often takes the pleasure out of work. People can become so accustomed to working that taking time off may become uncomfortable, even foreign, to them. When these people are asked, "What do you do in your spare time?" they respond, "I work."

On the other hand, many people enjoy their work because it is like play to them. A recent study by management experts Warren Bennis and Burt Nanus of corporate presidents and outstanding public leaders found that, almost without exception, successful leaders demonstrate "a sense of adventure and play in what they are doing." Furthermore, their success is largely due to "their felicitous fusion between work and play."[12]

Few of us are corporate presidents with the advantages of these positions, but still we look for pleasure and meaning in our work. Walt Disney enjoyed his work partly because his mission—to bring happiness to millions of people—was one he could accomplish. His creations, including Mickey Mouse and Donald Duck, and his famous cartoons, such as *Cinderella*, *Peter Pan*, and *Snow White and the Seven Dwarfs* are known around the world. Through them, Disney brought fable and fantasy to life. Knowing that there is a child in every grown-up, he appealed to both young and old. In doing so, Walt Disney "probably did more to heal or at least soothe troubled human spirits than all the psychiatrists in the world."[13]

Like Disney, we all want to do work that has meaning and provides opportunities for pleasure. We can do this, philosopher

Alan Watts believed, if we become "completely engaged in what we are doing and instead of calling it work, realize it is play."[14]

THE PLAYFUL SPIRIT

Physicists play with mathematical formulas while architects play with order, form, and space. Real estate brokers play with personalities, properties, and proposals; researchers with computers, software, and data bases; and musicians with notes, rhythm, and harmony. More personally, when any of us write a letter or a business report, we play with words, themes, and ideas. In cooking we play with recipes, tastes, and textures; while paying the bills we may play with numbers, priorities, and percentages. In fact, a great deal of what we do is creatively playing with something, no matter how serious we imagine it to be at the time.

Play is a basic component of work and relationships. It is one of the most poignant ways of expressing a passion for life. Furthermore, it is a natural behavior. Watch a kitten pounce on a ball of yarn or two puppies or children wrestle and the natural instinct to play is obvious.

Research psychologist Harry Harlow did some famous studies with monkeys in which he concluded that play enables monkeys to develop the necessary social and emotional skills required for successful functioning. He also found that monkeys that are prevented from playing with other monkeys become seriously ill.[15] And Gregory Bateson, a biologist and anthropologist, tells of a strategy he used to discover whether or not animals would initiate play with humans. He sat quietly in a pool and watched as a dolphin started playing with him by putting her beak under his arm. Next she swam around to sit on his lap to initiate their playing and swimming together.[16] Evidently animals have an urge to enjoy and show it by playing in ways that are similar to ours.

Humans also play naturally. Babies play in bathtubs with rubber duckies; children swing in the parks. Teenagers at dances and adults at barbecues frequently end up smiling, joking, and having fun with each other. Even at work, the tendency to play often surfaces with jokes around the water cooler or coffeepot due to the playful spirit within each of us.

When people experience their playful spirit within, they take an almost childlike delight in life. They are open to the unexpected in the present moment and are optimistic about the future. When in touch with the playful spirit, they have a sense of humor, can laugh at themselves and even laugh in tough situations. When people let their playful spirits out, they are trusting enough to be spontaneous without acting artificial or defensive. They feel confident and comfortable and enjoy playful interchanges with others.

This playfulness is an expression of the natural Child within that enjoys laughter and joy without planning and practice. The inner Child, doing what it wants to do, naturally enjoys fooling around, acting silly, joking, and laughing. It has a lightness that can bring a breath of fresh air to an otherwise tense or serious moment. This lightness reflects the spirit of play.

Each of us has a naturally playful spirit within, regardless of how we experience or express it. Some people are playful no matter what they are doing. They joke and laugh while driving across town or cleaning up after dinner. They make light of temporary setbacks and are able to share a smile even when working fast and furiously. Of course, some others overdo playfulness. They joke at inappropriate times or use ridicule and sarcasm under the guise of a friendly joke. They may use humor to distract from a difficult conversation, laugh when they feel uncomfortable or in pain, or make fun of something that is a very serious matter to someone else.

On the other hand, many people are uncomfortable letting their playful spirit out. Taking life too seriously, they consider playfulness to be frivolous and a waste of time. They feel compelled to keep busy instead of enjoying the momentary interactions and distractions. Pushing to make every moment productive, they may block their creativity, drain their energy, and decrease their sense of enthusiasm for life. For them, life is serious work and not all that pleasant.

Playfulness is also difficult for those who compulsively try to be perfect. Always needing to have things organized, whether it is a tidy desk or a spotless house, they prefer order and predictability in relationships and life in general to flexibility and joy.

Still others disdain playfulness because they find it a bit scary. Possibly they were ridiculed as children or rejected as adults, so they shy away from encounters they imagine could be embarrassing. They often try to be overly pleasing and helpful, or overly controlling and in charge, as a way to protect against the fears in the inner Child. Yet according to Erik Erikson, one of the world's experts on psychological development, play is "the most natural, self-healing measure" life can offer.[17]

In spite of these hesitations, the natural playfulness within each person can be seen in any situation where people express their basic urges. In expressing the urge to live, some people are lighthearted and friendly with hospital staff while taking a treadmill exam or having a few stitches put in a cut finger. Similarly, people who are playful while expressing their urge to create may scribble, doodle, or draw cartoons during a playful moment, or let their imaginations run free to daydream while searching for a creative solution to a problem. Similarly, when the playful spirit arises in people who are seeking to express their urge for understanding, they may make funny connections between ideas, or make puns that bring laughter to others in class. The spirit of play and enjoyment usually shows the most when we laugh.

THE JOY OF LAUGHTER

Laughter is part of being whole and thus a part of being holy. Laughing and holiness have a long history. The phrase, "laughter of the gods," is rooted in ancient cultures. Jupiter (or Jove), chief god of the ancient Romans, stood for mirth, joy, and humor; people born under the planet Jupiter are expected to be jovial. Buddhists often show Buddha laughing, and in Chinese writing, laughter is depicted by a human with arms and legs flung wide apart, head up to the sky, vibrating with mirth like bamboo leaves in the wind.[18]

The Old Testament story of Abraham says that when he was ninety-nine years old, God appeared and told him that he and his wife, Sarah, who was ninety years old at the time, would have a son to be named Isaac. Abraham, it says, found this so hard to believe that he fell down laughing. When Sarah gave birth to Isaac, she boasted, "God has made laughter for me."[19]

Many psalms speak of laughter and joy, of one who sits in the heavens and laughs, and of people so fortunate that "their mouths were filled with laughter and their tongues with shouts of joy."[20] A New Testament story speaks of the prodigal son who, after living a dissolute life and squandering his inheritance, is nevertheless welcomed home by his father; a celebration is held with music, dancing, and laughter.[21]

Celebrations with laughter and music are important in all religious traditions, and also outside of them as well. The wonder of laughter is that it can lighten up dismal situations and break tension in uncomfortable ones. Laughter attracts people to each other and, furthermore, is healing. More and more hospital personnel and others in the helping professions are finding laughter of immense value. For example, an increasing number of specially trained clowns are invited to go into children's medical wards and make funny faces that lift the spirits of the young patients.

Laughter activates the chemistry of the will to live and increases the capacity to fight against disease. The chest expands when laughing, respiration increases and forces exhausted air from the lungs. Laughing relaxes the body and stimulates the balance of health. Problems associated with high blood pressure, strokes, arthritis, ulcers, and heart disease are sometimes reduced when laughter releases the urge to enjoy life.

One of the most dramatic cases of the curative effects of laughter is that of Norman Cousins, editor and professor who laughed his way out of the hospital and out of a very serious, crippling collagen illness that doctors believed to be irreversible. Cousins, in excruciating pain, refused to give up. He decided to take more responsibility for his own cure with the ancient theory that laughter is good medicine. His rationale for laughing was

IF NEGATIVE EMOTIONS PRODUCE NEGATIVE CHEMICAL CHANGES IN THE BODY, WOULDN'T THE POSITIVE EMOTIONS PRODUCE POSITIVE CHEMICAL CHANGES? IS IT POSSIBLE THAT LOVE, HOPE, FAITH, LAUGHTER, CONFIDENCE, AND THE WILL TO LIVE HAVE THERAPEUTIC VALUE?[22]

He arranged for a movie projector to be set up in his hospital room and watched the humorous TV series, "Candid Camera," every day. In doing this he discovered that ten minutes of genuine belly laughter had an anesthetic effect that gave him at least two hours of pain-free sleep. In addition to watching funny programs, Cousins turned to books of humor. Although his high sedimentation rate dropped only a little after each laughter session, the effect was cumulative and it stayed down. Many years later, he has remained cured and active.

A different use of laughter was suggested by psychiatrist Viktor Frankl, who incorporated it into his system of "logotherapy." His belief was that laughing at oneself and one's predicament can be especially useful in treating psychological problems, especially for persons with obsessive-compulsive patterns or phobias. Frankl believes that a patient needs to "develop a sense of detachment toward his neurosis by laughing at it."[23] To facilitate this, his patients are encouraged to exaggerate their psychological symptoms briefly, not avoid them or control them, and to do this until they burst out laughing as they gain insight on how ridiculous their compulsions often are.

Any of us can laugh at our own absurdities and also encourage others to laugh. Martin Buber said it well:

> THERE ARE THOSE WHO SUFFER GREATLY AND THEY GO THEIR WAY FULL OF SUFFERING. BUT IF THEY MEET SOMEONE WHOSE FACE IS BRIGHT WITH LAUGHTER, HE CAN QUICKEN THEM WITH GLADNESS. AND IT IS NO SMALL THING TO QUICKEN A HUMAN BEING.[24]

Mimes and clowns at circuses, rodeos, or street fairs show us without words how to enjoy life by laughing at it. Marcel Marceau, one of the world's greatest mimes, uses exaggerated facial expressions and bodily actions to reveal the personalities of people, the existence of objects, even abstract concepts such as good and evil. His skill in this apparently comes from a playful spirit, his ability to use and control his face and body, his highly developed powers of observation, and the desire to bring laughter to others.[25] For any of us to bring laughter and enjoyment to others is a special and simple way to heal the spirit.

❦ RELEASING YOUR URGE TO ENJOY————————

Following are optional exercises to assist you in your search for happiness.

❦ CONTEMPLATE YOUR ATTITUDES. Think about your expressions of joy, laughter, and fun. Take a few moments and reflect on the following:

WHERE WERE YOU . . . WHEN THE MORNING STARS SANG TOGETHER,
AND ALL THE SONS [AND DAUGHTERS] OF GOD SHOUTED FOR JOY?
—JOB 38: 4–7

THE BURDEN OF THE SELF IS LIGHTENED WHEN I LAUGH AT MYSELF.
—RABINDRANATH TAGORE[26]

FUN CAN BE THE DESSERT OF OUR LIVES BUT NEVER ITS MAIN
COURSE.

—HAROLD KUSHNER[27]

A CHEERFUL HEART IS A GOOD MEDICINE,
BUT A DOWNCAST SPIRIT DRIES UP THE BONES.
—PROVERBS 17:22

MY MOTHER HAD A GREAT DEAL OF TROUBLE WITH ME, BUT I THINK
SHE ENJOYED IT.

—MARK TWAIN[28]

THE CONTEMPORARY FORM OF TRUE GREATNESS LIES IN A CIVILI-
ZATION FOUNDED ON THE SPIRITUALITY OF WORK.

—SIMONE WEIL[29]

❦ REMEMBERING THE JOY. There are many ways to remember and re-experience past joys. Some people return to a place where they once knew happiness. Others reread letters from lovers, friends, spouses, or children. Looking through photograph albums can also bring back special moments. List some of your most joyful moments in life. Now look at your list and consider, What made them joyful? Is there any pattern of what creates joy for you?

Joyful moments.   What made them joyful?
_____   _____

❦ CHILDHOOD FUN. One way to release your urge to enjoy is to recover your sense of playfulness from childhood. Relax and remember what you did for fun as a child. Did you fly kites, roller skate or ice skate, draw pictures, or what? Visualize yourself doing it again.

❦   DO IT AND ENJOY IT. There are four attitudes that people can take in dealing with tasks.[30] They can do them or not, and they can enjoy doing them or not. Think of activities you commonly do or avoid doing and consider which of these four attitudes applies:

I do it and enjoy it
I do it and don't enjoy it
I don't do it and enjoy not doing it
I don't do it and don't enjoy not doing it.

❦   THE PLEASURE OF YOUR WORK. Do you enjoy what you are doing at work? Are you enthusiastic about it? Does it feel like a path with heart for you? If not, are there any changes you might want or need to make in your job or how you do your work?

❦   FROM THE PITS TO THE PEAKS. What in your life pulls your spirits down? How do you act when you're in the pits? What do you do when you're on a plateau of boredom or peace? Is there anything you could do that might lead to more peak experiences in your life?

❦   FOR FURTHER THOUGHT. What are some questions or concerns you have about your urge to enjoy, your search for happiness, or your need for enthusiasm?

9

THE URGE TO CONNECT

THE WORLD IS NOT COMPREHENSIBLE, BUT IT IS EMBRACEABLE:
THROUGH THE EMBRACING OF ONE OF ITS BEINGS.

—MARTIN BUBER[1]

MARCHING TO DIFFERENT DRUMMERS

Everything is connected to everything else—either in observable
or nonobservable ways. Parades are observable ways of connecting
with others. The famous Easter parade in New York City, the St.
Patrick's Day parade in Boston, or the New Year's Rose Bowl parade
in Pasadena bring hours of joy to thousands of people. So do the
Mardi Gras parade in Rio, the Bastille Day parade in Paris, and the
Cinco de Mayo parade in Mexico City.

When Scottish bagpipers play "Bonnie Prince Charlie" or
"Scotland the Brave," when a Dixieland band swings out with
"When The Saints Go Marching In," when a marching band plays
"The Stars and Stripes Forever," when any band beats out the
cadence for a parade, hearts lift with excitement and joy.

While waiting for a parade, strangers may connect with each
other spontaneously and informally as they talk about the weather
and their anticipation of what's to come. As the parade marches
by they may cheer because of the spirit of the occasion. In the
parade itself, the marchers are in different groups with different

leaders, yet a feeling of unity develops among them during a parade.

Parades come in many forms, and life itself is like a parade. This parade may seem solitary as we toot our own horns or bang our own drums while no one is paying attention. Or the parade of life may seem like a massive group of people moving in the same direction. It may seem like a tightly controlled march with little opportunity for spontaneity. Or perhaps the parade is more like a joyful procession that allows flexibility and independence.

Henry David Thoreau once wrote, "If a man does not keep pace with his companions, perhaps it is because he hears a different drummer. Let him step to the music which he hears, however measured or far away."[2] When we experience life as a parade, we may wonder if we should go along with the crowd or be our own drummers.

THE URGE TO CONNECT

It is not possible to exist without connecting with other people. Before birth we are connected by an umbilical cord, and until death we continue to need each other. We feel the urge to connect physically, psychologically, and spiritually. *The urge to connect is the desire to relate to someone or something in life-enhancing ways.*

Everyone has a need for physical contact with others, although people vary a great deal in their comfort or discomfort with touching and being touched. The medical research of Rene Spitz, Harry Harlow, and others has repeatedly shown that warm, caring touch stimulates growth and physical health, just as withholding normal human contact and physical affection leads to physical and emotional deterioration, a process called the "marasmus effect."[3] The results of physical deprivation can be seen in infants who are neglected and become retarded in their physical growth.

Loving physical connections are being made when a child snuggles up for a bedtime story or holds up a hurt finger to be kissed "to make it better." When shaking hands with a stranger, hugging a friend, or kissing a lover, we are also meeting the need for physical connection.

Psychological connections exist when we work and share

ideas, play and laugh together, or help and comfort each other. Even the brief hellos and goodbyes exchanged when we enter or leave a job provide important psychological contact.

We can see the hunger for psychological connection in the desire we all feel to belong to a group, whether it is a family, a work team, or a community organization. In the midst of group activities, intellectual and emotional interaction occurs that reminds us of our value to others. Similarly, we all hunger for recognition from authorities and peers. Without such social contacts, we become lonely. Our self-esteem and confidence fall. Conversely, positive connections with others raise our self-esteem and lead to a sense of belonging.

Being spiritually connected is to have a deep awareness of or a personally moving experience with the holiness of life. This can occur when we share a deeply moving experience, such as hearing a superb symphony concert, assisting with the birth of a baby, or helping others during an unexpected crisis. We can also feel spiritual connections to others when standing before a veterans memorial together or joining others in worship and prayer.

Since the advent of mass communication, especially TV, we can even feel deeply connected to those who live far away. We are more aware of their fears and joys and, consequently, feel a deeper sense of unity and sympathy with them. There was worldwide rejoicing when the barriers fell between Eastern and Western Europe and broken connections were restored. Just watching it was like being part of an enormous meeting of loving friends.

Contemplating and studying the nature of the universe also leads to feeling spiritually connected. Theoretical physicist Stephen Hawking has devoted his life to uncovering the principles of the universe and cosmic connections. He battles for his intellectual freedom while being physically trapped in his body by "Lou Gehrig's disease." This is a progressive deterioration of the central nervous system that almost always causes death within three or four years. Yet Hawking has suffered from this disease for over twenty years.

Almost completely paralyzed, Hawking communicates using a voice synthesizer and a one-finger-operated computer built into his wheelchair. Unable to write down his thoughts, he is forced to work things out in his mind. Yet in spite of these handicaps, he gives his time, talent, and waning strength lecturing to many uni-

versity groups on his theories as best he can.[4] His spiritual search
is for a "grand unification" of the theories of relativity and quantum
mechanics. Intensely concerned with investigating cosmic connections, he also wonders why we exist and "what breathes fire
into the universe? If we find the answer to that," he says, "it would
be the ultimate triumph of human reason—for then we would know
the mind of God."[5]

Albert Einstein had a similar intention, of which he wrote:
"I want to know how God created this world. I am not interested
in this or that phenomenon, in the spectrum of this or that element;
I want to know His thoughts; the rest are details."[6]

SEVEN MOTIVATIONS FOR CONNECTING

The human spirit, with its marvelous creative energy, finds reasons
to connect physically, psychologically, and spiritually. Some are
positive and healthy; others are destructive. Seven motivations for
people to connect are corruption, cowardice, courtesy, cooperation, companionship, compassion, and communion.[7]

The least healthy motivation for connecting is when the
intent is the *corruption* of others. Giving drugs to teenagers to get
them hooked is a corrupt way to make contact. So is enticing
people into prostitution with promises of love and protection. People make corrupt connections when they act friendly in order to
climb a corporate ladder or when they act helpful as a way to curry
political favors.

Bribes are corrupt connections given to gain some kind of
control or advantage over others or to appear generous and elicit
praise or favors. The receivers of bribes may be unaware of the
givers' reasons until it is too late and the payback is requested or
demanded in some form of blackmail.

We may make contact with others out of *cowardice* because
we fear what might happen if someone else is displeased. A
spouse, for example, who is not in the mood to be affectionate
may be asked for a kiss and give it purely to avoid a confrontation.
Or children who are fighting may be manipulated with, "You know
you should love your little brother, don't you?" and act affectionate
out of fear of punishment.

Making connections out of cowardice is common with people who go to family gatherings, office parties, or committee meet-

ings that they feel they should attend and don't want to but just lack the courage to say no. Then, when they go out of cowardice, they act affable while feeling bored, act friendly while feeling resentful, or act distant while feeling angry at whoever invited them and angry at themselves for the lack of courage that got them there.

Doing things we don't want to do is not necessarily cowardice. We may choose this behavior out of a sense of politeness or *courtesy*. Politeness is doing what one should do according to what is considered to be good manners; courtesy is doing things to make someone genuinely comfortable. One can be devastatingly polite without being courteous. Courtesy comes from the human spirit and is respectful but not servile.

Courteous connecting includes the "hello," "how are you?" and "thank-you" that are considered polite with family, friends, acquaintances, and strangers. A smile and a warm "thank-you" can salvage a tough day for a grocery clerk, an elderly man pumping gas, or a beleaguered teacher after class.

Different cultures have different ways of expressing courtesy. With acquaintances, for example, a small, formal bow is considered courteous in many parts of the world, a small kiss on each side of the face is courteous in others, while a handshake is expected elsewhere.

Connecting for *cooperation* is working together as a team, like an orchestra playing in harmony. Some of the most dramatic examples of cooperation are found in space exploration. *Sputnik I,* the first satellite launched by the Soviets in 1957, caught the world's attention; twelve years later, Neil Armstrong held the world spellbound as he walked on the moon. In 1975, Soviet cosmonauts and American astronauts linked spacecrafts in an event of international cooperation. The launching of satellites and space shuttles has required an enormous amount of cooperation in bringing together many of the world's greatest scientists for some of the greatest adventures in history.

Companionship is coming together of friends. This brings enjoyment and eases loneliness. When companions get together, something special and memorable often occurs that binds them even closer.

A dramatic example of this occurred to John Muir, a naturalist and conservationist who was once climbing a high mountain in Alaska with a friend. Muir's friend was handicapped by arms that would often became dislocated because of previous injuries. As the two men were climbing along a narrow shelf of ice, Muir's companion fell and slid down the mountain to the edge of a cliff that dropped one thousand feet to a glacier. His feet hung off the ledge and he was trying to hold on with his chin and his nearly useless arms when Muir appeared. Holding his comrade's collar between his teeth, Muir pulled him to safety then carried him a thousand feet down the mountain.[8] Companionship such as this often brings out the best in people.

Compassion, which is a sympathetic concern for others and a desire to help them, is another reason for connecting. Compassion is the motive for helping strangers and friends, the homeless or helpless, those who are sick, lonely, or downtrodden. It is expressed in many ways. Volunteers who work without pay, compassionately doing things such as answering crisis intervention phone lines or caring for patients in hospices, make an enormous difference in the world because of their willingness to care.

This was the case in 1987 when Jessica McClure, one and a half years old at the time, was trapped in an abandoned well for fifty-eight hours. Her entire community of Midland, Texas, rallied to help her. While some people gathered equipment and supplies, others worked tirelessly to get air into the well and dig her out. Still others prepared and served food to those who were working nonstop. With prayers and hard work, they finally rescued Jessica from the dark, narrow shaft. During her long ordeal, she cried for her mother and sang "Winnie the Pooh" songs. Jessica survived because of the loving compassion shown her.

Similarly, during the catastrophic earthquakes in Mexico City in 1986 and in Armenia in 1988, distinctions between rich and poor, educated and uneducated, were forgotten in the common effort to save the lives of those caught in the rubble. The same was true in Chernobyl in 1986 when 90,000 people had to be evacuated because of an accident in a nuclear power plant.

In cases such as these, genuine compassion is often expressed by relative strangers. People share shelter and clothing. They sit and talk and break bread together. They smile with relief and hold those who are hurt or grieving. They do what they can to get money and supplies to those who have to live through the tragedy. When the crisis passes, they return to the everyday world which may seem more sacred because of their shared experience.

Another motivation for connecting arises from the need to be in *communion* with others. Historically, communion has referred to a gathering of religious believers who experienced themselves as part of a close community, often sharing a common meal. In a broader sense, however, communion refers to those moments when we let go of preconceived ideas about each other and communicate as openly and authentically as we can. Thus, communion is a two-way connection, an exchange of thoughts and feelings at a deep level with mutuality and equality.

Kahlil Gibran, author of *The Prophet*, enjoyed this kind of connection with his companion-secretary, Barbara Young. They had a ritual in which they would sit together at a table and with a spoon he would draw an imaginary line through a bowl of soup while saying, "This is your half of the soup and your croutons, and this other is mine. See to it that neither one trespasses upon the soup and croutons of the other."[9] Then both would laugh, celebrating the absurdity of dividing what they shared.

This communion was also the case for Benjamin Franklin and some of his friends who formed "a club of mutual improvement," which they named "the Junto."[10] They met every Friday evening to discuss ideas, politics, and philosophy. The members inspired each other to read, write, and speak in public, and the group maintained this communion for almost forty years!

Relationships ranging from brief acquaintances to lifelong friendships are often formed when people come together in communities that care. The word *community* springs from the same root word as communion. A community is a group of people living in a specific location or a group with a common interest. In universities, the faculty is sometimes called the academic community. Groups such as Alcoholics Anonymous, Narcotics Anonymous, and similar self-help groups become communities in this sense because the members share an interest in helping each other. Because of this common interest, the potential for communion is frequent. As Martin Buber writes, "Community is where community happens."[11] The communion that occurs when people come together in community is a powerful testimony to the wonder of the human spirit and the universal desire for connection.

This kind of enduring connection is wonderful to have, yet difficult to create. The difficulty of finding compatible people with whom to connect can be a major stumbling block to developing satisfying relationships. More often difficulties arise from the hesitancies and cautions we have about getting close to other people.

DECIDING TO CONNECT

Some people are very trusting and open to connecting, while others are not. In part, these differences reflect differences in basic character. For example, some babies seem to be more outgoing while others are quieter at birth. A study done by Alexander Thomas, Stella Chess, and Herbert Birch followed a group of children from birth to adulthood and, from this research, they concluded that the temperament of a child at birth tends to remain basically the same throughout life, although it may be strengthened or diminished by situational circumstances.[12]

In response to circumstances, the many ways we relate to other people often reflect the psychological decisions we made at a previous time. Psychological decisions are self-chosen beliefs we develop about ourselves, other people, and life in general in response to our internal wants and needs and to external influences. These decisions work like filters that color our perceptions, our judgments of people or events, and our responses to them. One person may meet a stranger at a party and hope to make a new friend, while another may meet someone and be afraid of being rejected. The first person may be living by a decision such as, "People are interesting and fun to get to know," whereas the second may be living by a decision that "You can't trust strangers" or "Once people get to know me they won't like me."

It is during infancy that we unknowingly begin to make such decisions. The cuddling, cooing, and caring we may receive from loving parents invites us to trust others because contact with people has been pleasurable.[13] Neglect, abuse, or simply harsh or inconsistent parenting leads us to decide that getting close is uncomfortable and risky.

When we move out into the wider world and interact with other children at school or around the neighborhood, and with other adults who are teachers, family friends, or strangers, these early decisions are often reinforced. If we have good friends to play with, we may decide that "Friends are worth the effort it takes to make them." Or from sexually unhealthy experiences with other children or adults, we may decide "To stay safe, I'd better be careful and not trust people, even if they act friendly at first."

Decisions about life are not always made in ideal circumstances. Growing up in environments that limit or inhibit positive social contacts, living in war zones or refugee camps, being impoverished and forced to work instead of attending school, growing up lonely because of physical or psychological handicaps, not knowing the language or customs when emigrating to a foreign country, or being raised by parents who are abusive or neglectful for whatever reasons—all contribute to the difficulty of making positive decisions about relationships. Children with these experiences have more than their share of pain, and learning to love is difficult. Some fall prey to their surroundings and are unable to transcend their conditions. Others succeed in spite of harsh realities. When they do, these children are eloquent testimonies to the triumph of the human spirit and the passion for life.

As adults we continue to make important decisions about who we are and what to expect from others. Fortunately, friendships can make up for some of the deficiencies of childhood. Success in school or in careers can also lead us to decide "The good life is possible" or "It's important to work with good people if I want to get ahead."

Marriage relationships also play a major role in the decisions we make. Finding someone who is loving and caring, we may decide that "I'm lovable" or "Dreams do come true." On the other hand, as a consequence of an unhappy marriage, we may decide "It's too painful to get close then have your dreams shattered, so I won't get that close to anyone again." Similar decisions can be made on the strength of a friendship or the loss of one. In fact, any adult relationship can have an effect on the decisions we make about life and love.[14]

Our positive decisions are like springboards propelling us into healthy connections. On the other hand, our overly cautious or blatantly distrustful decisions are like tethers that prevent us from getting close to others.

The decisions we live by are powerful forces that shape our relationships. Although they can become fairly fixed in our minds, they can be changed. Redecisions can be made spontaneously as a result of positive, healing interactions with others, or they can be made intentionally. We can redecide to be more open or more trusting or more responsive at any time. To do so requires a strong desire to change, accompanied by a clear plan of action. Sometimes we can make decisions on our own, other times a counselor or therapist's help can make a big difference in reopening paths that lead to love.[15]

THE SEARCH FOR LOVE

Love is the ultimate connection between people, and the search to find it often has two aspects: to find someone to love and to find someone who will love us. It is the motivating force that inspires us to meet people, make contact, become acquaintances, colleagues, friends, and even lovers.

The word *love* is used in many ways. It has been defined as a many-splendored thing, as eros or agape, as desire, deep affection, or unconditional approval. People speak of loving their children, their dog, their garden, even loving a new car or a new job. They speak of loving friends or a loving community or even self-love. With so many different ways of using the word, where can we start? Perhaps with oneself.

Self-love means self-acceptance to some people and self-centeredness to others. Yet self-love is a necessary element in each of our lives. Self-love does not mean complete acceptance of any behavior, belief, or desire; that is self-indulgence. *Healthy self-love is accepting the positive essence of ourselves and working to change those aspects of our behavior that get in the way of love.*

When people accept themselves, they recognize their natural capabilities, learned skills, and unique personalities. They do not ignore themselves, nor are they overly indulgent or overly fascinated by their own inner world. Rather they appreciate their deep urges to live, to be free, to create, understand, and enjoy, and they seek positive ways to express these urges.

The search for love is, for many, a search for romantic love. Romantic love is usually intense, possessive, and based on sexual attraction and the belief in being able to live happily ever after. In romantic love, each person cherishes the other for unique, positive attributes. Negative characteristics are ignored or seen through rose-colored glasses as charming idiosyncrasies. Romance usually begins with infatuation that may or may not deepen into lasting love. However, romantic love, with its roller coaster ups and downs, is so exciting that some people prefer it to commitment.[16]

The search for a loving family is another ongoing quest. We hunger for a family that will provide safety, be encouraging of growth, and supportive of change—without being possessive or domineering. Becoming part of a community, an extended family, or a close circle of friends can meet this need, as well.

The most common form of lasting love is friendship. The original meaning of the word *friendship* comes from the Old English word *freo,* meaning noble, glad, not in bondage. This word developed into *freon,* which means to love. Later this came to be *freond,* which in modern English is friend.

Friends, in the basic sense of the word, do not feel in bondage to each other. Instead, they are in the relationship voluntarily, as free to go as to stay. Such friends are glad, not jealous, over the other person's happiness; and the relationship has a quality of nobility to it, not one of master and slave.

The love of a friend can be what we need to get through a hard time, just as a friend can make a good time even better. A good friendship brings love with few strings attached and many benefits included. However, some people find their lives going so fast that friendships take second place to jobs, families, and chores. If a "friendship deficit" develops, people may feel isolated and experience a gradual fading of their spirits. On the other hand, when new friendships bloom—and they can at any moment—a spark of pleasure is ignited and life is once again filled with laughter and camaraderie.

In addition to searching for love in friendship, many people search for the love of God. For example, the great Dutch painter Vincent Van Gogh, whose work was virtually unknown until after his death, was always poor, lonely, and severely depressed. In his younger years, Van Gogh wanted to be a minister, yet he was in conflict with the church over doctrinal beliefs. So he decided his mission would be to bring compassion and hope to others through his art. In some of his letters, he wrote that he thought the best way to find the love of God was to "love a friend, a wife, something." He went on to explain:

SOMEONE WHO LOVES REMBRANDT WOULD SURELY KNOW THERE IS A GOD, AND SOMEONE WHO STUDIES THE FRENCH REVOLUTION

WILL SEE A SOVEREIGN POWER MANIFESTING ITSELF. AND WHEN
ONE FEELS LIKE A PRISONER, LOVE IS WHAT OPENS THE PRISON BY
SOME SUPREME POWER, BY SOME MAGIC FORCE.[17]

THE NEED FOR CARING

Love is shown in many ways, and one of the most important is in
the caring we show each other. To care is to be concerned with,
or interested in, someone or something. Caring reflects the pro-
tective, tender aspects of love. It is needed between children and
parents, friends and lovers, even between humans and animals
and all of nature. The process is:

Urge of the Human Spirit	Goal of the Search	Power Needed for the Search
to Connect	Love	Caring

People are biologically programmed to be caring. Psychologist Willard Gaylin observed that we instinctively want to take
care of the weak and helpless, the child and the childlike, whether
animal or human.[18] Although brutality, deprivations in early life,
and cultural values may interfere with some people's capacity to
care, this ability remains with most of us and is what sustains our
species.

In addition to caring for others, we all want to receive care.
Everyone wants to be nurtured from time to time. What a relief
when we can count on someone in time of need. It's nice to know
that someone will bring you some soup when you're sick. Or that
someone will cheer you up when you're depressed. Or that someone will help you to get back on track and get moving when you're
discouraged. Caring reassures us that we are not alone on an
island.

However, caring is not just tender words and gentle hugs.
It is not merely helping others or comforting them. *Genuine caring
is doing what needs to be done to help others grow.* It may require
speaking up or taking some kind of action in another person's
behalf. Someone who has been out of a job for several months,
for example, can become discouraged and resist going job hunting.
At times like this, a friend's pressure may be needed in order to
help the person get moving and go looking for work.

The urge to connect

*Looking for
the cosmic connection*

The love of a pet

DUNCAN JAMES

JOHN JAMES

IAN JAMES

Looking for Utopia

Shared excitement

DAVID M. ALLEN

DAVID B. REED

MURIEL JAMES

Connecting with oneself

Commitment to love

If caring is to have impact, it needs to be respectfully offered so that the receiver can feel free to accept or reject the help. We shouldn't imagine that, just because we care, others will appreciate our help. In fact, many don't. Albert Schweitzer warned, "Anyone who proposes to do good must not expect people to roll stones out of his way, but must accept his lot calmly if they even roll a few more upon it."[19]

The healthiest caring relationships are two-way streets. He gets up in the middle of the night to get her a glass of water because he likes her to be comfortable. She goes with him to a doctor's appointment because she cares about his health and wants to support him in this way. She puts up with visits from his grouchy parents because she knows it is important for him to spend time with them. He talks to her about the death of a close friend because he wants to help her in this time of grief and sorrow. Because they care, they are there for each other. However, if one person is consistently the giver and the other consistently the receiver, the giver grows tired and the receiver ungrateful. This doesn't work. Mutual caring can lead to long-lasting relationships.

ALTRUISTIC CARING

Altruism is one of the most profound ways people can show they care. *Altruism is giving without expecting anything in return.* It is the selfless concern for the well-being of others.

Altruism is sometimes expressed as humanitarianism, philanthropy, or just plain kindheartedness. It is often one-sided, and is readily apparent when someone takes care of an autistic child, a handicapped spouse, or a frail and elderly parent. It is seen in other kinds of helping relationships—between a teacher and a student, a nurse and a patient, a therapist and a client. It is even present on the job when experienced employees go out of their way to help newcomers.

Samuel and Pearl Oliner recently completed a study of 700 people living in Europe during the Nazi occupation who, although exposed to great personal danger, nevertheless rescued Jews. They did this voluntarily and without reward, as did over 50,000 others who similarly risked their lives. Many of the rescuers said they were not influenced by religious upbringing, but they grew up in homes where they had been taught care, compassion, and social responsibility.[20] Generally modest, they did not believe they had any choice except to rescue, feed, house, clothe, and hide those who needed it.[21]

In contrast to the rescuers without religious affiliation, Corrie Ten Boom was a staunch Christian who lived in Haarlem, Holland, during World War II. She was also unable to turn away from Jews who were trying to escape. In her bedroom, a false wall was built so that they could hide behind it until safety could be found. When she was discovered, she and her sister and father were sent to a concentration camp. Her sister and father died there, but Corrie, prisoner #66730 at Ravensbruch, the extermination camp for women, was finally released due to a clerical error.

When the war was over in 1945, a wealthy woman who had had five sons serving in the Resistance gave her a large estate where released prisoners might find hope and health once more. Then in Germany, where 9 million people were without homes, Corrie Ten Boom was asked to help develop housing for the homeless. She directed rehabilitation of old factories and other buildings for families who had nothing. One of these buildings had been a former concentration camp. She knew what that bleakness was like, so the first thing she did was order the barbed wire removed and everything painted in bright colors with a window box to be placed in front of every window.[22]

While lifelong acts of altruism like Corrie Ten Boom's are unusual, momentary acts of altruism can be found around us every day. The person who delivers meals to the elderly, the neighbor who reaches out to an unhappy child, the religious group that gives money to support a battered women's shelter, the community groups that raise money for the blind, handicapped, or homeless—all can be found in every community.

The altruistic person is one who gives. Although the giving is done without thought of reward, research shows that, in fact, a reward is there. Improved physical and emotional well-being results from caring and helping others. Even the act of remembering the caring leads to calmness and lowered blood pressure for both the caretaker and the one who received care.[23]

Many businesses and government agencies are also altruistic, in that they provide leadership and resources for community programs or national concerns. Organizations such as the American Red Cross and Amnesty International are established purely out of the altruistic desire to bring hope and help to those in life-threatening situations. These kinds of groups are based on the truth expressed by one Amnesty International leader: "You and I both know that the individual human spirit is far more powerful than guns or torture chambers."[24]

QUALITIES OF ALTRUISM

Important research conducted by Pitirim Sorokin at the Harvard Center for Altruistic Studies led him to conclude that love and altruism have five qualities: intensity, extensity, duration, purity, and adequacy.[25] How each quality is expressed changes with time and circumstance.

Intensity of love is experienced as a powerful emotional involvement that is common when people fall in love. They often become obsessed with thoughts of the other and, like Romeo and Juliet, feel that life is impossible unless they are together. They may also search for this kind of love and want to be cared for so intensely that love takes on more meaning than life. This often leads to a codependent relationship in which one's identity and self-esteem is too closely entwined with the partner's.

Intensity is experienced not only between lovers. Family members and comrades sometimes give their lives because of the intensity of their caring. More frequently, family or friends sacrifice time, energy, even body organs, to save the life of someone they love. For example, David and Doug Franks are 35-year-old identical twins who were not close as children and often tried to differentiate themselves from each other. Doug is gay; David is not. When Doug became infected with the AIDS virus, David was physically healthy. At considerable risk, they both entered a National Institute of Health program in which a dangerously large amount of David's bone marrow was transplanted into Doug. It was hoped that this would boost Doug's immune system to fight AIDS. This life-threatening crisis reignited the intensity of these brothers' love, and, as David explained, "We have finally accepted each other as twins."[26]

Duration is the quality of love that survives over time, in spite of the crises and doldrums that relationships inevitably have to weather. Tom Dooley was often called the "jungle doctor" because he spent so much time helping people in the jungles of southern Asia throughout his life. His passion for life led him to become a volunteer in helping to evacuate more than 600,000 refugees from North to South Vietnam in 1954 and 1955. He also developed an organization of volunteers, "The Followship of Those Who Bear the Mark of Pain," who work under primitive conditions in many parts of the world giving medical care and hope to those where little help was available.

Tom Dooley took a path with heart. In fact, the hospital ship his group used was named the Project Hope. His philosophy was "He who has been delivered from pain must not think he is now free, at liberty to continue his life and forget his sickness. He is a man whose eyes are opened. He now has a duty to help others in their battles with pain and anguish. He must help to bring to others the deliverance which he himself knows."[27]

Purity in love is expressed altruistically, without bargaining or asking for a reward of any kind. Clara Hale is an example of a person who loves purely. Twenty years ago in New York City, she started taking in babies who were born with a heroin addiction. Since that time, she has taken in over 600 babies. Now eighty-three, she takes in babies who are born to mothers infected by AIDS. When asked why, she explained, "They live two years at best. The city doesn't want them, and the hospitals have no room. What else can we do?"[28]

Extensity in love refers to the number of connecting relationships a person is able to maintain. Jesus and Gandhi are notable examples of people with the ability to love many. Less well-known is Gladys Aylard, who decided at the age of fourteen that she would become a missionary in China. She had no money to pay her passage but was so determined to go that, while serving as a maid in London, she worked on her days off and carefully saved her small earnings for fourteen years. At last she was promised an unpaid position assisting an elderly missionary in Yang-cheng.

Life in Yangcheng was far from paradise. Often pelted with mud for being a foreigner, she had a difficult time gaining acceptance. However, she learned five Chinese dialects and established the Inn of Eight Happinesses, where leaders of mule trains could stay overnight, get inexpensive food, and hear free stories from the Bible. In 1938, the Japanese attacked China and there was little safety for anyone; so, for two weeks, she marched one hundred children from an orphanage through mountain passes to the safety of Thailand. Hungry and cold, she and the older children carried the youngest ones and sang songs for encouragement. To the Chinese she was "the small woman" whose faith and courage were boundless. To countless orphans whom she continued to care for throughout the rest of her life, her love had no limits.[29]

Adequacy of love is the ability to do what needs to be done to help others succeed. For love to be adequate, two things are required. We need to feel love deeply and to express it caringly. To *feel* loving and not express it, or to *act* loving and not feel it are inadequate. Adequate love is both felt and expressed in ways that help other people to grow. Adequate love brings positive results. It unites friends, bonds couples, and builds happy families. It can also extend beyond the family circle to include many people. This was the case for Jane Addams, who was a leading spirit in the field of social settlement work in America.

Jane Addams described herself as ugly, both as a child and as a woman. She never married or had children of her own. In 1889, she founded Hull House in Chicago for orphans. The program expanded quickly until it included a thirteen-building complex and daily served 2,000 underprivileged people. Many immigrants came to Hull House for job training and other kinds of help. A pacifist, Addams fought for the legal protection of immigrants, for child labor laws, and for women's suffrage. She was awarded the Nobel Prize, and she gave all her prize money to improving the lives of others. President Theodore Roosevelt called her "the most useful citizen in America."[30]

We must find cooperative ways of dealing with the overwhelming social problems of today. Intense commitment is needed, a commitment that will endure for a sustained period of time. Love needs to be expressed altruistically. It needs to be extended to all, not only to a select group. For this to happen, we need continuing education in how to understand other people and cultures, and also how to improve our communication skills so that we can enter into an authentic dialogue with each other.

DIALOGIC CONNECTIONS

Love, caring, and altruism—whether initiated by an individual or a private or public group—are primarily rooted in person-to-person relationships that spring forth from the willingness to be in genuine dialogue with other people.

The word *dialogue* comes from the Greek word meaning to discuss. A dialogue is usually a conversation, an exchange of ideas, a sharing of opinions, beliefs, and dreams. Philosopher Martin Buber speaks of three kinds: technical dialogue, genuine dialogue, and monologue disguised as dialogue.

Technical dialogue is the clear exchange of information that results in an objective understanding. It includes sharing information about a project of mutual interest at work, asking and receiving information about schedules and responsibilities at home, or giving instructions and getting questions answered in a classroom. In a technical dialogue, people speak clearly and listen attentively. They express appreciation for others' values and accomplishments. Blaming and complaining are at a minimum because each person is "all there" and paying attention to the process, as well as to the content, of the conversation.

Genuine dialogue is the open give and take of ideas, feelings, joys, hopes, and fears. This is what Buber calls "the sphere of the between" where people meet, truly meet, without the sham of masks and facades. Genuine dialogue occurs between one open-hearted person and another open-hearted person. In this kind of dialogue, people talk with each other, not at or past each other. They look and speak directly without evading or diluting issues. They listen to the other's feelings as well as words, instead of planning what they are going to say when the other person stops talking.

The intent of genuine dialogue is to establish a relationship that is honest, alive, and vibrant. That is not easy as the demands are great. Consequently, some people shy away from this kind of interaction and find themselves moving from technical dialogue to monologues disguised as dialogue.

Monologue disguised as dialogue occurs when two or more people speak without concern for the other. Each is so preoccupied with what he or she wants to say that neither can hear nor make a significant connection with the other. They do not see or hear things from the other person's perspective. They talk only to confirm their own points of view. They do this by self-talking, emoting, advising, and debating.

Self-talking is when people talk just to hear themselves. They do not listen, although they may take turns when speaking. In this style of monologue, both try to confirm themselves in order to make an impression on the other. They are not on the same wavelength. They use each other as audiences or as backboards against which to throw their ideas, not caring about the ideas of others. A conversation like this is like talking to yourself in a mirror without noticing that someone else is looking into the same mirror.

Emoting is another form of monologue disguised as dialogue. This is when people go on and on talking about their own glorious experiences. They have little interest in other people's experiences except as they serve as catalysts for their own. Emoting is being on center stage saying, "Look how exciting I am," or "Listen to how wonderful my experience or insight was."

When people emote, each has a lot of energy in the self-centered Child ego state and looks for attention and applause from others.

Advice-giving is another inadequate monologic connection in which the advice giver does not make the effort to understand what the other person needs or wants. Advisers often try to confirm themselves by being helpful when their help has not been requested or is not necessary. The mask of helpfulness sometimes covers a determined effort to control the behavior, thoughts and feelings of others. Parents are prone to connect this way. So are spouses and close friends. Advice-giving often sounds like, "I think you should . . ." or "Why don't you . . ."

Debating occurs when thoughts are pointedly expressed to prove something, said in a way to strike home, sharply, without consideration for the other person. The other is only an opponent, to be won over or vanquished. Trying to get a point across, the debater wants to get the other person to agree, and is busy rehearsing a rebuttal while the other person is talking.

Debaters sometimes seem tough, stubborn, and thick skinned because they are so hard to reach. However, some debaters use a different style and manipulate by acting helpless and shaming their opponents into disarmament. Debaters often disguise criticism, pretending it is an open exchange of information until others admit defeat.

In each of these forms of monologue, people are more concerned with the image they project than with the essence they could freely share. When primarily concerned with their image, people worry about the impression they make on others; they tend to be cautious and show only the sides of themselves that they believe are acceptable. Other sides are kept private out of fear of criticism, rejection, or misuse. They often wonder, "How do I look? How do I sound? Will people like me?" Like politicians, they constantly try to project a favorable image and, to do this, they don psychological masks to hide behind. They erect psychological walls that give off subliminal signs, "Leave me alone," or "Don't get too close." These people avoid direct, open dialogue.

In contrast, when people share the essence of who they are, when they share from the depths of their human spirit, they act naturally and let themselves be known just as they are, not as they believe they should be. They simply give all of themselves to the interaction, knowing that their basic responsibility is to respond to others with as much honesty and openness as they can muster. They do this hoping that others will also feel invited to share of their essence. This kind of giving is an art, and we are all potential artists.

To give oneself does not mean forfeiting one's identity or getting lost in or swallowed up by the feelings, thoughts, or actions of another. To give oneself is to live through the common event from both sides—from one's own standpoint and from that of the other.[31] It means to recognize the other person's point of view, to acknowledge that it is of equal importance with one's own. Two astronauts experienced this and reported: "We went to the moon as technicians; we returned as humanitarians."[32]

Even in the most committed relationships, people move back and forth between monologic and dialogic conversations. It is impossible to live continually in dialogic relationship; the world of everyday activities requires too much objective interaction with other people. However, people who live exclusively in the world of monologic conversations do not really live.

Dialogic moments bring something special to relationships—they transform routine conversations into encounters that make a difference. It is in this spirit that humanitarian Albert Schweitzer advised: "Impart as much as you can of your spiritual being to those who are on the road with you, and accept as something precious what comes back to you from them."[33]

People who share of themselves honestly are open to life and can easily enter into dialogic encounter with others. This can be diagrammed:

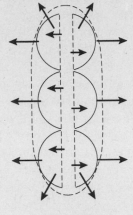

AN OPEN SPIRIT

THE IDEAL COMMUNITY

Because of the urge to connect with others in dialogic ways, people dream of ideal communities, write about them, and sometimes even try to construct them. Writers such as B. F. Skinner in *Walden Two*, Aldous Huxley in *Island*, and Hermann Hesse in *The Glass Bead Game* are a few of the writers that explore the possibilities and impossibilities of developing ideal communities.

The word for such a community is *utopia.* It was coined by Sir Thomas More in 1516 to refer to an ideal island where people lived in perfect conditions. Utopia comes from the Greek word meaning nowhere. In spite of the fact that they are nowhere and not possible, we yearn for them.

When refugees or pioneers and explorers search for new lands they are often searching for some form of utopia. Religious settlements have been organized, rural communities have been established, towns have been built, communes formed, and cults created, often with the goal of establishing an ideal community.

In addition to such theological views, political theories such as socialism, communism, and democracy have developed as constructs for social utopias. The elimination of class structure, freedom to worship as one pleases, and the rights to life, liberty, and the pursuit of happiness are only a few ideas that are associated with utopian dreams.

Dreams such as these are wonderful to imagine. Sometimes they come true; sometimes they do not. There are times when life seems to be almost perfect; other times it brings unexpected difficulties that pose major challenges. A natural tendency is to look to the future and hope for a better day, to look over the fence to where we imagine the grass is greener. Imagining a better world can be highly motivating and inspire us to do more or reach for more than we have. It can also be disappointing if we expect too much or find we are looking in the wrong direction.

When aware of this, we turn to friends, family, or extended family for such close and committed connections. We may also turn to God for assurance of an ideal life. In Christian tradition, for example, the Kingdom of God is often used as a theological term for utopia, with an emphasis on social responsibility and an expectation that this heavenly condition will definitely come at a certain time in history.

This belief has been widespread throughout the centuries. In fact, during the seventeenth and eighteenth centuries, various religious groups settled in the United States in anticipation of this event. Shortly thereafter German emigrants went to Russia for the same purpose. Even today groups isolate themselves from others while waiting for the end of the world when they expect overwhelming destruction and they hope to be among the chosen survivors.

Some Christians, however, have considered the Kingdom of God to be a condition that can be realized in any moment, in any relationship. Meister Eckhart, a thirteenth century theologian, believed the Kingdom of God to be the divine presence found "in all things and in all places," that it is here and now and we only need to "wake up" and be receptive to this blessing.[34] He wrote, "God is at home. It is we that have gone out for a walk."[35] Furthermore, the Kingdom of God is realized when we come home, meaning when we act with compassion and justice toward all. This tradition has continued through to the present and is expressed by theologian Matthew Fox in his concept of "creation-centered spirituality." Fox explains that it is "in this life we are to become heaven so God might find a home here."[36]

❦   RELEASING YOUR URGE TO CONNECT——————————

You may want to take a little time now to think about your urge to create and your relations with others.

❦   FOR CONTEMPLATION ON CONNECTING. For contemplation, read the following quotes and consider if any have meaning for you.

> IT IS AN ETERNAL OBLIGATION TOWARD THE HUMAN BEING NOT TO LET HIM SUFFER FROM HUNGER WHEN ONE HAS A CHANCE OF COMING TO HIS ASSISTANCE.
>
> —SIMONE WEIL[37]

> THE THING THAT LIES AT THE FOUNDATION OF POSITIVE CHANGE, THE WAY I SEE IT, IS SERVICE TO A FELLOW HUMAN BEING.
>
> —LECH WALESA[38]

> LIFE COMES FROM PHYSICAL SURVIVAL; BUT *THE GOOD LIFE* COMES FROM WHAT WE CARE ABOUT.
>
> —ROLLO MAY[39]

> YOU MAY CALL GOD LOVE, YOU MAY CALL GOD GOODNESS. BUT THE BEST NAME FOR GOD IS COMPASSION.
>
> —MEISTER ECKHART[40]

> COMPASSION AUTOMATICALLY INVITES YOU TO RELATE WITH PEOPLE BECAUSE YOU NO LONGER REGARD PEOPLE AS A DRAIN ON YOUR ENERGY.
>
> —CHOGYAM TRUNGPA[41]

> WE CANNOT AVOID USING POWER, CANNOT ESCAPE THE COMPULSION TO AFFLICT THE WORLD, SO LET US, CAUTIOUS IN DICTION AND MIGHTY IN CONTRADICTION, LOVE POWERFULLY.
>
> —MARTIN BUBER[42]

❦   THE ESSENCE OF CARING. Think of five different relationships in which you frequently act as a helper. List several ways you show you care for these people. How are these relationships turning out?

Persons	Ways I Show I Care	Results

❦   PROJECTS AND PROBLEMS. Select a specific interpersonal problem you now have. Are you involved in some kind of monologue disguised as dialogue? Is it self-talk, emoting, advising, or debating? Do you need to change your style of interacting in any way to get better results?

❦   CLOSE OR NOT-SO-CLOSE CONNECTIONS. On the diagram below, use initials to represent your family, friends and associates. Put their initials according to how close or distant you feel to them. Separate them by sex to see if you have any patterns of preference. Is there anyone on the outer circles that you'd like to invite to be closer to you? If so, how might you do that?

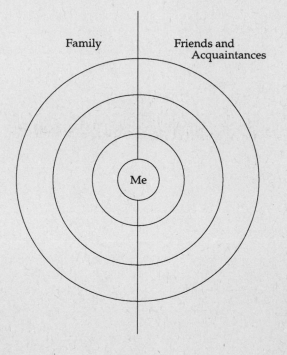

❦   CONNECTING WITH LOVE. What are the challenges of love that you are experiencing now? What questions do these challenges raise in your mind?

❦   DESIGN YOUR IDEAL. Imagine you have unlimited power and resources. How would you design your utopia? What would be its basic principles? How would people connect with each other?

10

THE URGE TO TRANSCEND

THROUGH STARS AND STONES, TREES AND ANIMALS; THROUGH
TOOLS AND HOUSES, SCULPTURE AND MELODY, POEMS AND PROSE;
THROUGH FAMILY RELATIONS AND VOLUNTARY COMMUNITIES, THE
HOLY CAN ENCOUNTER US.

—PAUL TILLICH[1]

REACHING FOR THE STARS

Stars have always had a special attraction for people—so beautiful,
impartial, ageless, and transcendent. From the earth, it is possible
to see about eight thousand stars; scientists say that there are
actually more than six trillion out there!

Children, as awestruck as their parents when looking at
them, often repeat the nursery rhymes "Twinkle, twinkle little star,
how I wonder what you are," and "Star bright, star light, first star
I see tonight, I wish I may, I wish I might." Poets have often written
of stars. Keats's last sonnet, "Bright Star," reveals his longing to
be as steadfast as a star, and Robert Frost wrote that we should
"choose something like a star" to follow instead of being swayed
by mobs who carry praise or blame too far. No wonder stars appeal
to us. Life may be so unpredictable that their steadfastness provides
us with a sense of security.

The origin of stars has been debated since the beginning
of time and all cultures have tried to explain them. As early as
4000 B.C. the ancient Mesopotamians and Egyptians were charting

them scientifically, and they were significant in magic, prophecy, and worship.

The Bible has frequent poetic references to stars. In the Psalms they were said to be fashioned by God's fingers and counted and named by God.[2] "The day star rising in men's hearts" is a symbolic way of pointing to hope, and Jesus was described as "the bright morning star."[3]

In the ancient world, the six-pointed star was widely used by both Jews and non-Jews as a symbol of strength and also as a decorative motif. In Jewish tradition it is called the "magen David," meaning shield of David, in honor of their second king. It was not until the nineteenth century that it became closely identified with Judaism, much as the cross symbolizes Christianity.

The story of the Star of Bethlehem has great meaning for Christians. The star appeared in the heavens at the time of the birth of Jesus and guided wise men to the stable where he was born. Astronomers have tried to identify this star and concluded it could have been a meteor, a comet, a nova, or an unusual grouping of planets. Regardless of what it was, some of the most loved Christmas carols are about this star-announced birth.

Whether scientists or not, whether we believe in a particular tradition or not, we reach for the stars in one way or another. They invite us to transcend our human limitations and feel at one with life and the cosmos.

THE URGE TO TRANSCEND

The urge to transcend who we are and what we do is a continuing desire of the human spirit. *To transcend is to rise above or pass beyond a human limit, to move beyond the everyday dimensions of life and its usual limitations.* The word *transcend* comes from the latin *transcendere, trans-* meaning over and *scendere* meaning to climb. Therefore, when we transcend something, we climb over it. We go beyond or rise above real or imagined limitations.

The urge to transcend is experienced in many ways, often as a yearning to expand ourselves and our potentials. These potentials include our qualities and capabilities that are latent and still-to-be-discovered, or that we are aware of but have not expressed, or that are partially developed and can be improved. The desire to transcend ourselves—whether physically, intellectually, emotionally, or otherwise—is a powerful motivator we all experience.

We want to transcend physical limitations. When weak, we want to be strong; when sick, we want to be well; when imprisoned, we want to be free. We want to transcend intellectual inadequacies. When confused, we want to be able to think more clearly. When feeling ignorant, we want more information. And when intellectually stimulated, we want to learn even more and put what we know into action. It is also part of human nature to want to transcend emotional problems. When sad, we want to be happy. When unsure, we want to feel confident. When lonely, we want to be loved; when alienated, we want to be reconciled.

We also want to go beyond restrictive cultural barriers. When forced into a role, we want to be ourselves; when held back by restrictive traditions, we want to do as we choose; when discriminated against, we want equality. When blending into a new culture, we want to retain some of our old traditions; when new to a community, we want to be accepted.

In addition, it is natural to want to transcend spiritual frustrations. When doubting, we want to have faith; when seeking we want to find; when despairing, we want hope; when in chaos, we want peace; when fragmented, we want to be whole.

The desire to expand our understanding of life is the same. We may want to learn a new idea or update an old one, challenge commonly accepted beliefs or embrace new ones. Transcending old mind-sets by expanding our information, values, and world views often motivates us to go beyond the familiar. Similarly, we may want to expand our lives by doing something that adds to the quality of life. In planting a tree or a garden, we may feel as if we are transcending the world of asphalt and concrete, of alarm clocks and highways, getting back in touch with nature and the heartbeat of life.

The urge to transcend is also expressed as a yearning to transform our routine, habitual responses to ones that come more from the depths of our spirit. This happens when we appreciate the good that surrounds us, whether it is listening to the voices of children on a playground, watching the patterns of the rain rush down a window, or enjoying the brief encounters we have with different people throughout the day. Transcending the ordinary may also occur when we go somewhere that is peaceful and quiet.

Calm reflection can overcome the tendency to see things piecemeal rather than as part of the whole, and we may feel a sudden appreciation of the oneness of everything.

The urge to transcend ourselves and our environments continually motivates us to go beyond barriers and limitations, whether real or imagined. Awareness of this urge can emerge at any time and often comes unexpectedly. Walking down a busy city street or along a quiet river bank, driving down the freeway in commuter traffic or watching TV at home, we may become aware of barriers we face in trying to live happily and work purposefully. Listening to a favorite piece of music or enjoying a quiet meal alone, we may become aware of the frustrating aspects of a relationship and yearn for ways to transcend them. Awareness may come in the middle of a meeting or while grocery shopping when we may wonder about what we'd rather be doing instead. Even while on vacation or lying sick in bed, we may recognize barriers we need to transcend if we want to express ourselves more fully and find a sense of oneness with life.

THE SEARCH FOR UNITY

To feel whole is to feel "at one" and undivided; it is to experience, at least for a moment, a unity and harmony with life. It is to feel at peace with ourselves and others, and to have a sense of our place in the larger scheme of things. This experience of unity affirms that life is worth living and that loneliness, grief, and other heartaches can be transcended.

The crisis of our time is the lack of a sense of unity and consequent feelings of fragmentation and alienation. Many people feel at odds with themselves, wanting "this" but doing "that." Or they may feel scattered and unfocused at times, without a sense of personal direction, following a path of convenience rather than one with heart. Yet, in the midst of this, they may also hunger to "get it all together" and know a sense of peace and clarity.

We also experience the crisis of fragmentation in unsatisfying relationships that lead us to conflict or alienation. When we are alienated from friends or family isolated from people in general, we may feel disconnected, angry, indifferent, or lonesome. We may yearn to cross the bridges that separate us from others.

Feeling separated from the universe may also lead to a

search for unity or oneness. Being cooped up in an office all day, without sun or fresh air, stifles the mind as well as the body. Not spending enough time outdoors or living in a city and never being in touch with nature can also lead to deep discomfort.

For some people, feeling alienated from God or the spiritual dimension of life is most painful. It is like the "dark night of the soul" when little comfort is to be found.

The desire to overcome any kind of separation or alienation and to recover a sense of oneness—whether personal or interpersonal, whether personal or interpersonal, whether with the cosmos or with God—is the prime motivator in a spiritual search for unity. This search takes many forms. The individual searches for a oneness within. The lover searches for oneness with a beloved. The nature lover searches for oneness with the universe. The religious person searches for oneness with God. For many who search for oneness, these quests often overlap. When we search for oneness and transcend the real or imagined barriers that keep us apart, we discover the principle of inseparability, that things do not exist in isolation.

This principle of inseparability is central to most religious traditions. Christianity, for example, uses the metaphor of the human body to highlight this belief. "Just as the body is one and has many members, and all the members of the body, though many, are one body. . . . If one member suffers, all suffer together; if one member is honored, all rejoice together."[4] An old Hasidic saying puts it differently, "All souls are one. Each is a spark of the original soul, and this soul is inherent in all souls."[5]

This principle is also at the roots of Hinduism, which points to the essence from which all apparent plurality or diversity of the world arises and leads to compassion. This is true for Taoism as well, which understands that "all things are one in Tao" and that a "still-point" exists when there is no separation between "this" and "that."[6]

This same principle of inseparability is what humanitarian John Gardner calls the wholeness incorporating diversity. "Today," he writes, "we live with many faiths. We must nurture a framework of shared secular values (justice, respect for the individual, tolerance, and so on) while leaving people free to honor diverse deeper faiths that undergird those values."[7]

This principle of inseparability unites us, as no one can live entirely alone. We need our children as much as they need us as parents. What would life be without relatives, spouses, or friends? We need to share the long journey of life with them. Similarly, the people we work with are dependent on our efforts and cooperation, and we are likewise dependent on them. Further, the global economy has made us realize that we are inextricably linked and, in some way, belong to each other. This is also what author and Nobel Peace prize-winner Alexander Solzhenitsyn meant when, after surviving the prison camps of the Gulag Archipelago, he wrote of his lifelong search for the oneness of a world community. He believed that this oneness already existed because of growing unity among people united in hope and danger through the international press and radio. This oneness, he said, is so tangible that "a wave of events washes over us and, in a moment, half the world hears the splash."[8]

This oneness that we share also extends to our earth and the environment. Acid rain, deforestation, global warming, and massive oil spills are calamities that remind us of our inseparability and interdependence. In similar fashion, knowing that everyone on earth lives by the warmth of the same sun and stands at night looking at the same moon and stars, reminds us of our shared reality. The words of Chief Seattle, a Native American, point to this profound unity we share with all life:

> EVERY SHINING PINE NEEDLE, EVERY SANDY SHORE, EVERY MIST IN THE DARK WOODS, EVERY MEADOW, EVERY HUMMING INSECT. ALL ARE HOLY IN THE MEMORY AND EXPERIENCE OF MY PEOPLE. . . . THIS WE KNOW: THE EARTH DOES NOT BELONG TO MAN, MAN BELONGS TO THE EARTH. ALL THINGS ARE CONNECTED LIKE THE BLOOD THAT UNITES US ALL. MAN DID NOT WEAVE THE WEB OF LIFE, HE IS MERELY A STRAND IN IT.[9]

SACRED OR PROFANE

Appreciation for the unity of life is the primary religious experience according to Mircea Eliade, a professor of the history of religions. It arises from an awareness that the universe and the earth are sacred and that the holy is manifested in everything. When the world is experienced as sacred, places become special—the place where one was born, or fell in love, or had a transcendent experience—and may even seem holy. The tree is no longer just a tree; it is a living monument to the magnificence of life. The mountain is no longer just a mountain; it is a special place because of the moment of illumination or peace.

Eliade proposed that there are two existential ways of addressing the world—as sacred and as profane.[10] Everything—from food and dance to music and words to pets and people—may be objectified and treated simply as objects to be used or abused or may be recognized as manifestations of the holy.

To treat something as profane is to show indifference and irreverence toward it. Treating anyone we encounter—whether rich or poor, educated or not, professors or service station attendants, secretaries or executives, spouses, parents, children, or friends— as if they exist only to serve a function, is to deny their basic sacredness and to miss the opportunity to be at one with them.

The same is true if we profane the earth by littering and using materials that are not biodegradable or recyclable. Ignoring the mistreatment of animals and endangered species is to profane another part of life and to lose a part of ourselves, for as an old Jewish tale advises, "Do not tell yourself in your heart of hearts that you are . . . more admirable than the worm, for it serves its Maker with all its power and strength."[11]

On the other hand, to treat people, places and things as sacred is to treat them with honor and respect, to recognize that there is a potential within them that can be brought out and enjoyed. In doing so, we find a greater value and sense of oneness with life.

SPHERES OF UNITY

It is possible to transcend ourselves and experience a sense of the sacred in five different spheres of existence: (1) with the inanimate world that reaches from stones to stars; (2) with the living world of plants and animals; (3) through the world of things that people create—everything from hovels to palaces, from primitive tools to sophisticated computers; (4) in relationships in which we meet person to person; and (5) within the inner world of the self.[12]

The first sphere in which moments of unity may occur is when we enter into a special, wordless *relationship with inanimate forms of creation*—everything from stones to stars. Most often this sphere is first perceived through our senses. We experience that special moment when we feel sand between our toes when walking on a beach, or hear a brook rippling over rocks, or feel the gentle warmth of the sun on our skin. Seeing a glowing sunset, a vast ocean, a towering cliff, a still and starry night—all invite a sense of awe and wonder when the whole universe seems sacred.

These moments are very different from times when we objectify the inanimate world. To objectify is to analyze, describe, and measure like scientists who are recording data. This is often what we need to do to deal with the world in a practical way. Yet there are times when we can feel a profound sense of oneness with life, when we experience the seemingly inanimate universe as alive and feel like poets moved beyond words or worshipers filled with awe and respect. It is with this deep sense of oneness that photographer John Pearson wrote, "Once in a lifetime, if one is lucky, one so merges with sunlight and air and running water that whole eons . . . pass in a single afternoon."[13]

Transcendent moments of unity may occur in *relationships with living forms of nature*, which includes everything from plants to animals. People who love plants or animals speak of special moments with them. Most of us can remember times when we felt at one with an animal, connected to it in a profound way that defies description. Or, coming upon an injured pet, we may have experienced the injury as though it happened to us and felt a deep compassion for the animal.

Like botanists and zoologists, we may name, analyze, and use plants and animals as if they were only for our benefit and consumption. Then there are times when we may feel more at one with them, like a child who is fascinated by watching a group of ants carrying their burdens, or an adult fascinated with the beauty of a plant. This must be what led agricultural scientist George Washington Carver to write, "When I touch that flower . . . I am touching infinity."[14]

The third sphere in which transcendent moments of union may occur is in *relationships with other people through their "works."* These works touch us deeply, whether a great painting by a famous artist or the simple drawing of a kindergarten child, a great statue or a bookcase laboriously built by a novice carpenter. The birthday cake cooked with love, the party planned with joy are creative works that come from the spirit within reaching for unity with others. Any piece of work can be just a piece of work, or it can be a deep expression of the human spirit. This expression of the spirit is what artist Corita Kent affirmed, "A painting is a symbol for the universe. Inside it, each piece relates to the other. . . . That's why people listen to music or look at paintings. To get in touch with that wholeness."[15]

Great ideas have similar effects. In reading an author's words, we may encounter the essence of that author, though we meet only through a book. In hearing someone speak words of hope or issue a call to action, we may be moved in the depths of being to respond in some positive and unified way.

Union may also occur in the sphere of *direct relationships with other people*—when we meet them as they really are and allow them to meet us in the same way, without sham or pretense. This kind of meeting is not limited by age, sex, or culture. It can happen at any time with anyone. It is possible, for example, to meet a stranger and, in a brief exchange, somehow connect in a very personal and open-hearted way. Transcendent moments of union are even more likely to occur, however, with people we feel close to and are willing to be ourselves with and to accept as they are. These moments, when two souls meet heart to heart, are so profound that they lead to strong bonds. This is the message of the statement on fellowship found in the *I Ching:*

WHEN TWO PEOPLE ARE AT ONE IN THEIR INMOST HEARTS,
THEY SHATTER EVEN THE STRENGTH OF IRON OR OF BRONZE.
AND WHEN TWO PEOPLE UNDERSTAND EACH OTHER IN THEIR
    INMOST HEARTS,
THEIR WORDS ARE SWEET AND STRONG, LIKE THE FRAGRANCE OF
    ORCHIDS.[16]

We cannot force a sense of unity and harmony to happen, but we can increase the possibility for such moments to occur. To do this is to be open to others without judgment or expectation and to be open ourselves, willing to share ourselves honestly and humbly.

The fifth sphere in which a sense of unity can be felt is the *relationship of "I" with "Me"* that can take place within the self. When we stop and listen to our thoughts and feelings, we can sometimes understand who we are and why we are here. In wrestling with ideas and imaginings, dreams and doubts, we encounter ourselves in new ways. In discovering some previously unknown strength within, we can experience moments of exaltation or peace. In all these ways, we learn to appreciate the amazing powers that emerge from our own inner core.

We may also experience moments of inner unity in the midst of an activity. Becoming immersed in a task, such as trimming the hedges or vacuuming the house, we may find ourselves forgetting other cares that hold us down and feeling glad to be alive. Seeing the results of a long-term project or a long day's work, we may find a sense of pride and satisfaction, enjoying our competence and capabilities. To feel at one with ourselves is to feel a sense of self-appreciation for who we are and what we do. It is to feel at peace and harmony within. Yet because self-interest and inner reflection can be overdone, the advice of the Jewish sage, Hillel, is worth keeping in mind, "To begin with oneself, but not to end with oneself; to start with oneself, but not to aim at oneself; to comprehend oneself, but not to be preoccupied with oneself."[17]

Awareness of each of the five spiritual dimensions is not constant. It comes and goes. Sometimes we feel the magic of the stars and other times are dead to their mystery. Sometimes we stop to smell the flowers and other times we only sneeze.

It is when we become aware of missing the flowers or being insensitive to the beauty of the heavens, of ignoring our inner selves or feeling isolated or angry at others, that our yearning for oneness and unity may grow in intensity. When it does, we may deliberately seek opportunities to know, once more, the transcending spirit of life.

OPPORTUNE MOMENTS

Because of the universal urge to transcend restrictions and limitations, people search for opportunities. An opportunity is a promising combination of circumstances or a favorable condition in time. They look for ways of improving their economic condition; they pursue chances to meet new friends; they search for opportune times to take vacations.

Astronauts refer to a "window of opportunity," in which all the conditions are right to launch or land a spacecraft. Using these opportunities, the space program has evolved by both planned and fortuitous events. Anthropologist Carlos Castaneda called this the "cubic centimeter of chance."[18] It pops up from time to time as a moment when we can reach for some desired result—if we are ready, willing, and able to do so.

Some opportunities appear suddenly and apparently by chance. "A stroke of luck" or "a lucky break" are phrases often used when something positive and totally unexpected happens, such as finding a twenty-dollar bill on the sidewalk. This sort of opportunity is spoken of around the office in comments such as, "All of a sudden, there I was, sitting on the plane next to the president of the company . . ." or "There was an unexpected vacancy in the company and it just happened that I applied there the day before." We don't create these sort of opportunities; they just happen by fortunate circumstance. Our hope is that we will be alert and ready to capitalize on them when they arise.

Other opportunities are created. A determined person, wanting to make connections with someone in particular, may arrange for an opportunity to be introduced. An enthusiastic salesperson with a new product to sell will hope to create a market of interested buyers.

Some opportunities are created out of desperation. Street vendors may see no other way to make a living, so seek ways to place themselves and present their wares as favorably as possible. Similarly, someone who is homebound may create an opportunity to earn money at home by starting a telemarketing or word processing business.

In addition to creating some opportunities, we search for those that might already exist though we have not yet found them. Looking for a place to live, we may read the want ads; looking for a job, we may go to an employment agency. In searching for further education, we may look for a scholarship; in planning a community project, we may search for a foundation grant. The place to live, a job or grant may all be out there and available, we may just need to find them.

At an even more significant level, if we are caught in a dangerous situation, we look for an opportunity to escape; if seriously ill, we search for an opportunity to be cured; if trying to help others, we search for opportunities to serve.

Some opportunities are always available, such as the opportunity to treat others with loving kindness, or the opportunity

The urge to transcend

A spirit of openness

DAVID B. REED

Unity with life

IAN JAM

*Transcending
hard realities*

BRIDGET SMEETON

Transcending the ordinary

DUNCAN JAMES

VID M. ALLEN

FRANK JARRETT

In touch
with the spirit

Evolving as persons

to develop a new interest, or the opportunity to understand ourselves and others at a deeper level. We don't have to go anywhere
to find them, they are with us all the time. This is what is meant
by the old Jewish saying, "The place where treasure can be found
is in the place on which one stands."[19] Opportunity abounds and
surrounds us—the challenge is to be open to it.

THE NEED FOR OPENNESS

Openness to all that is and all that could be is an important quality
that can make transcendence possible. It is that wonderful feeling
of being free of restrictive boundaries or limitations. *To be genuinely open is to be openminded and openhearted.* When feeling
like this, people walk with a bounce that expresses the freedom
they feel. Their faces often glow and their eyes sparkle as they
anticipate the possibilities ahead. They feel free to think, to speak
out, and to move ahead openly without fear. They do not hide or
pretend to be other than who they are. This process can be
understood:

Urge of the Human Spirit	Goal of the Search	Power Needed for the Search
to Transcend	Unity	Openness

Openness has two important aspects—receptiveness and
responsiveness. *To be receptive is to be openminded and unprej-
udiced.* It is to be open to whatever could happen without con-
cluding ahead of time, "This is the way it's going to be." When
receptive, we are not constantly wrapped up in our feelings or
preoccupied with past or future events. We are not constantly
turning something over in our minds; there is some open space
between our thoughts. We have trust and confidence in the positive
potential of the moment. This kind of receptiveness is often seen
in people who are sitting peacefully and looking relaxed instead
of looking harried and ready to run off to do something else.

The second aspect of openness is responsiveness. *Responsiveness is the willingness to embrace the positive as it occurs.*
To be responsive is to be sensitive to others and to reach out to
them rather than hold back. Martin Buber once wrote: "There are
no gifted or ungifted; there are only those who give and those who

withhold."[20] Responsiveness is the willingness to give instead of withhold.

Responsiveness requires a willingness to risk, to be vulnerable, and yet to reach out anyway. It is to be openhearted and openminded, looking for positive opportunities instead of expecting disappointments. This responsiveness is often shown in kindhearted people who go out of their way to respond to others in need. Because they are open to the whole human race, they don't prejudge on the basis of race, nationality, or socioeconomic background. To the responsive person, these things are not barriers but windows of opportunity.

A healthy balance of receptiveness and responsiveness to others is essential. Balance makes possible the dance of life and the sharing of that experience with others.

As we become more aware of the value of openness to others, we also need to be receptive and responsive to ourselves. To be receptive is to listen to ourselves and our yearnings and to be aware of how we hunger for opportunities to experience and express the urges of the human spirit on a path with heart.

This was true for Wilma Rudolph, who transcended the limitations of polio she had as a child. "Around age nine the braces came off, and now I can't remember which leg I wore my braces on. Once I discovered I could run, I spent all of my extra time running." Rudolph went on to win three gold medals in track and field events in the 1960 Olympics. She remembers that she used to ask God: "Why was I here? What was my purpose? Surely it wasn't just to win three gold medals."[21]

Each of us has a unique pattern of being receptive or rejecting of our inner yearnings. Some people pay close attention to the inner messages that come from their bodies; others pay closer attention to their feelings, or to what they think. Yet sooner or later, the various pieces that they have ignored call out for attention, pleading, or shouting, "Notice me. I'm here. I'm part of you."

When we pay attention to what we have put aside or ignored, then we can consciously decide what to do. A healthy goal is to be open to all parts of ourselves, learning ways to feel at one rather than fragmented or scattered.

Some people, however, are *too* receptive and take in anything that comes along from outside or from within. They don't maintain sufficient self-regard to filter out the good from the not-so-good. They become emotional mirrors of other people.

On the other hand, those who lack receptivity push away and close off possible opportunities. Being too focused on a task or a relationship, they miss out on what is going on around them. Or being too sure of their opinions and points of view, they close off other people and their understandings of life.

Similarly, to be too responsive is to miss the point. We can give all and save nothing for ourselves and end up exhausted and sick. Or we can be so oversensitive to emotions that we have no energy left for thinking or acting. In contrast, to be unresponsive is to be cold and distant, to seem aloof and uncaring. A healthy balance of receptiveness and responsiveness to ourselves and others leads to openness that becomes fertile ground for transcendence.

In addition to being open to ourselves and others, we need to be receptive and responsive to the process of life. This can be seen in people who do not despair when times get tough. When trying to transcend family problems, they stay open to each other. When trying to transcend on-the-job problems, they stay open to various options and other interpretations rather than making judgments about who is wrong and who is right.

As we become more receptive and responsive to ourselves and others, we open up to the possibility of transcendence in all spheres of our lives. An ancient Buddhist saying speaks of being open: When the eyes of an ox or mule are covered, it will go around and around turning a mill wheel, but if its eyes are open, it will not go around in circles. With awareness, we can open our eyes to the millwheel circles we follow and become free to choose new paths.

PERSONAL EVOLUTION

The biggest opportunity we all face is the opportunity to evolve. When we create an opportunity or seek one that is already present, we do so because we want to transcend something. In the process, we evolve into something or someone new. Opportunity opens the door for evolution.

To evolve is to become, to move from what is to what could be. Evolution is not something that is ever completed; it is constantly occurring. There are many kinds of evolution, and all involve change. Black holes, super novas, and exploding stars are all thought to point to cosmic evolution. The evolution of species, such as happens to viruses relatively quickly or plants or animals over eons, also reflects a process of biological change. A social evolution can be seen in the changing attitudes of people within a country, or a political evolution may occur when governments, national boundaries, and international conditions change. New communities evolve with changes in population or economic conditions.

Families also go through evolutionary processes. Couples alternate between closeness and distance. Children are born and everything changes. They grow up and eventually go their own ways. Illness, accidents, and aging add to the process, as do success and failure. These all challenge us to grow. And throughout the years, the drama of family life goes on, with its calms and crises, its moments of joy and sorrow.

Individuals also evolve. To evolve as people is to make a series of progressive changes in a new and positive direction. Individual evolution takes place on many levels. Physical well-being may evolve with exercise and healthy diet, just as athletic skills evolve with training and experience. Psychological insights may develop with psychotherapy, intellectual capacities increase with study, and spiritual understanding can expand with prayer.

As persons, we evolve in two primary ways—by gradual emergence and by deliberate efforts. To evolve gradually is to go through a series of insights or learning that eventually leads to some particular change. An adult on a job may gradually learn more about the subtleties involved in dealing with people and develop the finesse necessary to handle difficult situations adroitly. This is an unfolding or an awakening, much like what happens to a child growing up who becomes more aware of self, other people, and the world.

When we are deliberately evolving, we change because of the concerted efforts we make to achieve a desired goal. Sometimes we may not know exactly how to create the changes we hope for, so we flounder for a while. Other times, it is easier to set goals, make plans, and deliberately follow a path with heart. Either way, as we deliberately evolve, we develop new ideas, beliefs, attitudes, or behavior.

John Corcoran, for example, went through a dramatic personal evolution. While graduating from high school, getting a college degree, and teaching school, he hid the fact that he couldn't read. In childhood, Corcoran moved so often that his teachers did not realize this. Associating with people with good vocabularies, listening to radio and watching films, studying pictures in magazines and art galleries, he became well educated, though illiterate.[22] In college, he persuaded his professors to give him oral examinations and he won National Science Foundation grants for graduate studies. He then went on to become a popular teacher, never using a blackboard and frequently having students read aloud in class. Corcoran believed, "If you tell somebody you can't read, you're telling someone you're dumb."

Later, when he became a real estate developer, he surrounded himself with secretaries, lawyers, and other people to do all of his written work. Finally, at age forty-eight, his curiosity led him to take a fourteen-month course to learn to read. Now John Corcoran is an active speaker for Project Literacy, a continuing education program designed to overcome illiteracy among adults.

THE HEROIC ADVENTURE

Personal evolution is not easy and often requires an inward journey of heroic proportions. According to mythologist Joseph Campbell, the heroic adventure is the search to understand one's relationship with life.[23] It is a response to a call to know ourselves and to understand our relation to the holy. During this journey, Campbell believes we find powers within ourselves that have been hidden or ignored. This new understanding of ourselves and the holy becomes the cornerstone for further personal evolution.

The most common stimulus for beginning an inward journey is a gradual awareness that we are outgrowing our old ways of feeling, thinking, and behaving. The beliefs, ideals, relationships or emotional patterns we counted on for so long no longer fit with what we experience as reality. Something inside, almost like a gyroscope, tells us that our life is out of balance, and we feel compelled to do something about it.

Another stimulus is when some person or event awakens us from the trance of daily routines. Meeting someone who lives with a strong clarity of purpose and generosity of heart, we may become aware of our own inner poverty and wonder about the source of their strength. Or we may blunder into an experience that reveals unsuspected beauty in life that we do not understand and sparks our curiosity.

Whatever the catalyst, the call to transcend our old selves feels both necessary and disquieting. There is a natural tendency to resist the call and hold fast to the security and predictability of the status quo. This tendency is reinforced by others who want us to stay as we are. Campbell believes it is our reluctance to respond that is the first "dragon to be slain."[24]

When restlessness and attraction to the call overcome our fear of the unknown, we cross the threshold of adventure— leaving the comfort of the familiar for the challenge of the unknown.

In doing this, we inevitably meet with frustrations, temptations, and uncertainties that are difficult to understand. Things may get worse rather than better. Trials and tribulations may increase rather than get resolved. As the old saying goes, "When it rains, it pours." In fact, challenges may seem so great that even the most heroic of us may begin to wonder if we should have left well enough alone.

During this ordeal, Campbell believes that some form of guardian spirit may appear and offer help. It may be a teacher, therapist, or friend who points the way. It can be a spiritual leader or even an imaginary guide who helps us traverse the path of the inward journey.

If we are willing to stick with the process and search for the lessons to be learned, a metamorphosis begins to take place. Just as the pupa emerges from the cocoon as a butterfly, we begin to transform in some meaningful way. We evolve. Free of some restrictive mind-sets, we see the world with clearer eyes, think of people differently, and open our hearts and minds with compassion and gratitude.

According to Campbell, the goal of the heroic adventure is to discover that life is merciful and tolerable. By this he means that life is more good than bad, that even pain is a necessary part of existence, and that each person has the ability to tolerate and even enjoy the adventure of life. With this comes the realization of wholeness, the holiness of living, and oneness with God.

But personal evolution does not end here. The next challenge of the journey is to find ways to integrate these new insights into our relations with others.

TRANSCENDING CULTURAL DIFFERENCES

Spiritual adventures often lead us into contact with people from other cultures or subcultures—people with different ethnic and racial heritages, educational and economic backgrounds, social expectations, and behavior. When we are receptive and responsive to other people, we can transcend our cultural differences and be enriched by the contact.

By venturing across sometimes real, sometimes make-believe cultural boundaries, it is possible to discover a worldwide family. In most large cities, for example, there are ethnic neighborhoods with their enclaves of stores and restaurants catering to the local population. People with different languages, life-styles, even ways of eating live in close proximity. Some people sit on the floor, others on chairs. Some eat with their fingers, or use chopsticks, or hold knives and forks in one way or another.

However, some people don't like these differences. They identify themselves by saying "we" and other cultures or subcultures as "they." Suspicious or demeaning of "those people," they erect barriers and diminish opportunities for mutual benefit. Even worse, they block the natural flow of the human spirit in themselves and in "those people."

This kind of prejudice contaminates all societies. All too often whites distrust "people of color" and vice versa, or the poor distrust the rich, heterosexuals distrust homosexuals, labor distrusts management, and a lot of people distrust politicians and military leaders.

Too often, these kinds of cultural prejudices escalate to physical conflict. Catholics and Protestants fight in Ireland, Muslims and Jews in Israel, Hindus and Sikhs in India, and on and on. All of these cultural crusades or "holy wars" are the result of one culture attempting to gain superiority over the other, making judgments over who or what is good or bad, right or wrong. In doing so, they deny others the right to exist and seek to exclude them from positions of power.

No one wants to feel excluded or considered inferior in

some way. This must have been how Albert Einstein felt as a child. Growing up a Jew in a town where Jews were hated, he had no friends. Lonely and shy, he had an emotional breakdown in high school and was rejected as inadequate when he failed university entrance examinations. Feeling excluded, he was forced to turn inward to discover his own resources—to discover his own capacity to think in spite of the pain of exclusion.

To be included, on the other hand, is to feel welcomed in spite of our differences. Because we feel this, we are open to transcending our individual and cultural differences. Instead of feeling anxious, we feel confident, more trusting of others and our interactions with them. Instead of criticizing other cultures and customs, we find them interesting. Our lives are enriched, and we feel like sharing our experiences in exchange.

A big step in transcending religious animosities occurred in Assisi, Italy, in 1986 when one hundred and fifty-five leading figures from all of the world's major religions met for the first time in history. Their purpose for gathering was to pray for peace, as peace was a higher value to them than we-they distinctions.

Among the leaders were the Pope and the Dalai Lama. Also present were Mother Teresa, two American Indian chiefs, the Archbishop of Canterbury, and the Chief Rabbi of Rome. There were African and Sikh holy men, Muslim mullahs, and Japanese Shinto priests, as well as Baha'i, Hindu, Jain, and Zoroastrian spiritual leaders. Quakers, Mennonites, Methodists, Baptists, Lutherans, and the general secretary of the World Council of Churches were all present, and they were joined by 20,000 pilgrims and 24,000 residents who crowded the colorful chapels and narrow streets of the little town in Italy.

The urge to transcend differences was shown in many ways. Muslims chanted the Koran, Native Americans smoked a pipe for peace, and animists from Africa spoke of God as "the all-seeing Lord on high who sees even the footprints of an antelope on a rock mass."[25] A statue of the Buddha was placed on a Christian altar to symbolize their transcending of religious differences.

After the opening ceremonies, the groups went off to their own separate ceremonies to pray according to their own traditions. Later that day when they came together, Pope John Paul II summarized:

THE FORM AND CONTENT OF OUR PRAYERS ARE VERY DIFFERENT,
AND THERE CAN BE NO QUESTION OF REDUCING THEM TO A KIND
OF COMMON DENOMINATOR. YET WE ARE ABLE TO LET OUR HEARTS
RISE TOGETHER WITH A COMMON YEARNING.[26]

The ability to transcend and rise above such strong religious
and cultural differences is hopeful. In the process, a new world
culture is evolving because of similar expressions of openness.
This is happening in corporations with foreign investors and international markets demanding more cultural savoir faire. With
much of today's work force comprised of people from diverse
cultural backgrounds, dealing effectively with cultural differences
is a necessity in many positions. The worldwide trend toward political openness also encourages people to transcend their cultural
differences.

At an everyday level, satellite transmission of television is
reaching into millions of homes around the world, even to the
deepest jungles and most desolate corners of the earth. To sit in
one's own home and watch news events taking place on another
continent inevitably educates us to the multicultural aspects of
today's world. Switching channels and finding foreign-language
stations provides a similar opportunity.

Worldwide friendship seems not only possible, it seems
like a natural evolution, even between species. Recently in India,
for example, a herd of twenty-five elephants turned to humans for
help when an elephant calf was injured by a tiger. The herd literally
pushed the calf almost two miles in extreme heat to a ranger
station, apparently for help. The rangers were unable to save the
baby elephant's life, although several times the mother elephant
brought water to spray on the calf. After it died the rangers buried
it and, for two nights, the herd returned and trampled down the
earth, seemingly to protect the body from being ravished.[27]

We can no longer afford to ravish the earth and each other.
Hold up a kaleidoscope, and turn the tube. The same pieces of
glass are in every pattern, but the way they fall together is unique
each turn. Listen to a piece of music. Each piece can use the same
notes, yet the notes are put together into an endless variety of
melodies. And so it goes with people. When open to each other,
we can enjoy differences, have hope for today, and faith in the
future.

FAITH IN CRISIS

To have faith is to have confidence in the trustworthiness or truth of a person, idea, or thing, even if this confidence is not based on logical or material evidence. Simply put, *to have faith is to believe in something, even when it can't be proven.* In this way, faith is, according to poet Rabindranath Tagore, "like the bird that feels the light and sings when the dawn is still dark."[28]

When used in a religious context, faith usually means accepting a religious doctrine or believing in God. The way we feel about religious faith is often very strong. Some people accept what they have been taught without question and feel offended if others do not believe as they do. Other people struggle hard to understand religious beliefs and sometimes enjoy questioning and exploring their faith. Still others do not have such beliefs in God or a benevolent universal order and sometimes wish they did or reject those who do.

Faith pervades our lives, whether we think of it in religious or nonreligious terms. We have faith that our cars will not break down on the freeway or that our children will return home safely from school. We trust that our friends will stick by us in hard times and that someone will be there to wipe away our tears or encourage us to take charge of our lives. And, unless in deep despair, we have faith in our abilities to find hope, to be self-determined, to understand life, create something worthwhile, connect with others in meaningful ways, and generally enjoy life.

At one time or another, however, many of us experience a crisis in which we question or lose faith in our beliefs. We may have believed that we could live "happily ever after" and then find out that life doesn't go that way. We may have had faith in our abilities to move mountains or the equivalent and find our abilities to be inadequate. We may have trusted and had faith in someone and been let down. Events can be so unnerving that we doubt much of what we have staked our lives on. When this happens, we may question the wisdom of our beliefs and wonder, "Is this really the way I want to live?" Or we may feel discouraged and moan, "I don't know what to believe anymore." When old explanations no longer seem adequate and new ones are not yet in sight, this can feel like a spiritual crisis.

Four major faiths sprang from the lives of people who also

went through spiritual crises. The story of Moses tells that he went through a crisis when he killed an Egyptian who was beating a Hebrew laborer. To escape retaliation, he fled to a tribe of sheepherders, married, and had children. Then one day he experienced God telling him to return to Egypt to free the Hebrews. Moses protested because he felt inadequate for the task and doubted the wisdom of God's choice. However, excuses were not acceptable, so he ended up doing what he felt called to do.

Buddha's first spiritual crisis came with his dissatisfaction with life. Although he was a wealthy prince, he became aware of the emptiness of wealth, so he left all his earthly comforts to live a life of asceticism as a beggar. After long meditation and enlightenment, Buddha concluded that asceticism is not always necessary. What he found is necessary is doing good instead of evil and maintaining mental discipline and tranquility that can lead a person to intuitive wisdom and peace.

Among the many spiritual crises that Jesus had was the one at the end of his life when he was being crucified. According to the New Testament story, he first experienced himself as forsaken by God. When he transcended his doubt as he was dying, he was able to affirm his faith with "Father, into thy hands I commit my spirit."[29]

Muhammad, in his spiritual crisis, meditated for extended periods of time in caves near Mecca. An orphan from a poor family, he married a rich widow and had seven children by her. He also began to believe in the goodness of Allah and the responsibility to respond with gratitude and humility. However, when Muhammad began to preach about this, he became of threat to those who preferred the old gods. He was forced to flee and only after many years was he able to return to Mecca and rid it of idols.

In struggling to transcend everyday problems or crises in our own lives, we may, like Moses, discover the need to face life courageously even when feeling inadequate. Or like Buddha, we may learn that taking time to reflect on what is important can help resolve spiritual crises and answer questions about the meaning of life and faith. Or we may, like Jesus, reaffirm our faith in the midst of suffering, pain, and even death. Perhaps like Muhammad, we will discover that reaching a spiritual goal may take many years and that others may be resistant or even hostile to our goals but that the journey is worth the effort.

The spiritual crises that we confront challenge us to clarify what we believe in and what we are committed to doing. When we respond to the challenge and find our paths that have heart, we are likely to discover that our faith in life is strengthened and our passion for life released. We will find ourselves in touch with the incredible powers of the human spirit—the powers to live with hope, courage, curiosity, imagination, enthusiasm, caring and openness to whatever is and to the good that can be.

❦ RELEASING YOUR URGE TO TRANSCEND————————————

Following are optional exercises to assist you in your spiritual search for oneness and unity.

❦ CONTEMPLATION ON ONENESS. Take time to reflect on the meaning of oneness and faith in your life through the following quotes.

ENLIGHTENMENT MUST COME LITTLE BY LITTLE—OTHERWISE IT WOULD OVERWHELM.

—IDRIES SHAH[30]

TO ACHIEVE THE MOOD OF A WARRIOR IS NOT A SIMPLE MATTER. IT IS A REVOLUTION. TO REGARD THE LION AND THE WATER RATS AND OUR FELLOW MEN AS EQUALS IS A MAGNIFICENT ACT OF A WARRIOR'S SPIRIT. IT TAKES POWER TO DO THAT.

—CARLOS CASTANEDA[31]

MAYBE WE ARE LESS THAN OUR DREAMS, BUT THAT LESS WOULD MAKE US MORE THAN SOME GODS WOULD DREAM OF.

—CORITA KENT[32]

THE FARTHER WE GO, THE MORE THE ULTIMATE EXPLANATION RECEDES FROM US, AND ALL WE HAVE LEFT IS FAITH.

—VACLAV HLAVATY[33]

JUST AS A SMALL FIRE IS EXTINGUISHED BY THE STORM WHEREAS A LARGE FIRE IS ENHANCED BY IT—LIKEWISE A WEAK FAITH IS

WEAKENED BY PREDICAMENT AND CATASTROPHES WHEREAS A
STRONG FAITH IS STRENGTHENED BY THEM.
                                              —VIKTOR FRANKL[34]

I HOPE FOR THE DAY WHEN EVERYONE CAN SPEAK AGAIN OF GOD
WITHOUT EMBARRASSMENT.
                                               —PAUL TILLICH[35]

❦ ON FEELING WHOLE. Each of us searches for oneness. When we
find it, we feel whole. You have probably had many moments like
this. Get relaxed. Close your eyes. Take some time to review your
life as if you were watching a movie. See yourself in special moments when you felt at one with the universe, or with others, or
with yourself.

   Now focus on these five spheres of transcendence and recall
special moments that stand out in your memory.

From stones to stars:

With plants and animals:

Through creative works of others:

In interpersonal relationships:

In my own inner world:

❦ TRANSCENDING YOUR PERSONAL LIMITATIONS. Everyone has the urge
to transcend some personal limitations. What limitations have you
already transcended? What limitations do you want to transcend
now or in the future?

❦ PERSONAL EVOLUTION. When you think back over your life, you
are probably aware of evolutionary epochs or phases in your life.
What were they? What events caused you to change and move on
to another phase in your personal evolution?

❧ A SPIRITUAL CRISIS. Have you ever gone through what you would call a spiritual crisis? Can you remember what it was like and how you resolved it? What did you learn from that journey into darkness?

❧ LOOKING AHEAD. When you ponder over your future, what questions do you have about your urge to transcend, your search for unity, or your need for openness?

11

MISSION OF THE HUMAN SPIRIT

WE SHALL NOT CEASE FROM EXPLORATION AND THE END OF ALL
OUR EXPLORING WILL BE TO ARRIVE WHERE WE STARTED AND KNOW
THE PLACE FOR THE FIRST TIME.

—T. S. ELIOT[1]

COMING HOME

The process of coming home after years of being away is often an
exploratory process. The environment may have changed. The
neighbors may have moved. We may feel warm nostalgia, cold
resentment, calm indifference, or curious wonder. Yet going home
usually involves mixed feelings. What will it be like? Dare we hope
that it will be better than we remember? Will we be disappointed
or overwhelmed with joy? Is it possible that we may even experience some kind of spiritual moment and feel deeply moved by it?

In a sense, going on a spiritual search can be like a wonderful homecoming in which we get back in touch with ourselves
and what is important to us. However far-flung our journeys, we
may eventually go back home, back to the beginning, where we
can know ourselves and our world and explore both for the first
time.

Throughout this book, from beginning to end, the exploratory process has been highlighted in such phrases as "a path with
heart" and "the spiritual search." Although the word *spiritual* has
been defined by others in various ways, in this book it has been

used to refer to matters of ultimate concern that call for releasing the passions of the soul to search for goals with personal meaning.

Passions are activated by the release of seven basic urges that come from the depths of the human spirit and move us beyond the normal confines of life into wholeness and holiness. Although problems may interfere with expressing the urges of the human spirit, these powers cannot be held back indefinitely. The urges from the inner core are like embers always ready to flare up with fire and passion, and they can be directed in positive or negative ways, depending upon personal values.

Sometimes our values are traditional religious ones leading to the search for a personal God. Other times they are directed toward trying to understand the universe and other people. Values can inspire us to create a work of beauty that lifts the soul or commit us to living with integrity in some other specific way.

There are many kinds of spiritual searches. Because of the urge to live, we search for meaning, and for this we need hope. Out of the urge to be free we seek to be self-determining, and this requires courage. When we want to understand something, we seek knowledge spurred by our inherent curiosity. The goal of originality comes from the urge to create, which is fueled by our imagination. Because we want to enjoy life, we search for happiness; to do so requires enthusiasm. The urge to connect with each other is reflected in the search for love, and caring is needed for us to succeed. To be able to transcend ourselves and our environments, we seek for opportunities and find them when we are open and willing to both receive and to respond.

Let us take one final look at the urges that propel us to find and follow a path with heart—paths chosen because of the visions we have for the future and the missions we feel committed to.

MISSION TO ACCOMPLISH

The word *mission* is used in many ways. It can refer to people sent by one government to another to negotiate a matter of common interest. It is can be used in warfare to refer to a strategic objective. In religion, a mission may refer to a building where religious services are held or to evangelistic services or social welfare activities. In our own lives a *personal mission is a passionate desire to bring about a possible and positive future condition.* It is a willingness to make decisions, to act on the basis of them, and to remain committed until they become a reality. This commitment to act needs to come from the heart as well as from the head, for it is only when we care about something that we commit our urges to a passion for life.

People take on all kinds of causes as personal missions. Some become committed to global causes, such as working for world peace or preservation of rain forests. Others get involved in working for social causes, such as helping the mentally retarded or developing ways to prevent delinquency. Still others direct their energies toward more personal goals, such as raising a healthy family or assisting a long-ailing relative. Each of these missions and the variety of others we can pursue reflect what Martin Buber called "the mystery of a soul directed at a goal."[2]

Unfortunately, instead of engaging in a significant mission, we may take a path we think we "should" take or follow one that is exploitive or convenient instead of one that involves a spiritual search. In doing this, we may succeed yet still feel somewhat empty. We discover we have been on the wrong path and our enthusiasm wanes, yet deep in the human spirit our urges plead with us to find and follow a path with heart.

On the other hand, when we work toward causes that have meaning and significance, we mobilize a great deal of creative energy. The old motto "Where there's a will there's a way" is often true, and the results can be remarkable.

A group of space technologists were given the assignment of building the lunar excursion module for the mission of landing the first man on the moon. A remarkable change occurred when they realized they were taking part in a project that would fulfill one of mankind's oldest dreams.[3] This group of formerly lethargic workers was transformed into an inspired team by their mission. Psychologist Charles Garfield reported that those involved tapped hidden powers they had not known they possessed, the result being extraordinary accomplishments. Their excitement and pride came alive.

REVERENCE FOR LIFE

People with a mission often believe life is precious. Although there are moments when we may forget this, seeing the beauty of nature or experiencing the joy of a close relationship reminds us of the great gift of life and the need to commit ourselves to protecting it.

This was the case for Albert Schweitzer, a major humanitarian figure of the twentieth century. With doctoral degrees in medicine, music, philosophy, and theology, he decided that, instead of debating theological issues, he would live out his beliefs:

> I DECIDED I WOULD MAKE MY LIFE AN ARGUMENT. I WOULD ADVOCATE THE THINGS I BELIEVED IN TERMS OF THE LIFE I LIVED AND WHAT I DID. INSTEAD OF VOCALIZING MY BELIEF IN THE EXISTENCE OF GOD WITHIN EACH OF US, I WOULD ATTEMPT TO HAVE MY LIFE AND WORK SAY WHAT I BELIEVED.[4]

With this vision, Schweitzer went to the heart of the jungles of French Equatorial Africa and established a hospital and a leper colony where he treated more than one hundred thousand people and animals. While working with patients, he also searched for a universal ethic that would be inclusive of nature and of all peoples. He felt that without this ethic, he was wandering around in a thicket without a path or leaning against an iron door that would not yield.

One day on a river journey, the transcendent moment of insight happened; the iron door yielded. It was sunset and Schweitzer was passing through a herd of hippopotamuses when a phrase flashed into his mind: "reverence for life." To Schweitzer, this meant all of life is sacred, all is worthy of respect. This became his affirmation and his ethic. "Life," he said, "brings us into a spiritual relation with the world . . . and is renewed every time we look thoughtfully at ourselves and life around us."[5]

To Schweitzer, even killing an ant was anathema. To the Native Americans, animals were sacred and only killed when necessary, never for trophies to hang on the wall. Some Hindus will not eat fertile eggs or anything else that lives. They wait for the fruit to fall from the tree and the grain from the shaft because of their belief in the sacredness of all forms of life.

With a similar reverence for life, Mother Teresa found her commitment to bring life and love to the sickest of the sick and the poorest of the poor, including those without love:

> THERE ARE PEOPLE WHO HAVE NO ONE. THEY MAY NOT BE DYING OF HUNGER, BUT THEY ARE DYING OF HUNGER FOR LOVE. . . .

OFTEN IN BIG CITIES, BIG COUNTRIES, PEOPLE SIMPLY DIE OF LONE-
LINESS, UNWANTED, UNLOVED, FORGOTTEN. THIS IS A MUCH MORE
BITTER POVERTY THAN THE POVERTY NOT TO HAVE FOOD.[6]

Even in 1990, when her health was failing and her death
seemed imminent, her passion for life through helping others kept
her going.

FREEDOM AND CHOICE

Closely associated with reverence for life is the commitment to
freedom. Freedom is sometimes thought of as the freedom to act
as one wants to, without limitations or fear of consequences. Carried to extremes, this interpretation can be immoral. Thus the
choices we make about what to do with our freedom are crucial.

Philosophers have debated the concept of freedom of
choice for thousands of years, and psychologists have done so for
the past hundred and fifty. Philosopher Thomas Hobbes believed
that we are not really free because our acts are determined by
personality or necessity, by heredity and environment.

In contrast, philosopher René Dubos takes freedom for
granted, believing that everything is not predetermined, in spite of
the fact that there are certain aspects of life and the environment
we cannot control. He quotes two Nobel laureates in biology who
jointly stated:

UNDER THE MOST PERFECT LABORATORY CONDITIONS AND THE
MOST CAREFULLY PLANNED AND CONTROLLED EXPERIMENTAL PRO-
CEDURES, ANIMALS WILL DO WHAT THEY DAMNED WELL PLEASE
. . . COULD ONE ASK FOR MORE FREE WILL THAN THAT?[7]

Human freedom, according to philosopher Mortimer Adler,
is the freedom to act because we do have choices. "Freedom of
choice consists in always being able to choose otherwise, no matter what one has chosen in a particular instance."[8] In other words,
Adler believes that we are free, even free to make mistakes.

Psychologists have similar arguments. B.F. Skinner of Harvard University posed a deterministic point of view. He proposed
that although we may imagine we are free, we are not. Like Thomas
Hobbes, Skinner believed that our behavior is conditioned by phys-

ical, psychological, and social determinants, and that freedom is merely a myth and an illusion.[9]

In contrast, psychologist Carl Rogers believes in self-determination. His client-centered therapy, is based on the belief that people have the freedom to choose their own goals, that human beings constantly make choices, and that it is foolishness to believe in absolute biological and behavioral determinism.

Psychiatrist Eric Berne, originator of transactional analysis, also believed we make important life choices and have the freedom and power to change them. He wrote:

EACH PERSON DESIGNS HIS OWN LIFE. FREEDOM GIVES HIM THE POWER TO CARRY OUT HIS OWN DESIGNS, AND POWER GIVES THE FREEDOM TO INTERFERE WITH THE DESIGNS OF OTHERS. EVEN IF THE OUTCOME IS DECIDED BY MEN HE HAS NEVER MET OR GERMS HE WILL NEVER SEE, HIS LAST WORDS AND THE WORDS ON HIS GRAVESTONE WILL CRY OUT HIS STRIVING.[10]

If we believe in freedom of choice and in the concept of freedom for all, then we will fight against the four horsemen—war, pestilence, famine, and death. We will fight against cultural and personal apathy in matters of infant mortality, torture, and brutality. We will work toward improving world health and respond to those who suffer from famine. We will recognize the need for a just peace and seek ways to encourage it—in our own communities and internationally.

The four horsemen can be conquered. United States President Jimmy Carter, Egyptian President Anwar Sadat, and Israeli Prime Minister Menachem Begin attempted to do this when they met in 1978 at Camp David, Maryland. For days they had agonized over how to end the fighting between Egypt and Israel that had cost so many lives. As they attempted to negotiate freedom from hostilities and a just peace, they could not come to agreement.

Talks came to a stalemate. Failure seemed inevitable until they all pulled pictures of their grandchildren from their wallets and, as grandparents tend to do, talked with deep love about them. This led to speaking of their concerns for the world in which their grandchildren would grow up. With this, their commitment to the peace talks was renewed; they went back into negotiations that eventually led to the Camp David Accord, which created peace between Israel and Egypt.[11]

The urge for freedom and the passion to be self-determining and to allow others the same privilege often require courage, especially in international affairs. Yet, as pioneering aviator Amelia Earhart pointed out, "Courage is the price that life exacts for granting peace."[12]

FROM UNDERSTANDING TO WISDOM

Because of the urge to understand, we search for knowledge; yet knowledge is not the same as understanding or wisdom. We know the price in lives that war exacts and we understand that war is a poor way to settle disputes; yet we do not have the wisdom to avoid such conflicts. We know the importance of good medical care and have the medical technology to provide it, we even understand that a large percentage of the world's population is unable to afford such treatment, yet we do not have the wisdom to use our technology for the good of all.

We know about the value of certain relics to a native culture and understand the needs of a culture to have a heritage, but frequently we do not show the wisdom to leave sacred sites alone in respect for their tribal importance. We know about species becoming extinct and understand that wildlands and wetlands are needed for their survival, but we do not show the wisdom to protect them sufficiently.

It was this kind of wisdom that Rachel Carson was trying to promote in her work as a marine biologist and oceanographer. Carson developed a strong sense of mission because she saw the frightful possibilities of indiscriminate pesticide use.

Rachel Carson was a shy person who loved the earth and the sea and her work for the U.S. Fish and Wildlife Service. Her professional knowledge alerted her to new dangers to the earth and sea. In 1962, she wrote about the dangers of synthetic pesticides such as DDT and Chlordane that upset the natural ecological balance of the world. The title of her book *Silent Spring* was based on the possibility that the long-term effects of pesticides might "still the song of the birds" and spring would be silent. Her mission was to inform people so that they could understand the danger and act with wisdom.

Carson's book was a threat to the chemical industry because she courageously presented the facts about the dangers of pesticides. Chemical corporations and scientific organizations ridiculed her research and threatened to sue her. Fortunately, the public became involved in her cause, as did the federal government; and, in 1970, the Environmental Protection Agency was established, in part as a result of her writing.

Slowly we are learning how to live less destructively on the earth as we recognize our dependence on the ozone layer, clean air, and groundwater. Some species of wildlife that previously were endangered are now safe because one woman confronted big business in her spiritual battle to protect nature.

Wisdom is based on understanding life and how to live in harmony and balance with it. Wisdom is the ability to separate the important from the unimportant, the grain from the chaff, and to move toward that which is most worthwhile. It is this kind of wisdom that we, as individuals and as nations, need to put to use if we are to preserve life on our planet for our children and their children to come. The failure to do so is immoral and evil. As Carl Jung believed, "Understanding does not cure evil, but it is a definite help."[13]

CREATING IN ORIGINAL WAYS

Whatever does not yet exist is that which has not yet been born. Even before something is creatively born, our imaginations are active. We can imagine what a new baby will look like, what a song will sound like, what an orange will taste like. Imagination precedes creative action. First we imagine something, then we develop it—be it an idea, an object, a work of art, or a piece of junk. We do this because we are unique and want to create something original.

One of the most dramatic innovations in recent times is the widespread use of the computer. Yet it had its antecedents. Stonehenge, in England, was an ancient observatory made of four concentric circles of stones designed in such a way that remarkably accurate astronomical data could be obtained. It was a stone-age equivalent of the computer. Built around 3000 B.C. and used until

Missions of the human spirit

Working toward a mission

Taking a stand

Joining together in harmony

*Commitment
to recycling*

*The importance
of natural resources*

JANE SCHERR

JOHN JAMES

DAVID M. ALLEN

Let there be peace

Save the forests

JOHN JAMES

the first century, Stonehenge was partly destroyed by the Romans.[14] Yet what remains today reminds us of the powerful urge to create and the awesome nature of originality. In 1642, more than four thousand years after Stonehenge was built, a different kind of computer was constructed by Blaise Pascal, a mathematical genius and philosopher. He created a machine that could add and subtract by turning wheels, but it did not become popular with clerks because they were afraid it would take away their jobs.

The urge to create something innovative led Gottfried Leibnitz, thirty years later, to make a machine that multiplied. Two hundred years later, in 1882, Charles Babbage created a more complicated one called the "Difference Engine." Using her imagination, Ada Lovelace, a mathematician working with Babbage, went on to develop the very first computer program.[15] Since then, the speed and efficiency of computers has snowballed because of creative people such as these.

While many people are personally creative, some have a mission to help others also become creative. Maria Montessori was one. In 1894, the first woman to graduate with a medical degree from the University of Rome, she became director of the university psychiatric unit. There she developed an interest in the education of children and found that culturally deprived or mentally retarded children could be educated through specially designed materials. This discovery intrigued her so much that she began to study less disadvantaged children and, in doing so, came to believe that she was preparing herself for "an unknown mission."

Gradually Montessori developed a theory and techniques for releasing the natural creativity of children. In her school where neither grades nor other formal rewards or punishments were given, children became spontaneously creative as they discovered how to use materials without the interference or direction of teacher. They could then go on to more advanced academic learning. Today, Montessori principles and methods are used in schools throughout the world.[16]

Creativity—whether expressed in education, art, or inventions—reflects a universal search for originality fueled by the power of imagination. As playwright George Bernard Shaw explained, "Imagination is the beginning of creation. You imagine what you desire, you will what you imagine, and at last you create what you will."[17]

JOY TO THE WORLD

The urge to enjoy is a natural expression of the human spirit. It can be seen at every age. The infant who reaches up in awe toward a shaft of sunlight or reaches gleefully toward a mobile hanging over a crib is experiencing joy. The adolescent who smiles when finishing school assignments; the adult who sings along with a car radio or wanders through an art gallery and is awestruck by a picture is experiencing joy. So is the person who, after a long day of standing, soaks their tired feet in hot water or sits down in a comfortable chair to read a book.

There are innumerable ways we enjoy life, and each of us has our favorite ways. You may like one TV show and I prefer another; you may like to dress up and go out to dinner, and I might prefer to spend an evening at home. You may enjoy one kind of candy and I prefer another. You might be happier if a child acts one way; I might be happier if the child acts differently.

What people enjoy is often influenced by what they have been taught in the family or by cultural norms, as the anthropologist Margaret Mead has proven. For example, two primitive cultures in New Guinea in 1931 had very different opinions about whether or not children are a joy. Among the highly aggressive and competitive Mundugumors, infanticide by drowning was very common, with women throwing the girls into the river and men the boys. However, the Arapesh people, who lived nearby, were exactly the opposite; both fathers and mothers found their greatest happiness in nurturing their children.[18]

Most of us experience happiness when we are enjoying life and feeling free, enjoying the process and products of our creative and intellectual processes, enjoying the ecstasy of transcendent oneness with the universe. When feeling this way we often tell others about what we have enjoyed, hoping they can have similar experiences.

In addition to our own ways of enjoying life, enjoyment is an interpersonal process. It is natural to smile at others and receive a smile in return, to enjoy giving gifts and receiving them as well. Yet the finest gift we can give is to give of ourselves in such a way that the giving spreads tidings of comfort and joy and the possibility that joy and laughter, instead of tears and pain, can be our human destiny.

Composer and conductor Leonard Bernstein was able to do this. He found happiness by focusing his enthusiasm on music and sharing classical and popular music with millions. He had an enormous enthusiasm for life and a desire to share what he called "the joy of music" with others. Noted for both serious and light-hearted music, he enjoyed his work, whether he was composing an opera or conducting a children's concert.

Conductor of the New York Philharmonic for many years, and sometimes a soloist on the piano, he occasionally conducted the orchestra from the piano bench and held popular concerts in the Soviet Union, Middle East, Latin America, Europe, and Japan; his young people's concerts were always joyful occasions.

Among his compositions are Jewish and Christian liturgical themes in jazz, including a mass that was written for the opening of the John F. Kennedy Center for the Performing Arts in Washington, D.C. His musical, *West Side Story*, has become one of the most famous musicals of all time. Anyone who has seen it on stage or in film can recognize his gift to us in that composition alone.

Bernstein has been described as being like a tidal wave, crashing through life with incredible energy and playful exuberance. In doing what he loved to do, he would often send audiences home in a state of euphoria.[19]

In a state of euphoria, we often forget our cares and laugh with joy. Yet life is a precarious mixture of joy and sorrow, so the challenge is to find ways to live with both realities. When we can recognize suffering and still choose to be enthusiastic, life is tolerable and can open doors to joy.

CLOSER CONNECTIONS

Every day we become more aware of the millions of ways we connect with the universe and each other. International travel, student exchange, the study of languages, the growing use of television and computer networks all accelerate the process. Satellites now transmit symphonies from one nation to another or demonstrate new surgical techniques from one hospital to another. International exchanges of dance groups and choirs, business and professional associations, governmental agencies and relief groups, even efforts to control terrorism and the drug trade, all indicate that people of the world are moving toward closer connections.

These closer connections are making it more obvious that even though we appear to be separate, we are not. We are like trees walking. Because of our humanness, we are physically rooted in this earth and our roots intertwine. We breathe the same air and depend on the same sun. We all live on the same fragile earth and have more in common than is often acknowledged.

In a similar way, we intertwine at a spiritual level like the branches of a tree. We all experience the same spiritual urges and yearn to live lives that have meaning. We all have the potential to meet on the narrow ridge of love. In these ways, we are not separate.

Recognizing our connections is one thing; however, developing them is another. The bridge between I and Thou is difficult enough to cross. To bring entire communities or nations into closer connection can be even more challenging. Doing this requires people with visions of what can be who are willing to put forth a great deal of effort to bring them about. Even more, it requires people who are committed to causes that are greater than their own self-interests. This kind of personal commitment will be increasingly more important if we are to move beyond the sufferings and separations so frequent today.

It is this goal of encouraging close connections that lies at the core of many religious traditions. For example, one of the most moving statements was made by a Jew named Jesus of Nazareth to his disciples, who feared that if they did not see him for a long time they would not know him. To this Jesus replied,

OH, YES, YOU WILL KNOW ME. WHEN YOU WELCOME THE STRANGER, WHEN YOU CARE FOR THE HUNGRY AND THE HOMELESS, THE SICK AND THE LONELY, THE POOR AND IMPRISONED, I WILL BE THERE. FOR IN CARING FOR THEM, YOU WILL BE CARING FOR ME.[20]

Dorothea Dix, a semi-invalid teacher, took this injunction seriously. In 1841 she was asked to teach a class at the Massachusetts house of corrections where mentally ill people, irrespective of age or sex, were chained naked in cages and cellars and beaten into insensitivity and obedience. After a two-year investigation of how the mentally ill were treated, she made a moving presentation to the Massachusetts legislature against this treatment. Her plea was that they be treated in a humane way, that their care be supported by taxes, and that those in charge be intelligent personnel.

After Dorothea Dix's plea succeeded, she continued investigating and reporting, going from state to state, then to Canada and Italy. In Italy, she persuaded Pope Pius IX to personally investigate the conditions of the mentally ill there.[21] Justice William O. Douglas of the United States Supreme Court described her as one who lifted public consciousness to realize that,

THERE IS A SPIRITUAL QUALITY IN EVERY HUMAN BEING; THAT NO ONE IS BEYOND REDEMPTION; THAT OFTEN THOSE WHO HAVE BEEN CAST INTO THE OUTER DARKNESS OF "INSANITY" CAN BE RECLAIMED AND RESTORED TO HEALTH AND GOOD CITIZENSHIP.[22]

The power of love, similar to that shown by Dorothea Dix, is something we all need to express. Connecting with each other in genuine dialogue requires us to acknowledge our similarities and accept our differences. As J. Allen Boone explained, "All living things are individual instruments. . . . We are members of a vast cosmic orchestra, in which each living instrument is essential to the complementary and harmonious playing of the whole."[23]

BEYOND OURSELVES

In addition to closer connections between people, we have the potential for moving beyond ourselves and connecting with other forms of life.

We are becoming more alert to our need to take care of the cosmos, to respect its life-giving and life-taking capabilities. We are also realizing that we can no longer misuse the earth; it is our only home. Not only that, each day the earth and cosmos provide us opportunities to move beyond ourselves, to experience moments of joy, spellbound by magnificence. Who hasn't felt the glory of a golden red sunset or an invigorating breath of cold morning air. When we pay attention, we find the world we live in is alive with wonder.

We are also becoming more aware of the significance of our connections with plants and animals. Some of us have a green thumb and talk to our plants, worry if they show signs of stress, feel sad if one dies, and generally have a reverence for rooted things. Until recently these positive feelings for plants were thought to be one-sided, with the gardener doing all the caring and the plants all the receiving. Recently that idea has begun to change. By measuring responses on polygraph instruments, research now indicates that plants actually respond to different kinds of music, to potential danger, to the physical and emotional moods of people and other plants, even to words of love.[24]

Candelaria Villanueva responded to an unusual connection of a different kind. After a shipwreck off the Philippines in 1974 in which many passengers drowned and Mrs. Villanueva was lost at sea for two days, she was miraculously saved by a giant sea turtle. Normally these turtles do not stay on the surface long, but this one did as it bore Mrs. Villanueva on its back until she was sighted, haggard and hysterical. The naval lieutenant who found her verified the event, "I would not have believed it if I had merely heard about it. But I was an eyewitness myself, along with my shipmates. After the woman was pulled up onto the ship, the turtle circled the area twice before disappearing into the sea, as if to reassure itself that its former passenger was in good hands."[25]

Transcending boundaries with other forms of life is always possible. We are surrounded by a world teeming with life, and we are part of it.

THE EVOLUTION OF LOVE ————————————————————

Evolution involves change, whether it is an evolution of life forms or life-styles, theology or technology. Evolution is not sudden. It happens gradually, step by step, by chance or by choice.

Pierre Teilhard de Chardin believed in an evolution of love. He came to this connection after unearthing the famous prehistoric skeleton called Pekin Man. A paleontologist, theologian, and philosopher, his hypothesis was that in spite of the ignorance and brutality of our species, there is a natural evolution of the human race toward goodness, love, and the betterment of society. This is because of our capacities for self-determination and invention; it would be easier to stop the world's turning on its axis than to stop this evolution of the human race.[26]

Teilhard de Chardin reasoned that billions of years ago there was only inanimate matter. Yet ever-evolving love, imbedded in this matter, and the interplay of molecular forces led to a major breakthrough. Instead of continuing lifeless chemical interaction, life forms began to develop, and love began to evolve. Love was first manifested in the reproduction and proliferation of plants and fish, birds and animals.

The appearance of humans marked a new stage in the evolution of love. Families, tribes, and communities began to evolve and will continue to evolve until "someday after mastering the winds, the waves, the tides and gravity, we shall harness for God the energies of love, and then, for the second time in the history of the world, man will have discovered fire."[27]

Perhaps it is the Little Prince who can teach us what this can mean. This story by Antoine de Saint-Exupéry is of a little prince who lives on a small star where he can see the sunset forty-four times a day and is very lonely. The rose that he loves is too coquettish and has many thorny defenses. In desperation, the Little Prince goes to visit other stars. On one, he finds a king who will not tolerate any disobedience. On another is a conceited man who only wants to be admired. The third has a tippler who always drinks, and the fourth a businessman who is too busy for anything except counting. Then there is a lamplighter who is just obeying orders, and a scholar who is writing about things he's never experienced.

At last the Little Prince arrives on Earth where there are hunters, and a little fox. He becomes friends with the fox. One day, however, on seeing other roses, he decides he must return to his own rose. It is a sad leaving, yet the Little Prince leaves the fox the secret of transcendence: "At night you will look up at the stars. . . . They will be your friends. . . . In one of the stars I will be living. In one of them I will be laughing. And so it will be as if all the stars were laughing."[28]

To recognize the potential joy that surrounds us is to live in the love that was given in the beginning.[29] It is to enter into dialogic encounter with other people and all of existence. To live in love is to experience personal wholeness and integrity. It is to trust the eternal spirit, to listen when it speaks, to act when it calls, which is every minute of every day. To live in love is to be awestruck by the wonder of how all is interrelated—oceans crashing on the shore; yellow mustard fields blooming after the first spring rain; wind moaning through giant pines; a dog barking loudly to protect its master; the eyes of the sick, hurt and lonely pleading for help; the innocence of an infant reaching out in trust; and the tenderness of a hand responding in love.

Our mission is to remember that the boundaries that we imagine exist between us are not really there. We are uniquely different; we are also one. The passion for life urges us to take paths with heart and do so time and time again. Abraham Heschel spoke for all of us when he wrote, "What I look for is not how to gain a firm hold on myself and on life, but primarily how to live a life that would deserve and evoke an eternal Amen."[30]

NOTES

❦

INTRODUCTION

1. MURIEL JAMES, *Born to Love* (Reading, Mass.: Addison-Wesley, 1973), pp. 181–200. See also MURIEL JAMES and LOUIS SAVARY, *A New Self* (Reading, Mass.: Addison-Wesley, 1977), pp. 42–43, 323; MURIEL JAMES and LOUIS SAVARY, *The Power at the Bottom of the Well* (New York: Harper & Row, 1974), pp. 20–27; and MURIEL JAMES, "The Inner Core and the Human Spirit," *Transactional Analysis Journal* Vol. 11, January 1981, pp. 54–65.

1. A PATH WITH HEART

1. ROBERT FULGHUM, *All I Need to Know I Learned in Kindergarten* (New York: Villard Books, 1988), p. 161.
2. CARLOS CASTANEDA, *The Teachings of Don Juan: A Yaqui Way of Knowledge* (New York: Simon and Schuster, 1973), p. 122.
3. MICHAEL MCRAE, "Dilemma at Gombe," *San Francisco Chronicle*, 3 April 1988.
4. ROBERT SHORT, *The Parables of Peanuts* (New York: Harper & Row, 1968), pp. 199–200.
5. DAVID BAKER, *The History of Manned Space Flight* (New York: Crown Publishers, 1982), p. 316.
6. KEVIN KELLY, ed., *The Home Planet* (Reading, Mass.: Addison-Wesley, 1988), p. 70.
7. DAG HAMMARSKJOLD, *Markings* (New York: Ballantine Books, 1964), p. 3.
8. ABRAHAM HESCHEL, *The Wisdom of Heschel* (New York: Farrar, Straus and Giroux, 1975), p. 4.
9. MARTIN BUBER, *Tales of the Hasidim: The Early Masters* (New York: Schocken Books, 1968), p. 170.
10. NORMAN COUSINS, "What Matters about Schweitzer," *Saturday Review*, 25 September 1965.
11. MARIAN ANDERSON, *My Lord What a Morning* (New York, Viking Press, 1956), p. 312.

2. BEHOLD! THE HUMAN SPIRIT

1. MARTIN BUBER, *Between Man and Man* (New York: Macmillan Co., 1986), p. 102.
2. FRANCES MOSSIKER, *Napoleon and Josephine* (New York: Simon and Schuster, 1964), p. 222.
3. SIGMUND FREUD, "Femininity," *New Introduction Lectures on Psychoanalysis*, trans. James Strachey (New York: Norton, 1964), p. 135.
4. CARL JUNG, *Memories, Dreams, Reflections* (New York: Pantheon, 1963), p. 4.
5. ALFRED ADLER, *Understanding Human Nature* (New York: Fawcett Premier, 1954), p. 29.
6. VIKTOR FRANKL, *The Unconscious God* (New York: Simon and Schuster, 1975), p. 28.
7. GORDON ALLPORT, *The Individual and His Religion* (New York: Macmillan and Co., 1950), p. 60.
8. MURIEL JAMES AND DOROTHY JONGEWARD, *Born to Win* (Reading, Mass.: Addison-Wesley), 1971.
9. MURIEL JAMES, *Born to Love* (Reading, Mass.: Addison-Wesley, 1973), pp. 182–200.
10. ALBERT EINSTEIN, *Ideas and Opinions* (New York: Crown Publishers, 1982), p. 40.
11. HEINZ PAGELS, *The Cosmic Code: Quantum Physics as the Language of Nature* (New York: Bantam Books, 1982).
12. PAUL TILLICH, *Biblical Religion and the Search for Ultimate Reality* (Chicago: University of Chicago Press, 1955), p. 22ff.
13. JOHN MUIR, *My First Summer in the Sierra* (Boston: Houghton Mifflin, 1911), p. 146.
14. DONALD SANDNER, *Navaho Symbols of Healing* (New York: Harcourt Brace Jovanovich, 1979), p. 76.
15. TSUNETSUGU MURAOKA, *Studies in Shinto Thought*, trans. D. Brown and J. Araki (Tokyo: Japanese Commission for UNESCO, 1964).
16. MICAH 3:8.
17. I CORINTHIANS 3:16.
18. PAUL TILLICH, *The Eternal Thou* (New York: Charles Scribner's Sons, 1956), p. 86.
19. CARL JUNG, *Modern Man in Search of a Soul*, trans. W. S. Dell and C. F. Baynes (New York: Harcourt, Brace and Co., 1933), p. 282.
20. KEVIN KELLY, ed., *The Home Planet* (Reading, Mass.: Addison-Wesley, 1988), p. 38.
21. ERIC BERNE, *Principles of Group Treatment* (New York: Oxford University Press, 1966), p. 221.
22. VIKTOR FRANKL, *Man's Search for Meaning* (Boston: Beacon Press, 1962).
23. VIKTOR FRANKL, *The Doctor and the Soul* (New York: Bantam Books, 1967), p. 21.
24. PAUL TILLICH, *The Eternal Thou* (New York: Charles Scribner's Sons, 1956), p. 21.
25. ANNE MORROW LINDBERGH, *Gift from the Sea* (New York: New American Library, 1955), p. 17.
26. NIKOS KAZANTZAKIS, *Saint Francis*, trans. P. A. Bien (New York: Simon and Schuster, 1962).
27. MARGOT ASTROV, *American Indian Prose and Poetry* (New York: Capricorn Books, 1962), p. 279.
28. ALBERT SCHWEITZER, *Memories of Childhood and Youth*, trans. C. T. Campion (New York: Macmillan, 1931), p. 92.

3. PASSIONS OF THE SOUL

1. THOMAS MERTON, *The Wisdom of the Fathers* (New York: New Directions, 1960), p. ix.
2. MURIEL JAMES, "The Inner Core and the Human Spirit," *Transactional Analysis Journal* 11:1 (January 1981): pp. 54–64.
3. E. G. VALENS, *The Other Side of the Mountain* (New York: Warner Books, 1975).
4. JACOBO TIMERMAN, *Prisoner Without a Name, Cell Without a Number*, trans. Tony Talbot (New York: Random House, 1981).

5. *San Francisco Chronicle,* 16 December 1988.

6. ROBERT MCHENRY, ed., *Famous American Women* (New York: Dover Publications, 1983), p. 294.

7. DAN GOODGAME, "I Do Believe in Control," *Time* (28 Sept. 1987), pp. 62–64.

8. CARL ROGERS, *Client-Centered Therapy* (Boston: Houghton Mifflin, 1951); and CARL ROGERS, *On Becoming a Person* (Boston: Houghton Mifflin, 1961).

9. JAMES FOREST, *Thomas Merton: A Pictorial Biography* (New York: Paulist Press, 1980), p. 81. See also THOMAS MERTON, *No Man Is an Island* (New York: Harcourt, Brace and World, 1955).

10. "U-Thant Passes Away," *New Age Journal* 1:3 (February 1975): p. 11.

11. JOSEPH CAMPBELL, WITH BILL MOYERS, *The Power of Myth* (New York: Doubleday, 1988), p. xv.

12. NIKOS KAZANTZAKIS, *Report to Greco* (New York: Bantam Books, 1966), p. 197.

13. THOMAS MERTON, *The Way of Chuang Tzu* (New York: New Directions, 1965), p. 98.

14. EMMA STERNE, *Mary McLeod Bethune* (New York: Alfred A. Knopf, 1957), p. 247.

15. ROBERT LESLIE, *Jesus and Logotherapy* (Knoxville, Tenn.: Abingdon Press, 1965), p. 52.

4. THE URGE TO LIVE

1. MARGARET APPLEGARTH, *Men as Trees Walking* (New York: Harper Brothers, 1952), p. 24.

2. TED KAPTCHUK, *The Web That Has No Weaver: Understanding Chinese Medicine* (New York: Congdon & Weed, 1983), pp. 35–40.

3. JOHN ADAMS, *Dangling from the Golden Gate Bridge and Other Narrow Escapes* (New York: Ballantine Books, 1988), p. 132ff.

4. VIKTOR FRANKL, *Man's Search for Meaning* (New York: Washington Square Press, 1963).

5. MARGOT DOUGHERTY, and JACQUELINE SAVAIANO, "Though Tackled by Lou Gehrig's Disease, Coach Charlie Wedemeyer and Family Still Show How to Win," *People Weekly,* 18 December 1988, pp. 93–95.

6. ERIK ERIKSON, *Childhood and Society* (New York: W. W. Norton, 1963).

7. CHARLES GARFIELD, *Peak Performers: The New Heroes of American Business* (New York: William Morrow, 1986), p. 160.

8. CHARLES GARFIELD, *Peak Performance: Mental Training Techniques of the World's Greatest Athletes* (Los Angeles: Jeremy P. Tarcher, 1984), p. 133.

9. RICHARD LEAKEY, *One Life: An Autobiography* (Salem, N.H.: Salem House, 1984), pp. 182–202.

10. JACQUI SCHIFF, *Cathexis Reader* (New York: Harper & Row, 1975), p. 15.

11. M. A. MELINSKY, *Healing Miracles* (London: A. R. Mobray and Company, 1968), p. 4.

12. D. SCOTT ROGO, *Miracles: A Parascientific Inquiry into Wondrous Phenomena* (New York: Dial Press, 1982), pp. 262–264.

13. IBID., pp. 259–295.

14. DOLORES KREIGER, "Therapeutic Touch: The Imprimatur of Nursing," *American Journal of Nursing* 75: (May 1975), pp. 784–787.

15. O. CARL SIMONTON, STEPHANIE MATHEWS-SIMONTON, AND JAMES CREIGHTON, *Getting Well Again* (Los Angeles: Jeremy P. Tarcher, 1978).

16. BERNIE SIEGEL, *Love, Medicine, and Miracles* (New York: Harper & Row, 1986), p. 28.

17. ASHLEY MONTAGU, *Immortality, Religion, and Morals* (New York: Hawthorn Books, 1971), p. 29.

18. RAYMOND MOODY, *Life After Life* (New York: Bantam Books, 1975).

19. ELISABETH KÜBLER-ROSS, *On Children and Death* (New York: Macmillan, 1983).

20. JOHN BARTLETT, *Familiar Quotations* (Boston: Little, Brown, 1955), p. 300.

21. HENRY VAN DUSEN, "The Prayers of Dag Hammarskjold," *Presbyterian Life,* 15 January 1967, p. 15.

22. DAG HAMMARSKJOLD, *Markings,* trans. W. H. Auden and L. Sjoberg, (New York: Ballantine Books, 1964), p. 74.

23. T. C. MCLUHAN, *Touch the Earth: A Self-Portrait of Indian Existence* (New York: Promontory Press, 1971), p. 12.

24. THOMAS MERTON, *No Man Is an Island* (New York: Harcourt Brace Jovanovich, 1955), p. 24.

25. KAHLIL GIBRAN, *Sand and Foam* (New York: Alfred A. Knopf, 1926).

26. CHUNGLIANG AL HUANG, *Quantum Soup* (New York: E. P. Dutton, 1983), p. 19.

27. RABINDRANATH TAGORE, *Collected Poems and Plays of Rabindranath Tagore* (New York: Macmillan, 1974), p. 259.

28. A. J. UNGERSMA, *The Search for Meaning* (Philadelphia: Westminster Press, 1961), p. 43.

5. THE URGE FOR FREEDOM

1. PHILLIP BERMAN, ed., *The Courage of Conviction* (New York: Dodd, Mead and Co., 1985), p. 65.

2. RICHARD SCHNEIDER, *Freedom's Holy Light* (New York: Thomas Nelson, 1985), pp. 106–108.

3. ROLLO MAY, *The Courage to Create* (New York: W. W. Norton and Company, 1975), p. 100.

4. ABRAHAM HESCHEL, *The Wisdom of Heschel* (New York: Farrar, Straus and Giroux, 1975), p. 220.

5. RUTHE STEIN, "Whiz Kid Can't Forget Killing Fields," *San Francisco Chronicle,* 7 December 1987.

6. KEVIN JOHNSON, "On New Legs, New Life Starts Today," *USA Today,* 19 April 1988.

7. BETTY FORD, *The Times of My Life* (New York: Ballantine Books, 1979).

8. LECH WALESA QUOTED IN BERMAN, *Courage,* pp. 231–233.

9. MARTIN BUBER, *Between Man and Man* (Boston: Beacon Press, 1955), p. 92.

10. CARL JUNG, *Memories, Dreams, Reflections* (New York: Pantheon, 1963).

11. WILL DURANT, *Lessons of History* (New York: Simon and Schuster, 1968), p. 81.

12. LOUIS FISCHER, *Gandhi: His Message and Life for the World* (New York: New American Library, 1954), p. 47.

13. "KING IS THE MAN, OH, LORD," *Newsweek,* 25 April 1968, p. 35.

14. ELSIE BOULDING, *The Underside of History* (Boulder, Colo.: Westview Press, 1976), pp. 314–326, 595.

15. IBID., pp. 560–561.

16. IBID., pp. 590–591.

17. ABIGAIL ADAMS, *Letters of Mrs. Adams*, Third ed. (Boston: Little, Brown and Company, 1941), letter to John Adams, March 31, 1776.

18. ELEANOR FLEXNER, *Century of Struggle* (Cambridge, Mass.: Harvard University Press, 1968), p. 15.

19. MURIEL JAMES, *Hearts on Fire: Romance and Achievement in the Lives of Great Women* (Los Angeles: Jeremy Tarcher, 1990).

20. CAROLINE BIRD, *Born Female* (New York: David McKay, 1968), p. 7.

21. HERMANN BUHL, *Lonely Challenge,* trans. Hugh Merrick (New York: E. P. Dutton, 1956), p. 292.

22. O. CARL SIMONTON, STEPHANIE MATHEWS-SIMONTON, AND JAMES CREIGHTON, *Getting Well Again* (Los Angeles: Jeremy P. Tarcher, 1978).

23. CHARLES GARFIELD, *Peak Performers: The New Heroes of American Business* (New York: William Morrow, 1986), p. 160.

24. MARTIN BUBER, *Between Man and Man*, trans. R. G. Smith (London: Kegan Paul, 1947), p. 184.

25. GEORGE SELDES, *The Great Thoughts* (New York: Ballantine Books, 1985), p. 199.
26. ERIC BERNE, *What Do You Say after You Say Hello?* (New York: Grove Press, 1971), p. 31.
27. RABINDRANATH TAGORE, *Fireflies* (New York: Collier Books, 1975), p. 243.
28. SANG KYU SHIN, *The Making of a Martial Artist* (Detroit, Mich.: Sang Kyu Shin, 1980), p. 55.
29. DAG HAMMARSKJOLD, *Markings,* trans. W. H. Auden and L. Sjoberg (New York: Ballantine Books, 1964), p. 105.
30. MARTIN LUTHER KING, *The Strength to Love* (New York: Harper & Row, 1968), p. 136.
31. JOSEPH LASH, *Eleanor: The Years Alone* (New York: New American Library, 1972), p. 327.

6. THE URGE TO UNDERSTAND

1. PHILLIP BERMAN, *The Courage of Conviction* (New York: Dodd, Mead and Co., 1985), p. 48.
2. DEBBIE TOWNSEND, "Ida Beats Odds and the Breaks to Graduate," *Contra Costa Times*, June 24, 1989.
3. LIN YUTANG, *The Wisdom of China and India* (New York: Random House, 1942).
4. DANIEL BOORSTIN, *The Discoverers* (New York: Vintage Books, 1985), pp. 439, 465–76.
5. JENNIFER UGLOW, *The International Dictionary of Women's Biography* (New York: Continuum, 1985), pp. 191–192.
6. CHARLES PANATI, *Extraordinary Origins of Everyday Things* (New York: Harper & Row, 1987), p. 159.
7. CARL SAGAN, *The Dragons of Eden: Speculations on the Evolution of Human Intelligence* (New York: Ballantine Books, 1977), pp. 116–120. See also FRANCINE PATTERSON, and EUGENE LINDEN, *The Education of Koko* (New York: Holt, Rinehart and Winston, 1981).
8. This is also true for traditions that do not use the word *God.* For example, in Taoism it is said that "the nameless," which was "born before heaven and earth," cannot be seen or heard and is "forever undefinable." LAO TSU, *Tao Te Ching,* trans. D. C. Lau (New York: Penguin Books, 1963). See also ALAN WATTS, *TAO: The Watercourse Way* (New York: Pantheon, 1975), pp. 23–26.
9. LYNN GILBERT AND GALEN MOORE, *Particular Passions* (New York: Clarkson Potter, 1981), pp. 59–63.
10. JACQUES BARZUN AND HENRY GRAFF, *The Modern Researcher* (New York: Harcourt Brace and Jovanovich, 1977), p. 147.
11. HOWARD GARDNER, *Frames of Mind: The Theory of Multiple Intelligences* (New York: Basic Books, 1983).
12. IBID., p. 173.
13. VICTOR GOERTZEL AND MILDRED GOERTZEL, *Cradles of Eminence* (Boston: Little, Brown, 1962), p. 85.
14. CHUANG TSU, *Chuang Tsu: Inner Chapters,* trans. Gia-Fu Feng and Jane English (New York: Vintage Books, 1974), and WATTS, *TAO: The Watercourse Way;* and BENJAMIN HOFF, *The Tao of Pooh* (New York: Penguin Books, 1982).
15. PARAPHRASED FROM MARTIN BUBER, *The Way of Man* (New York: Citadel Press, 1967), p. 17.
16. SAGAN, *Dragons,* p. 34.
17. RUTH BLEIR, *Science and Gender: A Critique of Biology and Its Theories on Women* (New York: Pergamon Press, 1984), p.
18. ELSIE BOULDING, *The Underside of History* (Boulder, Co.: Westview Press, 1976), pp. 735–736. See also OCTAVIO PAZ, *Sor Juana* (Cambridge, Mass.: Harvard University Press, 1988).
19. BARBARA EHRENREICH AND DEIRDRE ENGLISH, *For Her Own Good* (Garden City, N.Y.), pp. 127–128.

20. RUTH ABRAMS, *Send Us a Lady Physician* (New York: W. W. Norton, 1985), p. 242.
21. ALFRED TENNYSON, "Locksley's Hall," *Tennyson's Poetical Works* (Boston: Houghton Mifflin, 1899), pp. 649–657.
22. BILL MOYERS, *A World of Ideas* (New York: Doubleday, 1989), p. 267.
23. RACKHAM HOLT, *Mary McLeod Bethune* (New York: Doubleday 1964), p. 17. See also HOPE STODDARD, *Famous American Women* (New York: Thomas Crowell, 1970), pp. 71–80.
24. MURIEL JAMES, *The Better Boss in Multicultural Organizations* (Walnut Creek, CA: Marshall Publishing, 1991).
25. MOYERS, *Ideas*, p. 267.
26. ELEANOR ROOSEVELT, *This Is My Story* (New York: Harper and Brothers, 1937).
27. JAMES CHRISTIAN, *Philosophy: An Introduction to the Art of Wondering* (New York: Holt, Rinehart and Winston, 1977).
28. PAUL TILLICH, *The Eternal Thou* (New York: Charles Scribner's Sons, 1956), p. 93.
29. CHUANG TSU, *Inner Chapters*, p. 22.
30. PEDRO CALDERON DE LA BARCA, *Life Is a Dream*, trans. William Colford (Woodbury, N.Y.: Barron's, 1958), p. 5.

7. THE URGE TO CREATE

1. BERGEN EVANS, *Dictionary of Quotations* (New York: Avenal Books, 1978), p. 340.
2. LADISLAO RETI, ed., *The Unknown Leonardo* (New York: McGraw-Hill, 1974), p. 174.
3. ROBERT CONAT, *A Streak of Luck* (New York: Bantam Books, 1980).
4. NIKOS KAZANTZAKIS, *Report to Greco*, trans. P. A. Bien (New York: Simon and Schuster, 1965).
5. MURIEL JAMES, *Hearts on Fire: Romance and Achievement in the Lives of Great Women* (Los Angeles: Jeremy P. Tarcher, 1990).
6. *Contra Costa Times*, 29 July 1988.
7. MURIEL JAMES AND LOUIS SAVARY, *The Heart of Friendship* (New York: Harper & Row, 1976), p. 158.
8. LOUIS MERTINS, *Robert Frost: Life and Talks* (Norman, Okla.: University of Oklahoma Press, 1965), p. 197.
9. CHARLES PANATI, *Extraordinary Origins of Everyday Things* (New York: Harper & Row, 1987), pp. 103–104.
10. IDRIES SHAH, *The Sufis* (London: W. H. Allen and Co., 1964), p. 97.
11. *San Francisco Chronicle*, 10 August 1988.
12. MIKE SAMUELS AND NANCY SAMUELS, *Seeing with the Mind's Eye* (New York: Random House, 1975), p. 263.
13. SILVANO ARIETI, *Creativity* (New York: Basic Books, 1976), p. 37.
14. HAROLD ANDERSON, ed., *Creativity and Its Cultivation* (New York: Harper and Bros., 1959), pp. 23–24.
15. ROBERT McKIM, *Experiences in Visual Thinking* (Monterey, CA: Brooks and Cole Publishing, 1980), p. 170.
16. PATRICIA GARFIELD, *Creative Dreaming* (New York: Simon and Schuster, 1974).
17. MURIEL JAMES AND DOROTHY JONGEWARD, *Born to Win: Transactional Analysis with Gestalt Experiments* (Reading, Mass.: Addison-Wesley, 1971).
18. GENESIS 28:10–22.
19. LOUIS SAVARY, PATRICIA BERNE AND STEPHEN WILLIAMS, *Dreams and Spiritual Growth: A Christian Approach to Dreamwork* (New York: Paulist Press, 1984), p. xi.
20. CARL JUNG, *Man and His Symbols* (New York: Doubleday, 1966), p. 102.
21. JOHN WHITE, *Rejection* (Reading, Mass.: Addison-Wesley, 1982), p. 92.
22. TERESA AMABILE, *Growing Up Creative: Nurturing a Lifetime of Creativity* (New York: Crown

Publishers, 1989). See also ALFIE KOHN, "Art for Art's Sake," *Psychology Today*, September 1987, pp. 52–57.

23. JOHN WHITE, *Rejection* (Reading, Mass.: Addison-Wesley, 1982), pp. 146–155.

24. A summary of many of these studies appears in Arieti, *Creativity*, pp. 354–359.

25. HAVELOCK ELLIS, *A Study of British Genius* (London: Hurst and Blackett, 1904).

26. EVA CURIE, *Madame Curie*, trans. Vincent Sheean (New York: Doubleday, 1937).

27. ERIC BERNE, *What Do You Do after You Say Hello?* (New York: Grove Press, 1972), p. 206ff.

28. MURIEL JAMES, "The Inner Core and the Human Spirit," *Transactional Analysis Journal* 11: 1 (January 1981), pp. 54–65.

29. R. BUCKMINSTER FULLER, *Synergetics: Explorations in the Geometry of Thinking* (New York: Macmillan, 1975).

30. ALDEN HATCH, *Buckminster Fuller: At Home in the Universe* (New York: Crown Publishers, 1974), pp. 194–195.

31. BLANCHE WILLIAMS, *George Eliot: A Biography* (New York: Macmillan, 1936), p. 276.

32. FRANCOIS GIROUD, *Marie Curie: A Life* (New York: Holmes and Meier, 1986).

33. VICTOR GOERTZEL AND MILDRED GOERTZEL, *Cradles of Eminence* (Boston: Little, Brown, 1962), p. 56.

34. R. BUCKMINSTER FULLER, *Operating Manual for Spaceship Earth* (New York: E. P. Dutton, 1978), p. 52.

8. THE URGE TO ENJOY

1. EVAN ESAR, *20,000 Quips and Quotes* (New York: Doubleday, 1968),

2. CLIFTON FADIMAN, ed., *The Little, Brown Book of Anecdotes* (Boston: Little, Brown and Company, 1985), p. 27.

3. DENNIS WHOLEY, ed., *Are You Happy?* (Boston: Houghton Mifflin, 1986), pp. 11–17.

4. ABRAHAM MASLOW, *The Further Reaches of Human Nature* (New York: Viking, 1971), p. 139.

5. HARRY STACK SULLIVAN, *The Psychiatric Interview* (New York: W. W. Norton, 1970), p. 207.

6. VALERIE CHANG AND MURIEL JAMES, "Anxiety and Projection as Related to Games and Scripts," *Transactional Analysis Journal* 17: 4 (October 1987), pp. 178–184.

7. ISAAC ASIMOV, *Biographical Encyclopedia of Science and Technology*, 2nd ed. (New York: Doubleday, 1982), p. 30.

8. I CORINTHIANS 12.

9. RENÉ DUBOS, *Pasteur and Modern Science* (New York: Doubleday, 1960), p. 146.

10. HANS SELYE, "On Stress," in Nathaniel Lande, *Mindstyles, Lifestyles* (Los Angeles: Price, Stern, Sloan Publishers, 1976), pp. 19–26.

11. BEVERLY SILLS AND LAWRENCE LINDERMAN, *Beverly: An Autobiography* (New York: Bantam Books, 1988).

12. WARREN BENNIS AND BURT NANUS, *Leaders* (New York: Harper & Row, 1985), p. 76ff.

13. BOB THOMAS, *Walt Disney* (New York: Simon and Schuster, 1976), p. 383.

14. ALAN WATTS, *The Essential Alan Watts* (Berkeley, Ca.: Celestial Arts, 1977), p. 92.

15. HARRY HARLOW, "Social Deprivation in Monkeys," *Scientific American* 207 (1962): 137–146.

16. GREGORY BATESON, *Mind and Nature: A Necessary Unity* (New York: Bantam Books, 1988), p. 148.

17. ERIK ERIKSON, *Childhood and Society*, 2nd ed. (New York: W. W. Norton, 1963), p. 222.

18. CHUNGLIANG AL HUANG, *Quantum Soup* (New York: E. P. Dutton, 1983), p. 7.

19. GENESIS 17; EXODUS 21.

20. PSALMS 2 AND PSALMS 126.

21. LUKE 15: 11–32.
22. NORMAN COUSINS, "Anatomy of an Illness (As perceived by the patient)," *New England Journal of Medicine* (December 23, 1976): 1458–1463.
23. VIKTOR FRANKL, *The Doctor and the Soul* (New York: Alfred A. Knopf, 1967).
24. MARTIN BUBER, *Tales of Rabbi Nachman* (New York: Avon Books, 1956), p. 40.
25. M. SIMMEL, "Anatomy of a Mime Performer," *The Justice* (Brandeis University), 6 May 1975, quoted in HOWARD GARDNER, *Frames of Mind: The Theory of Multiple Intelligences* (New York: Basic Books, 1983), p. 206.
26. RABINDRANATH TAGORE, *Fireflies* (New York: Collier Books, 1975), p. 69.
27. HAROLD KUSHNER, *When All You've Ever Wanted Isn't Enough* (New York: Simon and Schuster, 1986), p. 69.
28. EVAN ESAR, ed. *20,000 Quips and Quotes* (Garden City, New York: Doubleday, 1968), p. 269.
29. SIMONE WEIL, *The Need for Roots* (New York: G.P. Putnam, 1952), p. 97.
30. MARY GOULDING AND ROBERT GOULDING, *Not To Worry!* (New York: William Morrow, 1989).

9. THE URGE TO CONNECT

1. MARTIN BUBER, *Pointing the Way* (New York: Harper & Row, 1957), p. 27.
2. HENRY DAVID THOREAU, *Walden and Other Writings* (New York: Modern Library, 1937).
3. RENE SPITZ, "Hospitalism, Genesis of Psychiatric Conditions in Early Childhood," *Psychoanalytic Study of the Child* 1 (1945): 53–74.
4. LEON JAROFF, "Roaming the Cosmos," *Time,* 8 February 1988, p. 58.
5. STEPHEN HAWKING, *A Brief History of Time* (New York: Bantam Books, 1988), pp. 174–175.
6. "A Talk with Einstein," *The Listener,* September 1955, quoted in *Einstein: A Portrait* (Corte Madera, Calif.: Pomegranate Artbooks, 1984), p. 7.
7. ERIC BERNE related these to the sending of greeting cards and gifts at holidays, in "Games People Play at Christmas," *Transactional Analysis Journal* 8:4 (October 1978), pp. 322–325.
8. JOHN ADAMS, *Dangling from the Golden Gate Bridge and Other Narrow Escapes* (New York: Ballantine Books, 1988), pp. 28–33.
9. BARBARA YOUNG, *This Man From Lebanon: A Study of Kahlil Gibran* (New York: Alfred A. Knopf, 1950), p. 29.
10. MURIEL JAMES AND LOUIS SAVARY, *The Heart of Friendship* (New York: Harper & Row, 1976).
11. MARTIN BUBER, *Between Man and Man* (New York: Macmillan, 1986), p. 31.
12. ALEXANDER THOMAS, STELLA CHESS, AND HERBERT BIRCH, *Temperament and Behavior Disorders in Children* (New York: New York University Press, 1969).
13. For more on early decisions, see MURIEL JAMES, *Breaking Free* (Reading, Mass.: Addison-Wesley, 1981).
14. For more on adult relationships influencing life decisions, see JOHN JAMES AND IBIS SCHLESINGER, *Are You the One for Me? How to Choose the Right Partner* (Reading, Mass.: Addison-Wesley, 1988).
15. For more on how such change can be made, see MARY GOULDING AND ROBERT GOULDING, *Changing Lives through Redecision Therapy* (New York: Brunner/Mazel, 1979); MURIEL JAMES, *It's Never Too Late to Be Happy* (Reading, Mass.: Addison-Wesley, 1985); and ERIC BERNE, *What Do You Do after You Say Hello?* (New York: Grove Press, 1972).
16. JAMES AND SCHLESINGER, *Are You the One for Me?*
17. W. H. AUDEN, *Vincent Van Gogh: A Self Portrait* (Greenwich, Conn.: New York Graphic Society, 1961), pp. 52–56, 185–187.
18. WILLARD GAYLIN, *Caring* (New York: Alfred A. Knopf, 1976).
19. NORMAN COUSINS, "The Point about Schweitzer," *Saturday Review* (October 2, 1954).

20. From an interview on "Sonya Live," CNN-TV, 24 June 1988.

21. SAMUEL AND PEARL OLINER, *The Altruistic Personality* (New York: Free Press, 1988).

22. CORRIE TEN BOOM, *The Hiding Place* (New York: Bantam Books, 1971).

23. ALLAN LUKS, "Helper's High," *Psychology Today,* October 1988, pp. 39–42.

24. John Healy in his letter to the American public from Amnesty International U.S.A., September 1988, p. 5.

25. PITIRIM SOROKIN, *The Ways and Power of Love* (Chicago: Henry Regnery, 1967), pp. 15–35.

26. *San Francisco Examiner,* 10 January 1988, p. A-1.

27. THOMAS DOOLEY, *The Edge of Tomorrow* (New York: Farrar, Straus, and Cudahy, 1961), Foreword.

28. ANNETTE WINTER, "Spotlight," *Modern Maturity,* October–November 1988, p. 18.

29. ALAN BURGESS, *The Small Woman* (London: Evans Bros., 1957).

30. "Special Report," *Life,* April 1976, p. 113.

31. BUBER, *Between Man,* p. 97.

32. KEVIN KELLY, ed., *The Home Planet* (Reading, Mass.: Addison-Wesley, 1988), p. 137.

33. ALBERT SCHWEITZER, *Memoirs of Childhood and Youth,* trans. C. T. Campion (New York: Macmillan, 1931), p. 92.

34. MATTHEW FOX, *Breakthrough: Meister Eckhart's Creation Spirituality in New Translation* (New York: Doubleday, 1980), p. 139.

35. MATTHEW FOX, *Meditations with Meister Eckhart* (Santa Fe: Bear and Company, 1983), p. 15.

36. MATTHEW FOX, *Original Blessing: A Primer in Creation Spirituality* (Santa Fe: Bear and Company, 1983), p. 105.

37. SIMONE WEIL, *The Need for Roots: Prelude to a Declaration of Duties toward Mankind,* trans. Arthur Wills (New York: Harper Torchbooks, 1971), p. 6.

38. PHILLIP BERMAN, ed. *The Courage of Conviction* (New York: Dodd, Mead and Co., 1985), p. 188.

39. ROLLO MAY, *Love and Will* (New York: W. W. Norton, 1969), p. 286.

40. MATTHEW FOX, *Meditations with Meister Eckhart* (Santa Fe: Bear and Company, 1983), p. 111.

41. CHOGYAM TRUNGPA, *Cutting Through Spiritual Materialism* (Berkeley, Calif.: Shambhala, 1973), p. 99.

42. MARTIN BUBER, *A Believing Humanism,* trans. M. Friedman (New York: Simon and Schuster, 1967), p. 45.

10. THE URGE TO TRANSCEND

1. PAUL TILLICH, *Biblical Religion and the Search for Ultimate Reality* (Chicago: University of Chicago Press, 1955), p. 22ff.

2. PSALMS 8:3; PSALMS 147:4.

3. II PETER 1:19; REVELATIONS 22:16.

4. I CORINTHIANS 12:12–26.

5. MARTIN BUBER, *The Legends of the Baal-Shem* (New York: Schocken Books, 1969), p. 49.

6. LAO TSU, *Tao Te Ching,* trans. Gia-Fu Feng and Jane English (New York: Vintage Books, 1972, p. 53; and CHUANG TSU. *Chuang Tsu: Inner Chapters,* trans. Gia-Fu Feng and Jane English (New York: Vintage Books, 1974), p. 29.

7. JOHN W. GARDNER, *On Leadership* (New York: The Free Press, 1990), p. 115.

8. ALEXANDER SOLZHENITSYN, *Nobel Lecture,* trans. F. D. Reeve (New York: Farrar, Straus and Giroux, 1972), p. 13.

9. Chief Seattle's reply to President Fillmore in 1852.

10. MIRCEA ELIADE, *The Sacred and the Profane,* trans. Willard Trask (New York: Harper & Row, 1959), p. 204.

11. MARTIN BUBER, *Ten Rungs* (New York: Schocken Books, 1962), p. 101.

12. We are indebted to Martin Buber, who developed the concept of these first four spheres in *I and Thou* (New York: Charles Scribner's Sons, 1958), pp. 123–137. Based on our clinical experience, we have added the fifth sphere.

13. JOHN PEARSON, *The Sun's Birthday* (Garden City, N.Y.: Doubleday, 1973), p. 58.

14. PETER TOMPKINS AND CHRISTOPHER BIRD, *The Secret Life of Plants* (New York: Harper & Row, 1972), p. 142.

15. M. BRUNO, "Portrait of an Artist," *Newsweek,* 17 December 1984, p. 14.

16. SAM REIFLER, *I Ching: A New Interpretation for Modern Times* (New York: Bantam Books, 1974).

17. MARTIN BUBER, *The Way of Man* (New York: Citadel Press, 1963), p. 32.

18. CARLOS CASTANEDA, *Journey to Ixtlan: The Lessons of Don Juan* (New York: Simon and Schuster, 1972), p. 278.

19. MARTIN BUBER, *Hasidism and Modern Man,* trans. M. Friedman (New York: Horizon Press, 1958), p. 172.

20. MARTIN BUBER, *Between Man and Man,* trans. R. G. Smith (New York: Macmillan, 1965), p. 35.

21. BRIAN LANKER, "I Dream a World," *National Geographic,* August 1989, p. 213.

22. GARY LIBMAN, "The Millionaire Learns to Read," *San Francisco Chronicle,* 14 June 1988.

23. BILL MOYERS, "The Hero's Adventure—Part 5 of 6," *Joseph Campbell and the Power of Myth with Bill Moyers,* Public Affairs Television production, 1988, p. 2.

24. JOSEPH CAMPBELL, *The Hero with a Thousand Faces* (Princeton, N.J.: Princeton University Press, 1949), p. 337.

25. ROBERTO SURO, "Twelve Faiths Join Pope to Pray for Peace," *New York Times,* 28 October 1986; and PAUL CROW, "Assisi's Day of Prayer for Peace," *Christian Century* 103 (December 3, 1986): 1084.

26. POPE JOHN PAUL II, "The Challenge and the Possibility of Peace," *Origins* 17: 370.

27. *SAN FRANCISCO CHRONICLE,* 10 December 1988.

28. RABINDRANATH TAGORE, *Fireflies* (New York: Collier, 1975), p. 203.

29. LUKE 23:46.

30. IDRIES SHAH, *The Sufis* (London: W. H. Allen and Co., 1964), p. 124.

31. CARLOS CASTANEDA, *Journey to Ixtlan* (New York: Simon and Schuster, 1972), p. 151.

32. CORITA KENT and JOHN PINTAURO, *To Believe in Man* (New York: Harper & Row, 1970).

33. WILLIAM O. DOUGLAS, *An Almanac of Liberty* (Garden City, N.Y.: Doubleday, 1954), p. 383.

34. VIKTOR FRANKL, *The Unconscious God* (New York: Simon and Schuster, 1975), p. 16.

35. PAUL TILLICH, *The Eternal Thou* (New York: Charles Scribner's Sons, 1956), p. 93.

11. MISSION OF THE HUMAN SPIRIT

1. T. S. ELIOT, "Little Gidding," *The Complete Poems and Plays of T. S. Eliot* (New York: Harcourt, Brace, 1952), p. 145.

2. MARTIN BUBER, *Legend of the Baal-Shem* (New York: Schocken Books, 1969), p. 33.

3. CHARLES GARFIELD, *Peak Performance* (Los Angeles: Jeremy P. Tarcher, 1984), p. 66.

4. NORMAN COUSINS, *Albert Schweitzer's Mission* (New York: W. W. Norton, 1985), p. 125.

5. ALBERT SCHWEITZER, *Out of My Life and Thought* trans. C. P. Campion (New York: Holt, Rinehart and Winston, 1961).

6. COURTNEY TOWER, "Mother Teresa's Work of Grace," *Reader's Digest,* December 1987, p. 227.

7. RENÉ DUBOS, *Celebrations of Life* (New York, McGraw-Hill, 1981), pp. 38–39.

8. MORTIMER ADLER, *Ten Philosophical Mistakes* (New York: Macmillan, 1985), p. 147. See also MORTIMER ADLER, *The Idea of Freedom,* (Garden City, N.Y.: Doubleday, 1961).

9. JAMES CHRISTIAN, *Philosophy: An Introduction to the Art of Wondering* (New York: Holt, Rinehart and Winston, 1977), p. 283.

10. ERIC BERNE, *What Do You Do after You Say Hello?* (New York: Grove Press, 1971), p. 31.

11. JIMMY CARTER, *Keeping Faith* (New York: Bantam Books, 1982), p. 399.

12. ELAINE PARTNOW, *The Quotable Woman* (Los Angeles: Corwin Books, 1977), p. 262.

13. CARL JUNG, *Psyche and Symbol* (New York: Doubleday, 1958).

14. COLIN RONAN, *Lost Discoveries* (New York: McGraw-Hill, 1973), pp. 30–31.

15. CHARLES PANATI, *Browser's Book of Beginnings* (Boston: Houghton Mifflin, 1984), pp. 366–369.

16. RITA KRAMER, *Maria Montessori* (Reading, Mass.: Addison-Wesley, 1988).

17. JAMES SIMPSON, *Simpson's Contemporary Quotations* (Boston: Houghton Mifflin, 1988), p. 314.

18. MARGARET MEAD, *Blackberry Winter* (New York: Simon and Schuster, 1972), pp. 194–207.

19. MARK STEINBRINK, "Bernstein at Seventy," *Life,* September 1988, pp. 40–44. See also JOAN PEYSER, *Bernstein* (New York: Ballantine Books, 1987).

20. Paraphrase of Matthew 25: 34–40.

21. ROBERT MCHENRY, ed., *Famous American Women* (New York: Dover Publications, 1980), p. 102.

22. WILLIAM O. DOUGLAS, *An Almanac of Liberty* (Garden City, N.Y.: Doubleday, 1954), p. 281.

23. J. ALLEN BOONE, *Kinship with All Life* (New York: Harper & Row, 1954), p. 143.

24. PETER TOMPKINS AND CHRISTOPHER BIRD, *The Secret Life of Plants* (New York: Harper & Row, 1973).

25. Agence France-Presse, *San Francisco Chronicle,* 22 June 1974.

26. PIERRE TEILHARD DE CHARDIN, *The Nature of Man* (London: William Collins, 1964), p. 239.

27. JAMES SIMPSON, *Simpson's Contemporary Quotations* (Boston: Houghton Mifflin, 1988), p. 196.

28. ANTOINE DE SAINT-EXUPÉRY, *The Little Prince* (New York: Harcourt, Brace and Co.), 1943.

29. MURIEL JAMES, *Born to Love: Transactional Analysis in the Church* (Reading, Mass.: Addison-Wesley, 1973), p. 184.

30. ABRAHAM HESCHEL, *The Wisdom of Heschel* (New York: Farrar, Straus and Giroux, 1975), p. 3.

BIBLIOGRAPHY

Abram, Ruth. *Send Us a Lady Physician.* New York: W.W. Norton and Co., 1985.

Adams, Abigail. *Letters of Mrs. Adams.* 3rd ed. Boston: Little, Brown and Company, 1941.

Adams, Ansel. *Yosemite and the Range of Light.* Boston: Little, Brown and Company, 1982.

Adams, John. *Dangling from the Golden Bridge and Other Narrow Escapes.* New York: Ballantine Books, 1988.

Adler, Alfred. *Understanding Human Nature.* New York: Fawcett Premier, 1954.

Adler, Mortimer. *The Idea of Freedom.* Vol. 2. Garden City, New York: Doubleday, 1961.

———. *Ten Philosophical Mistakes.* New York: Macmillan, 1985.

Allport, Gordon. *The Individual and His Religion.* New York: Macmillan and Co., 1950.

Amabile, Teresa. "The Personality of Creativity," *Brandeis Review* 5 (Fall 1985).

Anderson, Harold, ed. *Creativity and Its Cultivation.* New York: Harper and Brothers, 1959.

Anderson, Marian. *My Lord What a Morning.* New York: Viking Press, 1956.

Applegarth, Margaret. *Men as Trees Walking.* New York: Harper and Brothers, 1952.

Arieti, Silvano. *Creativity.* New York: Basic Books, 1976.

Asimov, Isaac. *Biographical Encyclopedia of Science and Technology.* 2nd ed. New York: Doubleday and Co., 1982.

Astrov, Margot. *American Indian Prose and Poetry.* New York: Capricorn Books, 1962.

Auden, W.H., ed. *Vincent Van Gogh: A Self Portrait.* Greenwich, Conn.: New York Graphic Society, 1961.

Bainton, Roland. *Here I Stand: A Life of Martin Luther.* New York: Abingdon Cokesbury, 1950.

Baker, David. *The History of Manned Space Flight.* New York: Crown Publishing, 1982.

Bartlett, John. *Familiar Quotations.* Boston: Little, Brown and Company, 1955.

Barzun, Jacques, and Henry Graff. *The Modern Researcher.* New York: Harcourt Brace Jovanovich, 1977.

Bateson, Gregory. *Mind and Nature: A Necessary Unity.* New York: Bantam Books, 1988.

Bennis, Warren, and Burt Nanus. *Leaders.* New York: Harper and Row, 1985.

Berman, Phillip, ed. *The Courage of Conviction.* New York: Dodd, Mead and Co., 1985.

Berne, Eric. *Principles of Group Treatment.* New York: Oxford University Press, 1966.

————. *Transactional Analysis in Psychotherapy.* New York: Grove Press, 1961.

————. *What Do You Say After You Say Hello?* New York: Grove Press, 1972.

————. "Games People Play at Christmas," *Transactional Analysis Journal* 8 (October 1978).

Bird, Caroline. *Born Female.* New York: David McKay, 1968.

Bleir, Ruth. *Science and Gender: A Critique of Biology and Its Theories on Women.* New York: Pergamon Press, 1984.

Boone, J. Allen. *Kinship with All Life.* New York: Harper and Row, 1954.

Boorstin, Daniel. *The Discovers.* New York: Vintage Books, 1985.

Boulding, Elsie. *The Underside of History.* Boulder, Colorado: Westview Press, 1976.

Bruno, M. "Portrait of an Artist," *Newsweek* (December 17, 1984).

————. *A Believing Humanism.* Trans. Maurice Friedman. New York: Simon and Schuster, 1967.

Buber, Martin. *Between Man and Man.* Trans. Roger Smith. London: Kegan Paul, 1947. New York: Macmillan, 1965, 1986 with Maurice Friedman.

————. *Hasidism and Modern Man.* Trans. Maurice Friedman. New York: Horizon Press, 1958.

————. *I and Thou.* 2nd ed. Trans. Roger Smith. New York: Charles Scribner's Sons, 1958.

————. *Legend of the Baal-Shem.* New York: Schocken Books, 1969.

————. *Pointing The Way.* New York: Harper and Row, 1957.

————. *The Tales of Rabbi Nachman.* New York: Avon Books, 1956.

————. *Tales of the Hasidim: The Early Masters.* Trans. Olga Marx. New York: Schocken Books, 1968.

————. *Ten Rungs.* New York: Schocken Books, 1962.

————. *The Way of Man.* New York: Citadel Press, 1963.

Buhl, Hermann. *Lonely Challenge.* Trans. Hugh Merrick. New York: E.P. Dutton, 1956.

Burgess, Alan. *The Small Woman.* London: Evans Bros., 1957.

Burke, Thomas F., ed. *Einstein: A Portrait.* Corte Madera, California: Pomegranate Artbooks, 1984.

Calderon de la Barca, Pedro. *Life is a Dream.* Trans. William Colford. Woodbury, N.Y.: Barron's, 1958.

Campbell, Joseph. *The Hero with a Thousand Faces.* Princeton, N.J.: Princeton University Press, 1949.

————. *The Power of Myth.* With Bill Moyers. New York: Doubleday, 1988.

Carter, Jimmy. *Keeping Faith.* New York: Bantam Books, 1982.

Castaneda, Carlos. *Journey to Ixtlan.* New York: Simon and Schuster, 1972.

———. *The Teachings of Don Juan: A Yaqui Way of Knowledge.* New York: Simon and Schuster, 1973.

Chang, Valerie, and Muriel James. "Anxiety and Projection as Related to Games and Scripts," *Transactional Analysis Journal* 17 (October 1987).

Christian, James. *Philosophy: An Introduction to the Art of Wondering.* New York: Holt, Rinehart and Winston, 1977.

Chuang Tsu. *Chuang Tsu, Inner Chapters.* Trans. Gia-Fu Feng and Jane English. New York: Vintage Books, 1974.

Cornell, William, and Karen Olio. "Risks of Bodywork for Incest Survivors," *Association of Humanistic Psychology Perspective* (October 1990).

Cousins, Norman. *Albert Schweitzer's Mission.* New York: W.W. Norton, 1985.

———. "Anatomy of an Illness (As perceived by the patient)," *New England Journal of Medicine* (December 23, 1976).

———. *Head First: The Biology of Hope.* New York: E.P. Dutton, 1989.

———. "The Point about Schweitzer," *Saturday Review* (October 2, 1954).

———. "What Matters about Schweitzer," *Saturday Review* (September 25, 1965).

Crow, Paul. "Assisi's Day of Prayer for Peace," *Christian Century* 103 (December 3, 1986).

Dougherty, Margot, and Jacqueline Saviano. "Though Tackled by Lou Gehrig's Disease, Coach Charlie Wedemeyer and Family Still Show How to Win," *People Weekly* (December 18, 1988).

Douglas, William O. *An Almanac of Liberty.* Garden City, N.Y.: Doubleday and Company, 1954.

————. *Pasteur and Modern Science.* New York: Doubleday, 1960.

Dubos, Rene. *Celebrations of Life.* New York: McGraw-Hill, 1981.

Durant, Will. *Lessons of History.* New York: Simon and Schuster, 1968.

Ehrenreich, Barbara and Deirdre English. *For Her Own Good.* Garden City, New York: Anchor Books, 1979.

Einstein, Albert. *Ideas and Opinions.* New York: Crown Publishers, 1982.

Eliade, Mircea. *The Sacred and the Profane.* Trans. Willard Trask. New York: Harper and Row, 1959.

Eliot, T.S. "Little Gidding," *The Complete Poems and Plays of T.S. Eliot.* New York: Harcourt and Brace, 1952.

Ellis, Havelock. *A Study of British Genius.* London: Hurst and Blackett, 1904.

Erikson, Erik. *Childhood and Society.* 2nd ed. New York: W. W. Norton, 1963.

Esar, Evan. *20,000 Quips and Quotes.* New York: Doubleday, 1968.

Evans, Bergen. *Dictionary of Quotations.* New York: Avenal Books, 1978.

Fadiman, Clifton, ed. *The Little, Brown Book of Anecdotes.* Boston: Little, Brown and Company, 1985.

Fischer, Louis. *Gandhi: His Message and Life for the World.* New York: New American Library, 1954.

Flexner, Eleanor. *Century of Struggle.* Cambridge: Harvard University Press, 1968.

Ford, Betty. *The Times of My Life.* New York: Ballantine Books, 1979.

Forest, James. *Thomas Merton: A Pictorial Biography.* New York: Paulist Press, 1980.

Fox, Matthew. *Breakthrough: Meister Eckhart's Creation Spirituality in New Translation.* New York: Doubleday, 1980.

———. *Meditations with Meister Eckhart.* Santa Fe: Bear and Company, 1983.

———. *Original Blessing: A Primer in Creation Spirituality.* Santa Fe: Bear and Company, 1983.

Frankl, Viktor. *The Doctor and the Soul.* New York: Bantam Books, 1967.

———. *Man's Search for Meaning.* Boston: Beacon Press, 1962. New York: Washington Square Press, 1963.

———. *The Unconscious God.* New York: Simon and Schuster, 1975.

Freud, Sigmund. "Femininity," *New Introduction Lectures on Psychoanalysis.* Trans. James Strachey. New York: Norton, 1964.

Fromm, Erich. *The Fear of Freedom.* London: Routledge and Kegan Paul Ltd., 1942.

Fulghum, Robert. *All I Need to Know I Learned in Kindergarten.* New York: Villard Books, 1988.

Fuller, R. Buckminster. *Operating Manual for Spaceship Earth.* New York: E.P. Dutton, 1978.

————. *Synergetics: Explorations in the Geometry of Thinking.* New York: Macmillan, 1975.

Gardner, Howard. *Frames of Mind: The Theory of Multiple Intelligences.* New York: Basic Books, 1983.

Gardner, John W. *On Leadership.* New York: The Free Press, 1990.

Garfield, Charles. *Peak Performance: Mental Training Techniques of the World's Greatest Athletes.* Los Angeles: Jeremy P. Tarcher, 1984.

————. *Peak Performers: The New Heros of American Business.* New York: William Morrow and Company, 1986.

Garfield, Patricia. *Creative Dreaming.* New York: Simon and Schuster, 1974.

Gaylin, Willard. *Caring.* New York: Alfred Knopf, 1976.

Gibran, Kahlil. *Sand and Foam.* New York: Alfred Knopf, 1926.

Gilbert, Lynn, and Galen Moore. *Particular Passions.* New York: Clarkson Potter Publications, 1981.

Giroud, Francois. *Marie Curie: A Life.* New York: Holmes and Meier, 1986.

Goertzel, Victor, and Mildred Goertzel. *Cradles of Eminence.* Boston: Little, Brown and Co., 1962.

Goodgame, Dan. "I Do Believe in Control," *Time* (September 28, 1987).

Goulding, Mary, and Robert Goulding. *Changing Lives Through Redecision Therapy.* New York: Brunner/Mazel, 1979.

————. *Not To Worry!* New York: William Morrow, 1989.

Greer, K. "Are American Families Finding New Strength in Spirituality?" *Better Homes & Gardens* (January 1988).

Hammarskjold, Dag. *Markings.* Trans. W.H. Auden and L. Sjoberg. New York: Ballantine Books, 1964.

Harlow, Harry. "Social Deprivation in Monkeys," *Scientific American* 207 (1962).

Hatch, Alden. *Buckminster Fuller: At Home in the Universe.* New York: Crown Books, 1974.

Hawking, Stephen. *A Brief History of Time.* New York: Bantam Books, 1988.

Healy, John. "To the American Public." In letter from Amnesty International U.S.A., September 1988.

Heschel, Abraham. *The Wisdom of Heschel.* New York: Farrar, Straus and Giroux, 1975.

Hoff, Benjamin. *The Tao of Pooh.* New York: Penguin Books, 1982.

Holt, Rackham. *Marty McLeod Bethune.* New York: Doubleday, 1964.

Huang, Chungliang Al. *Quantum Soup.* New York: E.P. Dutton, 1983.

James, John. "Cultural Consciousness: The Challenge to TA," *Transactional Analysis Journal* 13 (October 1983).

————. "Grandparents and the Family Script Parade," *Transactional Analysis Journal* 14 (January 1984).

280 BIBLIOGRAPHY

James, John, and Ibis Schlesinger. *Are You the One for Me? How to Choose the Right Partner.* Reading, Mass.: Addison-Wesley, 1988.

James, Muriel. *The Better Boss in Multicultural Organizations.* Walnut Creek, California: Marshall Publishing, 1991.

————. *Born to Love: Transactional Analysis in the Church.* Reading, Mass.: Addison-Wesley, 1973.

————. *Breaking Free: Self-Reparenting for a New Life.* Reading, Mass.: Addison-Wesley, 1981.

————. "Cultural Scripts: Historical Events vs. Historical Interpretation," *Transactional Analysis Journal* 13 (October 1983).

————. "Diagnosis and Treatment of Ego State Boundary Problems," *Transactional Analysis Journal* 16 (July 1986).

————. "The Down-Scripting of Women for 115 Generations: A Historic Kaleidoscope," *Transactional Analysis Journal* 3 (January 1973).

————. *Hearts on Fire: Romance and Achievement in the Lives of Great Women.* Los Angeles: Jeremy Tarcher, 1991.

————. "The Inner Core and the Human Spirit," *Transactional Analysis Journal* 11 (January 1981).

————. *It's Never Too Late To Be Happy: The Psychology of Self-Reparenting.* Reading, Mass.: Addison-Wesley, 1985.

————. "Laugh Therapy: Theory, Procedures, Results in Clinical and Special Fields," *Transactional Analysis Journal* 9 (October 1979).

James, Muriel, and Valerie Chang. "Anxiety and Projection as Related to Games and Scripts," *Transactional Analysis Journal* 17 (October 1987).

James, Muriel, and Dorothy Jongeward. *Born to Win: Transactional Analysis with Gestalt Experiments.* Reading, Mass.: Addison-Wesley, 1971.

James, Muriel, and Louis Savary. *The Heart of Friendship.* New York: Harper and Row, 1976.

————. *The Power at the Bottom of the Well: Transactional Analysis with a Biblical Perspective.* Study Guide Edition. New York: Harper and Row, 1976.

Jaroff, Leon. "Roaming the Cosmos," *Time,* February 8, 1988.

Jung, Carl. *Man and His Symbols.* New York: Doubleday, 1966.

————. *Memories, Dreams, Reflections.* New York: Random House, 1963.

————. *Modern Man in Search of a Soul.* Trans. W. S. Dell and C.F. Baynes. New York: Harcourt, Brace and Co., 1933.

————. *Psyche and Symbol.* New York: Doubleday, 1958.

Kaptchuk, Ted. *The Web That Has No Weaver: Understanding Chinese Medicine.* New York: Congdon & Weed, 1983.

Kazantzakis, Nikos. *Report to El Greco.* Trans. P.A. Bien. New York: Simon and Schuster, 1965.

————. *Report to Greco.* New York: Bantam Books, 1966.

————. *St. Francis.* Trans. P. A. Bien. New York: Simon and Schuster, 1965.

Keller, Helen. *The Open Door.* New York: Doubleday, 1957.

Kelly, Kevin, ed. *The Home Planet.* Reading, Mass.: Addison-Wesley, 1988

Kent, Corita, and John Pintauro. *To Believe In Man.* New York: Harper and Row, 1970.

King, Martin Luther. *Strength to Love.* New York: Pocket Books, 1964.

Kohn, Alfie. "Art for Art's Sake," *Psychology Today* (September, 1987).

Kramer, Rita. *Maria Montessori.* Reading, Mass.: Addison-Wesley, 1988.

Kreiger, Dolores. "Therapeutic Touch: The Imprimatur of Nursing," *American Journal of Nursing* 75 (May 1975).

Kübler-Ross, Elisabeth. *On Children and Death.* New York: Macmillan, 1983.

Kushner, Harold. *When All You've Ever Wanted Isn't Enough.* New York: Simon and Schuster, 1986.

Lande, Nathaniel. *Mindstyles, Lifestyles.* Los Angeles: Price, Stern, Sloan Publishers, 1976.

Lanker, Brian. "I Dream a World," *National Geographic* (August 1989).

Lao Tsu. *Tao Te Ching.* Trans. D.C. Lau. New York: Penguin Books, 1963. Trans. Gia-Fu Feng and Jane English. New York: Vintage Books, 1972.

Lash, Joseph. *Eleanor: The Years Alone.* New York: New American Library, 1972.

Leakey, Richard. *One Life: An Autobiography.* Salem, New Hampshire: Salem House, 1984.

Leslie, Robert. *Jesus and Logotherapy.* Knoxville: Abingdon Press, 1965.

Life Magazine (April 1976).

Lindbergh, Anne Morrow. *Gift from the Sea.* New York: New American Library, 1955.

Luks, Allan. "Helper's High," *Psychology Today* (October 1988).

Maslow, Abraham. *The Further Reaches of Human Nature.* New York: Viking, 1971.

May, Rollo. *The Courage to Create.* New York: W.W. Norton and Company, 1975.

————. *Love and Will.* New York: Norton, 1969.

McDonnell, Colleen, and Bernhard Lang. *Heaven, a History.* Princeton, N.J.: Yale University Press, 1988.

McHenry, Robert, ed. *Famous American Women.* New York: Dover Publications, 1980.

McKim, Robert. *Experiences in Visual Thinking.* Monterey, California: Brooks and Cole Publishing, 1980.

McLuhan, Teri C. *Touch the Earth: A Self-Portrait of Indian Existence.* New York: Promontory Press, 1971.

Mead, Margaret. *Blackberry Winter.* New York: Simon and Schuster, 1972.

Melinsky, M.A. *Healing Miracles.* London: A.R. Mobray and Company, 1968.

Mertins, Louis. *Robert Frost: Life and Talks.* Norman, Oklahoma: University of Oklahoma Press, 1965.

Merton, Thomas. *No Man Is An Island.* New York: Harcourt Brace Jovanovich, 1955.

————. *The Way of Chuang Tzu.* New York: New Directions, 1965.

———. *Wisdom of the Desert Fathers.* New York: New Directions, 1960.

Moody, Raymond. *Life After Life.* New York: Bantam Books, 1975.

Mossiker, Frances. *Napoleon and Josephine.* New York: Simon and Schuster, 1964.

Moyers, Bill. "The Hero's Adventure," Part 5 of 6. *Joseph Campbell and the Power of Myth with Bill Moyers.* New York: Public Affairs Television production, 1988.

———. *A World of Ideas.* New York: Doubleday, 1989.

Muggeridge, Malcolm. *Something Beautiful for God.* San Francisco: Harper and Row, 1971.

Muir, John. *My First Summer in the Sierra.* Boston: Houghton Mifflin, 1911.

Muraoka, Tsunetsugu. *Studies in Shinto Thought.* Trans. D. Brown and J. Araki. Tokyo: Japanese Commission for UNESCO, 1964.

New Age Journal 1 (February 1975).

Newsweek, April 25, 1968.

Oliner, Samuel, and Pearl Oliner. *The Altruistic Personality.* New York: Free Press, 1988.

Pagels, Heinz. *The Cosmic Code: Quantum Physics as the Language of Nature.* New York: Bantam Books, 1982.

Panati, Charles. *Browser's Book of Beginnings.* Boston: Houghton Mifflin, 1984.

———. *Extraordinary Origins of Everyday Things.* New York: Harper and Row, 1987.

Parks, Gordon. *Gordon Parks: A Poet and His Camera.* New York: Viking Press, 1968.

Partnow, Elaine. *The Quotable Woman.* Los Angeles: Corwin Books, 1977.

Patterson, Francine, and Eugene Linden. *The Education of Koko.* New York: Holt, Rinehart and Winston, 1981.

Paz, Octavio. *Sor Juana.* Cambridge, Mass.: Harvard University Press, 1988.

Pearson, John. *Begin Sweet World.* Garden City, New York: Doubleday and Co., 1976.

———. *The Sun's Birthday.* Garden City, New York: Doubleday and Company, 1973.

Peyser, Joan. *Bernstein.* New York: Ballantine Books, 1987.

Pope John Paul II. "The Challenge and the Possibility of Peace," *Origins* 17 (November 6, 1986).

Robbins, Jhan. *Front Page Marriage.* New York: G.P. Putnam's Sons, 1982.

Rogers, Carl. *Client Centered Therapy.* Boston: Houghton Mifflin, 1951.

———. *On Becoming a Person.* Boston: Houghton Mifflin, 1961.

Rogo, D. Scott. *Miracles: A Parascientific Inquiry Into Wondrous Phenomena.* New York: Dial Press, 1982.

Ronan, Colin. *Lost Discoveries.* New York: McGraw-Hill, 1973.

Roosevelt, Eleanor. *This Is My Story.* New York: Harper and Brothers, 1937.

Russell, Jeffrey. *The Devil: Perceptions of Evil from Antiquity to Primitive Christianity.* Ithaca, N.Y.: Cornell University Press, 1977.

Sagan, Carl. *The Dragons of Eden: Speculations on the Evolution of Human Intelligence.* New York: Ballantine Books, 1977.

Saint-Exupéry, Antoine de. *The Little Prince.* New York: Harcourt, Brace and Co., 1943.

Samuels, Mike, and Nancy Samuels. *Seeing with the Mind's Eye.* New York: Random House, 1975.

Sandner, Donald. *Navaho Symbols of Healing.* New York: Harcourt Brace Jovanovich, 1979.

Savary, Louis, Patricia Berne, and Strephon Williams. *Dreams and Spiritual Growth: A Christian Approach to Dreamwork.* New York: Paulist Press, 1984.

Schiff, Jacqui. *Cathexis Reader.* New York: Harper & Row, 1975.

Schneider, Richard. *Freedom's Holy Light.* New York: Thomas Nelson, 1985.

Schweitzer, Albert. *Memories of Childhood and Youth.* Trans. C.T. Campion. New York: Macmillan, 1931.

———. *Out of My Life and Thought.* Trans. C.P. Campion. New York: Holt, Rinehart and Winston, 1961.

Seldes, George. *The Great Thoughts.* New York: Ballantine Books, 1985.

Shah, Idries. *The Sufis.* London: W.H. Allen and Co., 1964.

Shin, Sang Kyu. *The Making of a Martial Artist.* Detroit, Michigan: Sang Kyu Shin, 1980.

Short, Robert. *The Parables of Peanuts.* New York: Harper and Row, 1968.

Siegel, Bernie. *Love, Medicine, and Miracles.* New York: Harper and Row, 1986.

Sills, Beverly, and Lawrence Linderman. *Beverly: An Autobiography.* New York: Bantam Books, 1988.

Simonton, O. Carl, Stephanie Mathews-Simonton, and James Creighton. *Getting Well Again.* Los Angeles: J.P. Tarcher, 1978.

Simpson, James. *Simpson's Contemporary Quotations.* Boston: Houghton Mifflin Co., 1988.

Solzhenitsyn, Alexander. *Nobel Lecture.* Trans. F.D. Reeve. New York: Farrar, Straus and Giroux, 1972.

Sorokin, Pitirim. *The Ways and Power of Love.* Chicago: Henley Regnery, 1967.

Spitz, Rene. "Hospitalism, Genesis of Psychiatric Conditions in Early Childhood," *Psychoanalytic Study of the Child* I (1945).

Steinbrink, Mark. "Bernstein at Seventy," *Life* Magazine (September 1988).

Steinem, Gloria. *Outrageous Acts and Everyday Rebellions.* New York: Holt, Rinehart and Winston, 1983.

Sterne, Emma. *Mary McLeod Bethune.* New York: Alfred Knopf, 1957.

Stoddard, Hope. *Famous American Women.* New York: Thomas Crowell, 1970.

Sullivan, Harry Stack. *Interpersonal Theory of Psychiatry.* New York: W.W. Norton, 1953.

————. *The Psychiatric Interview.* New York: Norton & Co., 1970.

Tagore, Rabindranath. *Collected Poems and Plays of Rabindranath Tagore.* New York: Macmillan, 1974.

————. *Fireflies.* New York: Collier Books, 1975.

Teilhard de Chardin, Pierre. *The Nature of Man.* London: William Collins, 1964.

————. *The Phenomenon of Man.* New York: Harper and Row, 1959.

Ten Boom, Corrie. *The Hiding Place.* With John and Elizabeth Sherrill. New York: Bantam Books, 1985.

Tennyson, Alfred. "Locksley's Hall," *Tennyson's Poetical Works.* Boston: Houghton, Mifflin and Company, 1899.

The Holy Bible, Revised Standard Version. New York: Thomas Nelson, 1953.

Thomas, Alexander, Stella Chess, and Herbert Birch. *Temperament and Behavior Disorders in Children.* New York: New York University Press, 1969.

Thomas, Bob. *Walt Disney.* New York: Simon and Schuster, 1976.

Thoreau, Henry David. *Walden and Other Writings.* New York: Modern Library, 1937.

Tillich, Paul. *Biblical Religion and the Search For Ultimate Reality.* Chicago: University of Chicago Press, 1955.

————. *The Eternal Thou.* New York: Charles Scribner's Sons, 1956.

Timerman, Jacobo. *Prisoner without a Name, Cell without a Number.* Trans. Tony Talbot. New York: Random House, 1981.

Tompkins, Peter, and Christopher Bird. *The Secret Life of Plants.* New York: Harper and Row, 1972.

Tower, Courtney. "Mother Teresa's Work of Grace," *Readers Digest* (December 1987).

Trungpa, Chogyam. *Cutting Through Spiritual Materialism.* Boston: Shambhala Books, 1973.

———. *The Myth of Freedom.* Boston: Shambhala, 1988.

Uglow, Jennifer. *The International Dictionary of Women's Biography.* New York: Continuum, 1985.

Ungersma, Aaron J. *The Search for Meaning.* Philadelphia: Westminster Press, 1961.

Valens, E.G. *The Other Side Of The Mountain.* New York: Warner Books, 1975.

Van Dusen, Henry. "The Prayers of Dag Hammarskjold," *Presbyterian Life* (January 15, 1967).

Watts, Alan. *The Essential Alan Watts.* Berkeley, Ca.: Celestial Arts, 1977.

———. *Tao: The Watercourse Way.* New York: Pantheon Books, 1975.

Weatherhead, Leslie. *Prescription for Anxiety.* Nashville: Abingdon Press, 1956.

Weil, Simone. *The Need for Roots.* New York: G.P. Putnam, 1952.

———. *The Need for Roots: Prelude to a Declaration of Duties toward Mankind.* Trans. Arthus Wills. New York: Harper Torchbooks Edition, 1971.

White, John. *Rejection.* Reading, Mass.: Addison-Wesley, 1982.

Wholey, Dennis, ed. *Are You Happy?* Boston: Houghton Mifflin, 1986.

Williams, Blanche. *George Eliot: A Biography.* New York: Macmillan, 1936.

Winter, Annette. "Spotlight," *Modern Maturity* (October-November 1988).

Woodward, Kenneth. "Heaven," *Newsweek* (March 27, 1989).

Young, Barbara. *This Man From Lebanon: A Study of Kahlil Gibran.* New York: Knopf, 1950.

Yutang, Lin. *The Wisdom of China and India.* New York: Random House, 1942.

INDEX